"Any woman who chooses to behave like a full human being should be warned that the armies of the status quo will treat her as something of a dirty joke; that's their natural and first weapon." **from "Sisterhood" by Gloria Steinem.**

"Do you put down other women for being on welfare? . . . Stop for a minute and think what would happen to you and your kids if you suddenly had no husband and no savings." **from "Welfare Is a Women's Issue" by Johnnie Tillmon.**

"The first time we used tear gas in Vietnam, I couldn't say hello to women friends without being denounced for working in the Pentagon." **from "Women and War" by Daniel Ellsberg.**

"How can you raise kids to be free when they're so systematically shackled within the schools? The answer is, you can't . . . And that's why children's liberation is the next item on our civil rights shopping list." **from "Down with Sexist Upbringing" by Letty Cottin Pogrebin.**

THE FIRST

Ms.

READER

Edited by FRANCINE KLAGSBRUN

WARNER
PAPERBACK
LIBRARY

A Warner Communications Company

The First Ms. Reader

WARNER PAPERBACK LIBRARY EDITION
First Printing: September, 1973
Second Printing: November, 1973
Third Printing: July, 1974

Acknowledgments:
"The Shulmans' Marriage Agreement." *Ms., Spring 1972,* copyright © 1970, 1971 by Alix Shulman. Del Martin & Phyllis Lyon, "Lesbian Love & Sexuality, *Ms., July 1972,* from *Lesbian/Woman* by Del Martin & Phyllis Lyon, copyright © 1972 by Del Martin & Phyllis Lyon. By permission of Bantam Books, Inc. Harriet Rosenstein, "Reconsidering Sylvia Plath," *Ms., Sept. 1972,* copyright © Harriet Rosenstein. Angela Davis, "The Myth of the Black Matriarch," *Ms., Aug. 1972,* excerpted from "Reflections on the Black Woman's Role in the Community of Slaves," *The Black Scholar,* Dec. 1971, Reprinted by permission of *The Black Scholar.* Alice Schwarzer, "The Radicalization of Simone de Beauvoir," *Ms., July 1972,* copyright © 1972 Alice Schwarzer. "A Reading List for Free Children," copyright © 1971 Letty Cottin Pogrebin.

Gloria Steinem, "Sisterhood"; Jane O'Reilly, "The Housewife's Moment of Truth"; Judy Syfers, "I Want a Wife"; Vivian Gornick, "Why Women Fear Success"; Cellestine Ware, "The Black Family and Feminism"; Daniel Ellsberg, "Women and War"; Johnnie Tillmon, "Welfare Is a Women's Issue"; Cynthia Ozick, "We Are the Crazy Lady"; Susan Edmiston, "How To Write Your Own Marriage Contract"; Linda Francke & Dorothy Hughes, "How To Start a Child Care Center"; Anselma Dell'Olio, "The Sexual Revolution Wasn't Our War"; Letty Cottin Pogrebin, "Down With Sexist Upbringing"; Estelle Ramey, "Men's Monthly Cycles"; Nicholas von Hoffman, "My Mother, the Dentist": *Ms., Spring 1972.* Margaret Edmonson Sloan, "The Saturday Morning Nap-Conversion"; Harriet Lyons & Rebecca Rosenblatt, "Body Hair: The Last Frontier"; *Ms., July 1972.* Gloria Steinem, "Marilyn—The Woman Who Died Too Soon"; Susan Davis, "Organizing from Within"; Jennifer Macleod, "Rate Your Employer": *Ms., August 1972.* Cynthia Ozick, "The Hole/Birth Catalog": *Ms., Oct. 1972,* Erica Jong. "The Artist as Housewife": *Ms., Dec. 1972.* Jonathan Weigand, "The Single Father": *Ms., Jan. 1973.* Reprinted by Permission of the Authors.

Cover design by Bea Feitler, Art Director of Ms.

Text typography designed by Milton Batalion

Warner Paperback Library is a division of Warner Books, Inc.,
75 Rockefeller Plaza, New York, N.Y. 10019.

Printed in the United States of America

CONTENTS

INTRODUCTION

This is a book with a mind of its own. Even its creators hadn't thought that such an anthology would exist until much later; until that conventional point in the life of a magazine when articles have accumulated into neat categories.

But this *First Ms. Reader* really began the moment the first issue of *Ms.* appeared in 1972. It was a very fat, special issue designed to remain on the newsstands for at least two months, and it contained many different kinds of articles, from an analysis of the Sexual Revolution to the very personal story of a woman on welfare, from problems of the black family to problems of women in the suburbs and on campuses. It was an experiment: most opinion in the publishing world was pessimistic about magazines in general, and an unconventional one coming out of the Women's Movement in particular. Many women writers and editors disagreed, but had no way to prove that the publishing professionals were wrong. This preview issue was a test. If it worked, there was hope of building a new kind of women's magazine. If it didn't— well, we who worked on it would have to suffer the cries of "I told you so," and concede that much of our hope and effort had either been too soon or in vain.

The test *did* work. In fact, all 300,000 copies of that cherished preview issue sold out not in two months, but in just a few days. We celebrated, and then the enormity of the task we had undertaken began to sink in. A whole national magazine, from editorial ideas through production and distribution, had to be constructed in short order if we were to fulfill the promises the first issue had made.

Occasionally during that hectic period, we heard reports

of the first-born. Women's Studies courses on various campuses requested it. Somewhat absent-mindedly, we supplied the few copies we had left. Women from other countries wrote to order it, and we had to reply with regret. Even after we produced the first regular issue of *Ms.* six months later, the preview issue was being passed hand to hand. Finally it was sold underground—for $5 instead of the original $1.50. Then for $10 and $15 on the West Coast.

When the price reached $25, the *Ms.* staff finally began to understand that we had to do something about it. After all, one of the purposes of the magazine was to be as inexpensive as possible in order to be available to many women. The issue had turned itself into a book—and a very expensive one at that.

So this *First Ms. Reader* was planned to include all those first-issue articles that had not been outdated by time—and that has turned out to be most of them. It also includes twelve additional articles from subsequent issues, to round out the selection. Because the authors involved wanted a populist book too—one that would be available to most women—they agreed to smaller payments than usual. That has allowed us to produce this first paperback in large numbers, and for one-half to one-third the price that such a book would normally cost.

Of course, there are many kinds of articles that could not be included. The emphasis is more practical than philosophical, for instance. Future anthologies will include more articles on consciousness-raising groups, the economic implications of the Women's Movement, role-free stories for children, and the like.

But this collection does have a life of its own, and the many additions seemed to belong here. It is an introduction to *Ms. Magazine*; we hope it will encourage you to join us in the future.

Even more important, the book is an introduction to the great change that is happening in the hearts and minds of women. We are beginning, through insights like the ones in this book, to change our lives at last.

The editors of *Ms.*

I. Some Feminist Realizations

SISTERHOOD

GLORIA STEINEM

A very, very long time ago (about three or four years),
I took a certain secure and righteous pleasure in saying
the things that women are supposed to say.

I remember with pain—

"My work won't interfere with marriage. After all. I
can always keep my typewriter at home." Or:

"I don't want to write about women's stuff. I want to
write about foreign policy." Or:

"Black families were forced into matriarchy, so I see
why black women have to step back and let their men get
ahead." Or:

"I know we're helping Chicano groups that are tough
on women, but *that's their culture*." Or:

"Who would want to join a women's group? I've never
been a joiner, have you?" Or (when bragging):

"He says I write about abstract ideas like a man."

I suppose it's obvious from the kinds of statements I
chose that I was secretly non-conforming. (I wasn't married. I was earning a living at a profession I cared about,
and I had basically—if quietly—opted out of the "feminine" role.) But that made it all the more necessary to
repeat some Conventional Wisdom, even to look as conventional as I could manage, if I was to avoid the punishments reserved by society for women who don't do as
society says. I therefore learned to Uncle Tom with sub-

---

*Gloria Steinem has been a free-lance writer for more than
ten years. Since 1969, she has also traveled the country lec-
turing on the Women's Movement. She is an editor of "Ms."*

tlety, logic, and humor. Sometimes, I even believed it myself.

If it weren't for the Women's Movement, I might still be dissembling away. But the ideas of this great sea-change in women's view of ourselves are contagious and irresistible. They hit women like a revelation, as if we had left a small dark room and walked into the sun.

At first my discoveries seemed complex and personal. In fact, they were the same ones so many millions of women have made and are making. Greatly simplified, they went like this: Women are human beings first, with minor differences from men that apply largely to the act of reproduction. We share the dreams, capabilities, and weaknesses of all human beings, but our occasional pregnancies and other visible differences have been used—even more pervasively, if less brutally, than racial differences have been used—to mark us for an elaborate division of labor that may once have been practical but has since become cruel and false. The division is continued for clear reason, consciously or not: the economic and social profit of men as a group.

Once this feminist realization dawned, I reacted in what turned out to be predictable ways. First, I was amazed at the simplicity and obviousness of a realization that made sense, at last, of my life experience: I couldn't figure out why I hadn't seen it before. Second, I realized, painfully, how far that new vision of life was from the system around us, and how tough it would be to explain the feminist realization at all, much less to get people (especially, though not only, men) to accept so drastic a change.

But I tried to explain. God knows (*she* knows) that women try. We make analogies with other groups that have been marked for subservient roles in order to assist blocked imaginations. We supply endless facts and statistics of injustice, reeling them off until we feel like human information-retrieval machines. We lean heavily on the device of reversal. (If there is a male reader to whom all my pre-realization statements seem perfectly logical, for instance, let him substitute "men" for "women" or himself for me in each sentence, and see how he feels. "My work won't interfere with marriage. . . ." ". . . Chicano groups that are tough on men. . . ." You get the idea.)

We even use logic. If a woman spends a year bearing and nursing a child, for instance, she is supposed to have the primary responsibility for raising that child to adulthood. That's logic by the male definition, but it often makes women feel children are their only function or discourages them from being mothers at all. Wouldn't it be just as logical to say that the child has two parents, both equally responsible for child-rearing, and that therefore the father should compensate for that extra year by spending *more* than his half of the time with the child? Now *that's* logic.

Occasionally, these efforts at explaining succeed. More often, I get the feeling that we are speaking Urdu and the men are speaking Pali. As for logic, it's in the eye of the logician.

Painful or not, both stages of reaction to our discovery have a great reward. They give birth to sisterhood.

First, we share with each other the exhilaration of growth and self-discovery, the sensation of having the scales fall from our eyes. Whether we are giving other women this new knowledge or receiving it from them, the pleasure for all concerned is enormous. And very moving.

In the second stage, when we're exhausted from dredging up facts and arguments for the men whom we had previously thought advanced and intelligent, we make another simple discovery. Women understand. We may share experiences, make jokes, paint pictures, and describe humiliations that mean nothing to men, but *women understand*.

The odd thing about these deep and personal connections of women is that they often ignore barriers of age, economics, worldly experiences, race, culture—all the barriers that, in male or mixed society, had seemed so difficult to cross.

I remember meeting with a group of women in Missouri who, because they had come in equal numbers from the small town and from its nearby campus, seemed to be split between wives with white gloves welded to their wrists and students with boots who talked about "im-

6

perialism" and "oppression." Planning for a child care center had brought them together, but the meeting seemed hopeless until three of the booted young women began to argue among themselves about a young male professor, the leader of the radicals on campus, who accused all women unwilling to run mimeograph machines of not being sufficiently devoted to the cause. As for child care centers, he felt their effect of allowing women to compete with men for jobs was part of the "feminization" of the American male and American culture.

"He sounds just like my husband," said one of the white-gloved women, "only he wants me to have bake-sales and collect door-to-door for his Republican Party."

The young women had sense enough to take it from there. What did boots or white gloves matter if they were all getting treated like servants and children? Before they broke up, they were discussing the myth of the vaginal orgasm and planning to meet every week. "Men think we're whatever it is we do for men," explained one of the housewives. "It's only by getting together with other women that we'll ever find out who we are."

Even racial differences become a little less hopeless once we discover this mutuality of our life experience as women. At a meeting run by black women domestics who had formed a job cooperative in Alabama, a white housewife asked me about the consciousness-raising sessions or "rap groups" that are the basic unit of the Women's Movement. I explained that while men, even minority men, usually had someplace where they could get together every day and be themselves, women were isolated from each other. We had no street corners, no bars, no offices, no territory that was recognized as ours. Rap groups were an effort to create that free place: an occasional chance for total honesty and support from our sisters.

As I talked about isolation, the feeling that there must be something wrong with us if we weren't content to be housekeepers and mothers, tears began to stream down the cheeks of this dignified woman—clearly as much of a surprise to her as to us. For the black women, some barrier was broken down by seeing her cry.

"He does it to us both, honey," said the black woman next to her, putting an arm around her shoulders. "If it's

7

your own kitchen or somebody else's, you still don't get treated like people. Women's work just doesn't count."

The meeting ended with the housewife organizing a support group of white women who would extract from the husbands a living wage for domestic workers and help them fight the local hierarchy: a support group without which the domestic workers felt their small and brave cooperative could not survive.

As for the "matriarchal" argument that I swallowed in pre-feminist days, I now understand why many black women resent it and feel that it's the white sociologist's way of encouraging the black community to imitate a white suburban life style. ("If I end up cooking grits for revolutionaries," explained a black woman poet from Chicago, "it isn't my revolution. Black men and women need to work together for partnership, not patriarchy. You can't have liberation for half a race.") In fact, some black women wonder if criticism of the strength they were forced to develop isn't a way to keep half the black community working at lowered capacity and lowered pay, as well as to attribute some of black men's sufferings to black women, instead of to their real source—white racism. I wonder with them.

Looking back at all those male-approved things I used to say, the basic hang-up seems clear: a lack of esteem for women—black women, Chicana women, white women—and for myself.

This is the most tragic punishment that society inflicts on any second-class group. Ultimately, the brainwashing works, and we ourselves come to believe our group is inferior. Even if we achieve a little success in the world and think of ourselves as "different," we don't want to associate with our group. We want to identify up, not down (clearly my problem in not wanting to write about women, and not wanting to join women's groups). We want to be the only woman in the office, or the only black family on the block, or the only Jew in the club.

The pain of looking back at wasted, imitative years is enormous. Trying to write like men. Valuing myself and other women according to the degree of our acceptance by men—socially, in politics, and in our professions. It's as painful as it is now to hear two grown-up female human beings competing with each other on the basis of their husbands' status, like servants whose identity rests on the wealth or accomplishments of their employers.

And this lack of esteem that makes us put each other down is still the major enemy of sisterhood. Women who are conforming to society's expectations view the non-conformists with justifiable alarm. "Those noisy, unfeminine women," they say to themselves. "They will only make trouble for us all." Women who are quietly non-conforming, hoping nobody will notice, are even more alarmed because they have more to lose. And that makes sense, too.

Because the status quo protects itself by punishing all challengers, especially women whose rebellion strikes at the most fundamental social organization: the sex roles that convince half the population its identity depends on being first in work or in war, and the other half that it must serve as docile ("feminine") unpaid or underpaid labor. There seems to be no punishment inside the white male club that quite equals the ridicule and personal viciousness reserved for women who rebel. Attractive or young women who act forcefully are assumed to be male-controlled. If they succeed, it could only have been sexually, through men. Old women or women considered unattractive by male standards are accused of acting only out of bitterness, because they could not get a man. Any woman who chooses to behave like a full human being should be warned that the armies of the status quo will treat her as something of a dirty joke; that's their natural and first weapon. She will *need* sisterhood.

All of that is meant to be a warning but not a discouragement. There are so many more rewards than punishments.

For myself, I can now admit anger, and use it constructively, where once I would have submerged it and let it fester into guilt or collect for some destructive explosion.

I have met brave women who are exploring the outer edge of human possibility, with no history to guide them, and with a courage to make themselves vulnerable that I find moving beyond words.

I no longer think that I do not exist, which was my

version of that lack of self-esteem afflicting many women. (If male standards weren't natural to me, and they were the only standards, how could I exist?) This means that I am less likely to need male values to identify myself with and am less vulnerable to classic arguments ("If you don't like me, you're not a Real Woman"—said by a man who is Coming On. "If you don't like me, you are not a Real Person, and you can't relate to other people"—said by anyone who understands blackmail as an art).

I can sometimes deal with men as equals and therefore can afford to like them for the first time.

I have discovered politics that are not intellectual or superimposed. They are organic, because I finally understand why I for years inexplicably identified with "out" groups. I belong to one, too. It will take a coalition of such groups to achieve a society in which, at a minimum, no one is born into a second-class role because of visible difference, because of race or of sex.

I no longer feel strange by myself, or with a group of women in public. I feel just fine.

I am continually moved to discover I have sisters.

I am beginning, just beginning, to find out who I am.

THE HOUSEWIFE'S MOMENT OF TRUTH

JANE O'REILLY

Forty people were lying on a floor in Aspen, Colorado, floating free and uneasy on the indoor/outdoor carpet, eyes closed, being led through the first phase of a "Workshop in Approaching Unisexuality." It would turn out later that the aim of the exercise was not to solve the problem of who does what and to whom, but to reveal to the participants that adjectives such as warm, violent, soft, timid, peaceful, and aggressive are not necessarily definitions for male or female.

We closed our eyes and cleared our minds. Slowly we perceived a lake in the distance, and as we walked toward it, the surface became smooth as a mirror into which we could look and see our reflection. There was no reflection. Infinitely slowly, we began to evolve into the animal that most expressed our own ideas of ourselves—of our sensual selves. Minutes passed and we became aware of the other animals around us. At last we opened our eyes and those animals that felt like it did whatever seemed natural. Most of the women twittered or purred. Most of the men growled, or attempted to wag tails. I was a cat, black, with a lovely long tail, sitting under a red geranium in a sunny window. We formed groups in our part of the conference-room forest, and told each other what we had become.

"I was a snake," said a beautiful young woman, a pro-

Jane O'Reilly is a contributing editor of "New York" magazine and the mother of an eight-year-old son. She is currently writing a book called "The American Way of Love."

fessional designer. "As I was moving through the grass, enjoying my slithering, curving progress, I realized I had no fangs. No bite. I couldn't even hiss. My only protection was that I could change color in reaction to the people that passed by. I started to go through my garden and I saw that there were panthers draped over all the lawn furniture. I went into my house, and there were panthers everywhere, filling every chair, curled up in groups in all the rooms. They were eating, rather elegantly, and no one paid any attention to me, even when I asked if they wanted anything more to eat. I was interested, but I was different, and finally I withdrew."

The women in the group looked at her, looked at each other, and . . . click! A moment of truth. The shock of recognition. Instant sisterhood. "You became a *housewife*," we said, excited, together, turning to the men to see if they understood. "She is describing a housewife. Do you know that?"

"Hmm, yes, well, uh . . ." they said, sensitized for the morning, but eager to recount their own stories of becoming spotted leopards in green forests, of turning to griffins with human heads who know and see all. The next time, or perhaps the time after that, they will recognize the click! of recognition, that parenthesis of truth around a little thing that completes the puzzle of reality in women's minds—the moment that brings a gleam to our eyes and means the revolution has begun.

Those clicks are coming faster and faster. They were nearly audible last summer, which was a very angry summer for American women. Not redneck-angry from screaming because we are so frustrated and unfulfilled-angry, but clicking-things-into-place-angry, because we have suddenly and shockingly perceived the basic disorder in what has been believed to be the natural order of things.

One little click turns on a thousand others. I had been sitting in that Aspen room, feeling a very liberated cat—alone on my window sill, self-sufficient and self-enclosed, able to purr or scratch as I chose. I was fooling myself. If my free-association had had any connection with my actual life, I would have evolved as a pig. But I followed the pattern of my socialization: cued by the word *sensual*, I became a nice, domestic cat, sitting under a healthy well-

12

watered geranium, watching the sunlight fall through a clean window, over a dust-free window sill, across a polished floor. The room was cozy, with a tea tray by the fire. In another five minutes of meditating evolution, I would have jumped off the window sill and started curling around the leg of a dog.

In fact, parables are unnecessary for recognizing the blatant absurdity of everyday life. Reality is lesson enough. In Houston, Texas, a friend of mine stood and watched her husband step over a pile of toys on the stairs, put there to be carried up. "Why can't you get this stuff put away?" he mumbled. Click! "You have two hands," she said, turning away.

Last summer I got a letter, from a man who wrote: "I do not agree with your last article, and I am cancelling my wife's subscription." The next day I got a letter from his wife saying, "*I* am not cancelling *my* subscription." Click!

On Fire Island my weekend hostess and I had just finished cooking breakfast, lunch, and washing dishes for both. A male guest came wandeing into the kitchen just as the last dish was being put away and said, "How about something to eat?" He sat down, expectantly, and started to read the paper. Click! "You work all week," said the hostesss, "and *I* work all week, and if you want something to eat, you can get it, and wash up after it yourself."

In New York last fall, my neighbors—named Jones—had a couple named Smith over for dinner. Mr. Smith kept telling his wife to get up and help Mrs. Jones. Click! Click! Two women radicalized at once.

A woman I know in St. Louis, who had begun to enjoy a little success writing a grain company's newsletter, came home to tell her husband about lunch in the executive dining room. She had planned a funny little anecdote about the deeply humorous pomposity of executives, when she noticed her husband rocking with laughter. "Ho ho, my little wife in an executive dining room." Click!

Last August, I was on a boat leaving an island in Maine. Two families were with me, and the mothers were discussing the troubles of cleaning up after a rental summer. "Bob cleaned up the bathroom for me, didn't you

13

honey?" she confided, gratefully patting her husband's knee. "Well, what the hell, it's vacation,' he said, fondly. The two women looked at each other, and the queerest change came over their faces. "I got up at six this morning to make the sandwiches for the trip home from this 'vacation,'" the first one said. "So I wonder why I've thanked him at least six times for cleaning the bathroom?" Click! Click!

Attitudes are expressed in semantic equations that simply turn out to be two languages; one for men and another for women. One morning a friend of mine told her husband she would like to hire a baby sitter so she could get back to her painting. "Maybe when you start to make money from your pictures, then we could think about it," said her husband. My friend didn't stop to argue the inherent fallacy in his point—how could she make money if no one was willing to free her for work? She suggested that, instead of hiring someone, he could help with the housework a little more. "Well, I don't know, honey," he said, "I guess sharing the housework is all right if the wife is really contributing something, brings in a salary. . . ." For a terrible minute my friend thought she would kill her husband, right there at breakfast, in front of the children. For ten years, she had been covering furniture, hanging wallpaper, making curtains and refinishing floors so that they could afford the mortgage on their apartment. She had planned the money-saving menus so they could afford the little dinners for prospective clients. She had crossed town to save money on clothes so the family could have a new hi-fi. All the little advances in station—the vacations, the theater tickets, the new car—had been made possible by her crafty, endless, worried manipulation of the household expenses. "I was under the impression," she said, "that I *was* contributing something. Evidently my life's blood is simply a non-deductible expense."

In suburban Chicago, the party consisted of three couples. The women were a writer, a doctor and a teacher. The men were all lawyers. As the last couple arrived, the host said, jovially, "With a roomful of lawyers, we ought to have a good evening." Silence. Click! "What are we?" asked the teacher. "Invisible?"

14

In an office, a political columnist, male, was waiting to see the editor-in-chief. Leaning against a doorway, the columnist turned to the first woman he saw and said, "Listen, call Barry Brown and tell him I'll be late." Click! It wasn't because she happened to be an editor herself that she refused to make the call.

In the end, we are all housewives, the natural people to turn to when there is something unpleasant, inconvenient or inconclusive to be done. It will not do for women who have jobs to pretend that society's ills will be cured if all women are gainfully employed. In Russia, 70 per cent of the doctors and 20 per cent of the construction workers are women, but women still do *all* the housework. Some revolution. As the Russian women's saying goes, it simply freed us to do twice the work.

It will not do for women who are mostly housewives to say that Women's Liberation is fine for women who work, but has no relevance for them. Equal pay for equal work is only part of the argument—usually described as "the part I'll go along with."

We are all housewives. We would prefer to be persons. That is the part they *don't* go along with.

"That broad . . ." begins a male guest who Hasn't Thought.

"Woman," corrects the hostess, smiling meaningfully over her coffeepot.

"Oh, no," groans the guest. "Don't tell me you believe in this Women's Lib stuff!"

"Yes," says the hostess.

"Well, I'll go along with some of it, equal pay for equal work, that seems fair enough," he concedes. Uneasy now, he waits for the male hoots of laughter, for the flutter of wives rushing to sit by their husbands at the merest breath of the subject of Women's Liberation. But that was three or four years ago. Too many moments have clicked in the minds of too many women since then. This year the women in the room have not moved to their husbands' sides; they have . . . solidified. A gelid quality settles over the room. The guest struggles on.

"You can't tell me Women's Lib means I have to wash the dishes, does it?"

"Yes."

They tell us we are being petty. The future improvement of civilization could not depend on who washes the dishes. Could it? Yes. The liberated society—with men, women and children living as whole human beings, not halves divided by sex roles—depends on the steadfast search for new solutions to just such apparently trivial problems, on new answers to tired old questions. Such questions as:

Denise works as a waitress from 6 a.m. to 3 p.m. Her husband is a cabdriver, who moonlights on weekends as a doorman. They have four children. When her husband comes home at night, he asks: *"What's for dinner?"*

Jonathan and Joanne are both doctors. They have identical office hours. They come home in the evening to a dinner cooked by the housekeeper. When they go to bed he drops his clothes on the floor and she picks them up. In the morning he asks: *"Where is my pink and orange striped shirt?"*

In moments of suburban strife, Fred often asks his wife, "Why haven't you mended my shirt and lubricated the car? *What else have you got to do but sit around the house all day?"*

How dare he ask such a question? What sort of bizarre social arrangement is post-industrial-revolution marriage? What kind of relationship involves two people sharing their lives without knowing, or apparently caring, what the other does all day?

According to insurance companies, it would cost Fred $8,000 to $9,000 a year to replace Alice's services if she died. Alice, being an average ideal suburban housewife, works 99.6 hours a week—always feeling there is too much to be done and always guilty because it is never quite finished. Besides, her work doesn't seem important. After all, Fred is paid for doing whatever it is he does. Abstract statistics make no impact on Alice. "My situation is different," she says. Of course it is. All situations are different. But sooner or later she will experience—in a blinding click—a moment of truth. She will remember that she once had other interests, vague hopes, great plans. She will decide that the work in the house is less important than reordering that work so she can consider her own life.

16

The problem is, what does she do then?

The first thing we all do is argue. We present our case: It is unfair that we should bear the whole responsibility for the constant schema of household management; that this burden should be implanted, inescapable, like Mrs. Ramsey's boeuf bourguignon, in our minds.

Soon, we find out that argument serves no practical motivational purpose. We may get agreement, but we will never get cooperation or permission. Rebuttals may begin at the lowest level: "It is a woman's job to wash dishes." Men at a higher stage of enlightenment may argue, "Why do we need a washing machine? I wash my socks and we send everything out." They simply cannot understand that we are the ones who must gather and list and plan even for the laundry we send out. It is, quite simply, *on our minds*. And *not* on theirs. Evenings of explanation and understanding will still end with, "Honey, do I have any clean shorts for tomorrow?" Most women will decide that it is not worth making an issue out of shorts.

In fact, underwear is as good a place to begin as anywhere. Last summer I carried the underwear downstairs, put it in the hamper, sorted it, washed and dried it, folded it, carried it upstairs, and put it away. One day, I decided that as an act of extreme courage I would not carry the laundry upstairs. I put it on the couch in the room with the television set. The family moved it to one side of the couch so they could sit down. I left it there. I put more on the couch. They piled it up. They began to dress off the couch. I began to avoid the television room. At last, guilty and angry, my nerve failed and I carried the laundry upstairs. No one noticed. Out of that experience, I formulated a few rules, which I intend to follow as soon as I finish the painful process of thinking about the assumptions that make them necessary.

(1) *Decide what housework needs to be done. Then cut the list in half.* It is no longer necessary to prove ourselves by being in motion all day and all night. Beds must be made and food cooked, but it is unfair to demand that the family share the work if your standards include cooking like Julia Child and bouncing dimes on the bedspread. Beware of useless and self-defeating stand-

17

ards. It is preposterous and not unusual for a woman to feel her house must look as though no one lived there. Who's looking? Who cares?

(2) *Decide what you will and will not do.* Keep firmly in mind the notion of personal maintenance as an individual responsibility. If children cannot put away their clothes and therefore cannot find them and have to go to school looking like ragpickers—well, presumably they will learn from experience. Their appearance does not make *you* a bad person. (If you can acknowledge and act on that fact, you are becoming liberated.) If you spend four or five hours a day driving your children places, ask yourself why. Are they cripples? Are there no safe streets they can walk along? Why? Seizing responsibility from children has been women's way to compensate for their own lack of responsibility for themselves, and it has resulted in two generations of non-adults.

(3) *Make a plan and present it as final.* There will, of course, be democratic argument, but it is only fair to state your purpose. Not that anyone will pay attention. They will laugh nervously and expect life to go on as usual. Do not be distracted by sophisticated arguments, such as, "Well, let's take the relative value of our days." Yes. Let's. When your husband sits down at his desk after dinner, to use his brain, do you murmur, "Poor darling," as you wash up, tidy the living room, start the wash and check the bathroom for clean towels? Why? A game of role reversal can be most enlightening. A wife who figures out that his important business meeting is no different from her P.T.A. committee meeting may opt for equal hours—and quit her own work at five o'clock.

Another diversionary remark is: "But honey, this isn't a business agreement. This is a home. It is a question of helping each other reach fulfillment." In my home, when I am working against a deadline, I sit in front of a typewriter and shout, "More tea!" The whole family hustles in with more tea. I call out, "Go to bed," "Get some lamb chops." It is an emergency situation and they all spring to, helping me fulfill myself. But *I* am still in charge of remembering to get the lamb chops. It is a problem that may not be solved in my lifetime.

Almost equally difficult is deciding who does what.

18

Men will always opt for things that get finished and stay that way—putting up screens, but not planning menus. Some find washing dishes a peaceful, meditative experience. It has to be worked out. The important thing is to get the argument away from philosophy and onto assigned chores.

(4) *Think revolutionary thoughts*. The nineteenth century ended 73 years ago, but we are still trying to arrange our households according to that "ideal" image of family life. Think of something new. I know a man and woman who decided to stop eating dinner. She had been rushing around putting children to bed, and then laying on a candlelit dinner with three kinds of food on the plate for her husband. They liked chatting at dinner. He helped clean up. They never finished before ten. But one night they discovered that both were dreaming of long cozy evenings reading by the fire. So they have skipped the ritual feast—and replaced it with sandwiches. They get up earlier and have family talks at breakfast. Who knows what daring innovations may follow? He may demand an end to success based on overtime. Both may demand less homework so the children can assume some responsibilities.

This is, after all, part of the revolution we are talking about. The woman in Aspen who imagined herself a snake happened to be a nursing mother. One day a complaining note appeared on the conference bulletin board saying: "Why are there crying babies in the tent? Signed, Father of Five." The conference was discussing designs for the future, and Father of Five learned that in the future, children, and their mothers, will no longer be quarantined. Some*one* does not have to take care of the children, some*two* will share them.

(5) *Never give in*. Empty one dishwasher, and it leads to a lifetime of emptying dishwashers. Remember that nothing will ever get done by anyone else if you do it. If you are the only person who worries about it, perhaps it isn't worth worrying about. If it is very important to you that you not live in a sty, then you must persuade everyone else that what is important to you counts.

It is very hard not to give in. One evening recently two men came to our house for the weekend. "When shall we

19

eat?" they asked, beaming. "Whenever you want," I said, bravely. "I'm not cooking. I'm working tonight." They cooked, while I held myself in my chair by an incredible effort of will, the words blurring before my determined eyes. The next day, I expiated my guilt by going the whole route, including homemade bread. "Ah!" they said. "How wonderful! You are a real woman. And working, too."

(6) *Do not feel guilty*. I have never met a woman who did not feel guilty. We can post signs in our hearts and on our walls saying: "It is not wrong to inconvenience my family—it is making us all responsible, ego-strong adults." But when a man we are attached to goes out with a button off his coat, we—not he—feel feckless. The only near-cure is to have something more interesting to think about. Even if "something to do" means going back to easy courses in school—back to the point where we abdicated for marriage—it is a beginning, and we are older now and will learn rapidly, because at least we know we want things some other way.

(7) *Expect regression. And remember, the next step is human liberation.* The slightest mischance in my life makes me want to fling myself into the protection of someone else's bank account. And yet I still speak of "our money" as clearly separated from "my money." Occasionally, men become liberated and it is a dreadful shock. "I'm not going to work this year; I need to think," announced a friend's husband. She had spent seven years in his care and keeping and then, as she put it, "Finally I get my own business going and *he* wants to lie around all day." Why not? Women who say, "I like my freedom—I have my day organized and I can do what I like with my time," forget that men are entitled to some of that freedom. They are also prisoners of the rigid structure of their roles and jobs.

I cannot imagine anything more difficult than incurring the kind of domestic trauma I describe. It requires the conscious loss of the role we have been taught, and its replacement by a true identity. And what if we succeed? What if we become liberated women who recognize that our guilt is reinforced by the marketplace, which would have us attach our identity to furniture polish and confine our deepest anxieties to color coordinating our toilet paper and our washing machines? What if we overcome our creeping sense of something unnatural when our husbands approach "our" stoves? What if we don't allow ourselves to be treated as people with nothing better to do than wait for repairmen and gynecologists? What if we finally learn that we are not defined by our children and our husbands, but by ourselves? Then we will be able to control our own lives, able to step out into the New Tomorrow. But the sad and solemn truth is that we may have to step out alone.

The more we try, and argue, and change, the more we will realize that the male ego will be the last thing in this world to change. And the *last* place it will change is at home.

Some women pride themselves on the intransigence of their men. I have always taken pride in the liberated attitudes of mine. And yet, last weekend, when I buckled my seat belt in the car, he growled: "You don't have to do that with *me* driving." My God! We were back to Start; he was threatened by my safety measure. How do we argue with feelings like that? With the constant demands to bolster and boost egos grown fat and fragile, with the blocks and jealousies and petty meannesses that drain off our energies? Too often the only way to find ourselves is to leave.

Men's resistance is more subtle than simply leaving the dishes unwashed for a month. A woman I know was married for seventeen years to a man who threatened to smash her sculpture whenever they fought. He complained continuously about the cost of her tools, he laughed at her work in public. When she finally left, she was dazed to discover that the critics found her work excellent.

I have a friend in Cleveland who left high school to marry. She raised two children and worked nights in her husband's office. When she went back to college, it happened mysteriously that they had an exhausting fight the night before every exam. When she still got high marks, he took credit for encouraging her.

I know a writer whose husband never once read her work. She visited an analyst who declared her role conflict a character defect. Her husband told the analyst he wouldn't mind his wife's inadequacies so much if she did

21

something. "But she does write," said the doctor. "Oh. That," said the husband bitterly, dismissing the work he would eventually feel reflected credit on him, but only after their divorce.

No, the question of housework is not a trivial matter to be worked out the day before we go on to greater things. Men do not want equality at home. A strong woman is a threat, someone to be jealous of. Most of all, she is an inconvenience, and she can be replaced. They like things as they are. It's pleasanter.

I had never realized how seductive the role of master is until the other day. I was watering a plant, and the water began to run on the floor. I stood where I was and moaned about the puddle until the live-in babysitter dropped what she was doing and brought me the rag it would have been easier for me to get. She, at least, was not saying, "Don't worry darling, let me take care of it." But my excuse was . . . I have more important things to think about than housework.

I WANT A WIFE

JUDY SYFERS

I belong to that classification of people known as wives. I am A Wife. And, not altogether incidentally, I am a mother.

Not too long ago a male friend of mine appeared on the scene fresh from a recent divorce. He had one child, who is, of course, with his ex-wife. He is obviously looking for another wife. As I thought about him while I was ironing one evening, it suddenly occurred to me that I, too, would like to have a wife. Why do I want a wife?

I would like to go back to school so that I can become economically independent, support myself, and, if need be, support those dependent upon me. I want a wife who will work and send me to school. And while I am going to school I want a wife to keep track of the children's doctor and dentist appointments. And to keep track of mine, too. I want a wife to make sure my children eat properly and are kept clean. I want a wife who will wash the children's clothes and keep them mended. I want a wife who is a good nurturant attendant to my children, who arranges for their schooling, makes sure that they

---

Judy Syfers is married and has two children. To accompany this article, she wanted us to make the following statement: Ms. Syfers wishes to stress that "the problems of an American wife stem from the fact that we live in a society which is structured in such a way as to profit only a few at the expense of the many. As long as we women tolerate such a capitalist system, all but a privileged few of us must necessarily be exploited as workers and as wives."

have an adequate social life with their peers, takes them to the park, the zoo, etc. I want a wife who takes care of the children when they are sick, a wife who arranges to be around when the children need special care, because, of course, I cannot miss classes at school. My wife must arrange to lose time at work and not lose the job. It may mean a small cut in my wife's income from time to time, but I guess I can tolerate that. Needless to say, my wife will arrange and pay for the care of the children while my wife is working.

I want a wife who will take care of *my* physical needs. I want a wife who will keep my house clean. A wife who will pick up after me. I want a wife who will keep my clothes clean, ironed, mended, replaced when need be, and who will see to it that my personal things are kept in their proper place so that I can find what I need the minute I need it. I want a wife who cooks the meals, a wife who is a *good* cook. I want a wife who will plan the menus, do the necessary grocery shopping, prepare the meals, serve them pleasantly, and then do the cleaning up while I do my studying. I want a wife who will care for me when I am sick and sympathize with my pain and loss of time from school. I want a wife to go along when our family takes a vacation so that someone can continue to care for me and my children when I need a rest and change of scene.

I want a wife who will not bother me with rambling complaints about a wife's duties. But I want a wife who will listen to me when I feel the need to explain a rather difficult point I have come across in my course of studies. And I want a wife who will type my papers for me when I have written them.

I want a wife who will take care of the details of my social life. When my wife and I are invited out by my friends, I want a wife who will take care of the baby-sitting arrangements. When I meet people at school that I like and want to entertain, I want a wife who will have the house clean, will prepare a special meal, serve it to me and my friends, and not interrupt when I talk about the things that interest me and my friends. I want a wife who will have arranged that the children are fed and ready for bed before my guests arrive so that the children do not bother us. I want a wife who takes care of the needs of my guests so that they feel comfortable, who makes sure that they have an ashtray, that they are passed the hors d'oeuvres, that they are offered a second helping of the food, that their wine glasses are replenished when necessary, that their coffee is served to them as they like it.

And I want a wife who knows that sometimes I need a night out by myself.

I want a wife who is sensitive to my sexual needs, a wife who makes love passionately and eagerly when I feel like it, a wife who makes sure that I am satisfied. And, of course, I want a wife who will not demand sexual attention when I am not in the mood for it. I want a wife who assumes the complete responsibility for birth control, because I do not want more children. I want a wife who will remain sexually faithful to me so that I do not have to clutter up my intellectual life with jealousies. And I want a wife who understands that *my* sexual needs may entail more than strict adherence to monogamy. I must, after all, be able to relate to people as fully as possible.

If, by chance, I find another person more suitable as a wife than the wife I already have, I want the liberty to replace my present wife with another one. Naturally, I will expect a fresh, new life; my wife will take the children and be solely responsible for them so that I am left free.

When I am through with school and have a job, I want my wife to quit working and remain at home so that my wife can more fully and completely take care of a wife's duties.

My God, who *wouldn't* want a wife?

WHY WOMEN
FEAR SUCCESS

VIVIAN GORNICK

Girls get dumber and dumber as they get older and older.
We all know that. We have all *always* known that. The
girl child matures early, levels off fast, and then slowly
retrogresses. Thousands of females who are positively brilliant in grade school become merely bright in high school,
simply very good in college, and finally, almost mediocre
in graduate school. It is a curious pattern of human development familiar to all of us, one that has come under
formal observation very often in the past 75 years.

The explanation for this peculiar reversal has consisted of obscure references to something in the female
that turns inward, something that is repelled by competition, some natural lack of aggression. Freud said
it, Erikson says it, and the entirety of Western culture
repeats it. All of our observations and predilections have
traditionally supported the idea that women, in the long
haul, simply do not have the constitution for normal
competition; that, in women, the inner necessity to succeed which nourishes and sharpens the intelligence seems
to be missing. In all of the highly perceptive work done
on the relation between motivation and achievement,
none of the information contributed by women adds to our
understanding of this powerful dynamic in human lives, be-

*Vivian Gornick is a New York based writer formerly on
the staff of the Village Voice. She is co-editor of an anthology,
"Women in Sexist Society," and has recently completed a
book about Egypt.*

cause women seem unresponsive to the stimulus to achieve. In fact, they seem dominated by a profound wish to fail.

Eight years ago, Matina Horner,* an experimental psychologist working on the relation between motivation and achievement at the University of Michigan, was as puzzled as the men in her department by the irregular and disturbing results that came exclusively from female subjects. All sorts of data based on information given by the men were successfully fed into the carefully worked-out test model, but when it came to the women, the model went crazy. Nothing meshed; no two sets of women came up with the same kinds of results—ever. In addition, the women tested out abnormally high on anxiety. Bewildered and dissatisfied, the psychologists reluctantly dismissed the women's data as indicating a hopeless "will to fail," impossible to cope with in achievement-motivation work. Dr. Horner, however, sensed that this was not an adequate explanation for what she felt was going on with the women; she stumbled, ultimately, on the idea that the women involved were not exhibiting a will to fail, but rather an active, anxious desire to *avoid success*.

When I met her, Matina Horner, a dark-haired, dark-eyed woman in her early thirties, was assistant professor of clinical psychology at Harvard. She taught three courses in personality, one of them a graduate seminar in the personality development of women. Her office, in a new Harvard building, was a large, bright room overlooking the city of Cambridge. I spent a morning in that room with Dr. Horner. We discussed her work, and inevitably—as we were not only a psychologist and a journalist, but two women as well—we discussed our own lives. (After all, were they not proper subjects for a study of the fear of success in women?)

Dr. Horner spoke slowly; as she warmed to both her subject and her visitor she became more animated.

I asked Dr. Horner what had made her tumble to the idea that it was not the will to fail that was operating in the girl students she had tested, but rather the desire to avoid success.

---

* Since this article was written, Matina Horner has become president of Radcliffe College.

27

"Well," she said, smiling, "the desire to fail comes from some deep psychological conviction that the consequences of failure will be *satisfying*. These girls at Michigan were motivated by the opposite; they were positively anxiety-ridden over the prospect of success. They were not simply eager to fail and have done with it; they seemed to be in a state of anxious conflict over what would happen if they succeeded. It was almost as though this conflict was inhibiting their capacity for achievement."

Intrigued by the intellectual problem that these male-female sexual differences seemed to present, Dr. Horner had decided to work up another model for testing, one that would concentrate on discovering women's actual expectancies in relation to achievement. This approach made use of what is known in scientific jargon as an "expectancy-value theory of motivation." Here the experimenter aims to discover what a subject's expectations are regarding the consequences of an action he or she proposes to take. According to the theory, anxiety is aroused when one expects the consequences to be negative. Thus, anxiety acts as an inhibiting force and produces what scientists call an "avoidance motive." This motive doesn't tell us what someone *will* do, but it indicates clearly what he or she will *not* do.

Out of this approach came a theory Dr. Horner called "the Motive to Avoid Success." The compelling evidence for her theory came from a series of Thematic Appercep-tion Tests she administered to 90 girls and 88 boys, all undergraduates at the University of Michigan. Known to psychologists as T.A.T.s, these tests require the interpretation of a picture or the completion of a story line. The results of those T.A.T.s were startling. As Dr. Horner explains in her first study:

"We asked Phil, a bright young college sophomore . . . to tell us a story based on one clue: *After first-term finals, John finds himself at the top of his medical school class.* Phil writes:

John is a conscientious young man who worked hard. He is pleased with himself. John has always wanted to go into medicine and is very dedicated. . . . John continues working hard and eventually graduates at the top of his class.

28

"Now consider Monica, another honor student. She too has always done well and she too has visions of a flourishing career. We give her the same clue, but with 'Anne' as the successful student. . . . Instead of identifying with Anne's triumph, Monica tells a bizarre tale:

Anne starts proclaiming her surprise and joy. Her fellow classmates are so disgusted with her behavior that they jump on her in a body and beat her. She is maimed for life.

"Next we ask Monica and Phil to work on a series of achievement tests by themselves. Monica scores higher than Phil. Then we get them together, competing against each other on the same kinds of tests. Phil performs magnificently; Monica dissolves into a bundle of nerves.

"The glaring contrast between the two stories and the dramatic changes in competitive situations illustrate important differences between men and women in reacting to achievement . . .

"In response to the successful-male cue (*After first-term finals, John finds himself* . . .) more than 90 per cent of the men in the study showed strong positive feelings, indicated increased striving, confidence in the future and a belief that this success would be instrumental to fulfilling other goals such as providing a secure and happy home for some girl. . . . Fewer than 10 per cent of the men responded at all negatively. . . .

"On the other hand, in response to the successful-female cue, 65 per cent of the girls were disconcerted, troubled or confused by the cue. Unusual excellence in women was clearly associated for them with the loss of femininity, social rejection, personal or societal destruction or some combination of the above. Their responses were filled with negative consequences and affect, righteous indignation, withdrawal rather than enhanced striving, concern, or even an inability to accept the information presented in the cue. For example:

Anne will deliberately lower her academic standing the next term, while she does all she subtly can to help Carl. . . . His grades come up and Anne soon drops out of med school. They marry and he goes on in school while she raises their family.

Anne is a code name for a nonexistent person created

29

*by a group of med students. They take turns taking
exams and writing papers for Anne. . . .*

*Aggressive, unmarried, wearing Oxford shoes and hair
pulled back in a bun, she wears glasses and is terribly
bright.*

"In other words, women showed significantly more
evidence of the motive to avoid success than did men, with
59 of the 90 women scoring high and 8 of the 88 men
doing so."

"What was even more apparent," said Dr. Horner,
swiveling her chair around to face me more directly, "was
that the fear of success manifested itself mainly in women
of demonstrably high intelligence, coming from homes
where high achievement was much valued. Which makes
great sense, when you think about it. After all, a girl
who's not too bright and doesn't have much chance for
success to begin with is hardly likely to be frightened by
the prospect of success. Whereas, a bright girl from a
middle-class home, knowing she actually has it within
her possible grasp . . ."

What happens to most women of this type, continued
Dr. Horner, is simple. In this age of lip-service to equality
and self-realization for all, parents encourage their
daughters to fulfill their entire potential and allow them
some of the advantages given to men. The encouragement,
however, is essentially hollow. Somewhere around a girl's
junior year in college, if not before, the parents' strong desire surfaces: that the girl be securely married, rather than
take the unconventional and risky course of becoming
a serious working person. The contradictory message that
the girl gets, from society as well as from her parents, is
that if she is too smart, too independent, and above all,
too serious about her work, she is unfeminine and will
therefore never get married. (Speculation that the full
brunt of anxiety over femininity and academic achievement
begins to fall upon a woman student about halfway
through college is supported by special studies. For instance, one study revealed that the fear of success in
women ranged from a low 47 per cent in a seventh grade
junior high school sample to a high 88 per cent in a sample
of high-ability undergraduate students at a prominent
Eastern school.)

The woman student in her third year understands then —or primarily then—that she actually has been sent to college to find a husband and to fit herself out as an attractive and educated wife. The important aspect of this reversal of goals is the immediate capitulation in the girl's psyche, a capitulation that parallels the rapidity with which the fear of success then grows in the brightest women students. The implication, clearly, is that the girl is predisposed to accept this notion that femininity and academic achievement are incompatible; that some deep receptivity toward this idea has been developing in her personality almost from birth; some influence beyond the inauthentic encouragement of her parents to become an autonomously developed human being has caused her to internalize the traditional sexual stereotype of passive femininity. Once the thin crust of encouragement is broken, a deep well of social conditioning is discovered underneath. She goes into a tailspin of anxiety as she struggles to reverse her appetite for fulfillment, an appetite she now learns is in direct contradiction to her *feminine* fulfillment.

As Dr. Horner succinctly puts it in her study: "Our data indicate that the emphasis on the new freedom for women has thus far not been any more effective in doing away with this tendency [to avoid success] than were the vote, trousers, cigarettes, and even changing standards of sexual behavior. If anything, our most recent data indicate something of a backlash phenomenon since the mid-sixties. The negative attitudes we find expressed toward successful women have increased to a disproportionately greater extent than have the positive ones, and this is true of both male and female subjects."

Needless to say, such a contradictory state of being is unthinkable for a man, who is taught *from birth* that his human fulfillment and his masculine fulfillment are one and the same. While it is true that achievement-motivation work has raised the fear of success in men, that fear is always coupled with philosophical issues in the man's mind, i.e., an apprehension regarding the values of succeeding in a materialistic or socially amoral culture. It is never coupled with a deep conflict over the crucial and fundamental issue of his masculinity.

31

What happens inside the mind of a woman struggling with such a conflict? Since it has never been properly asknowledged until now, the question has remained unaddressed.

One day Dr. Horner separated out into two piles the results of one of her T.A.T.s. She separated them according to the data collected through other T.A.T.s which had identified some of these same subjects as low in fear of success, and others, as high in fear of success. The T.A.T. cue was *Anne is sitting in a chair with a smile on her face.* Those low in fear of success had responded to the cue with rather pleasant, neutral tales such as:

Anne is happy—she's happy with the world because it is so beautiful. It's snowing, and nice outside—she's happy to be alive and this gives her a warm feeling. . . .

Anne is alone in her room. It's a beautiful day. . . . Her two closet friends have just met marvelous people and believe they are in love. . . . The beautiful day and her nice friends' happiness create an aura of happiness about her. . . .

The stories written by the girls high in fear of success were startlingly different:

Anne is recollecting her conquest of the day. She has just stolen her ex-boyfriend away, right before the High School Senior Prom. . . . She wanted to hurt her friend, and succeeded by taking the boyfriend away underhandedly. . . .

Anne is at her father's funeral. There are over 200 people there. . . . Her mother, two brothers and several relations are there. Anne's father committed suicide . . . She knows it is unseemly to smile but cannot help it. . . . Her brother Ralph pokes her in fury but she is uncontrollable. . . . Anne rises dramatically and leaves the room, stopping first to pluck a carnation from the blanket of flowers on the coffin.

(Anne), a woman in her twenties, is sitting, smiling smugly, in a chair in a small restaurant in New York City. She has just successfully (so far) completed her first robbery (a jewelry store). . . . Gun in hand, she is waiting for her stepmother to return home. A short time earlier, her father was murdered and she believes her stepmother did it. . . .

To think seriously on the meaning of these fantasies in the minds of women who long for and are morbidly afraid of autonomous fulfillment is to come away with fear and sadness. Our culture has made a deep split in the souls of its women, and the result is insupportable anxiety which can bear up only by transforming itself into the malevolence of what is known as passive-aggressive behavior. Behind the "passive" exterior of many women there lies a growing anger over lost energies and confused lives, an anger so sharp in its fury but so diffuse in its focus that one can only describe it as the price society must pay for creating a patriarchal system in the first place, and for now refusing to let it go.

And make no mistake, it is not letting go.

In the summer of 1970 at Harvard University, Dr. Horner tested a group of undergraduate men in order to discover their genuine feelings about successful women. She gave them the T.A.T. cue that she had previously given to women at the University of Michigan, i.e., *After first-term finals, Anne finds herself at the top of her medical school class.* The answers, overwhelmingly, were along the following lines:

Anne is not a woman. She is really a computer, the best in a new line of machines. . . . Anne rushes out of her smelly formaldehyde laboratory, and runs to the university bar where she knows she will find Bruno! The perfect man!

Anne is paralyzed from the waist down. She sits in a wheelchair and studies for medical school. . . .

This from Harvard University. This from the men who will marry the girls at Michigan.

"How has this happened to women?" I asked Dr. Horner. "And how can it *un*-happen?"

"Those are both extremely difficult issues even to *speculate* about," Dr. Horner smiled. "How does it all happen? When does it begin to happen? So fast, so early that it is frightening. My daughter is five years old. One day she came into my room and said to me: 'Mommy, Daddy must love you very much.' 'Why do you say that?' I asked her, pleased that she had made such an assumption. 'Because he doesn't want you to be tired,' she said. 'He does the dishes so that you won't be tired.' . . . Now, it was very nice that the conclusion she came to was that my husband cared for me because he washed the dishes, but the point is, it was a *problem* in her mind, one she had to find a solution for. At five—without any help from us, I can assure you—she knows something is funny if her daddy is doing the dishes!

"The sexual stereotypes are fixed in the minds of girls and of boys almost from birth, and God, do they ever *stay* fixed. I've observed it repeatedly in *myself*. Look, when I was up for my prelims, I went into a state of anxiety like nothing I'd ever known before. I carried on so I frightened my husband and finally, in desperation, he yelled at me: 'For God's sake, maybe women *shouldn't* be in graduate school!' Now, what was I afraid of? I had designed my own prelim, I knew everything I was responsible for. There wasn't the *remotest* possibility of failure; and yet, I was shaking, throwing up, screaming I was stupid and now they'd all know I was stupid.

"Interestingly enough, there was only one time that I remember facing an audience calmly. I rose to speak and was amazed at how quiet and good I felt inside. Then I looked down at myself, and I understood. There I was, seven months pregnant. Nothing I was about to say could contradict *that*. It was my insurance—I was loved, I was about to have a baby, I was in there being a woman— nothing to be afraid of.

"To alter all this is the most complex problem we face now. And it's what we do here. We sit around and we think about these things. My students here at Harvard are marvelous: very bright, very quick, very much taken with these problems. We sit together in our seminars and we ask hard questions. It's exciting to see these ideas taking hold in their minds.

"What we have to do is to get to the bottom of what is genuinely natural in women. What we now call natural is only normative. It is what our culture has defined as normal for women and normal for men, but it sheds no light on what is *natural*. For instance the assertion that women have no natural aggression in them is absurd. Women can be very aggressive even while using 'passive' methods. Silence can be used aggressively. Two little girls getting together in a schoolyard and saying to each

34

other: 'You be my friend and I'll be yours, and we won't be *her* friend'—that's aggressive! Aggression is a desire to exercise will. Passivity is not. Well, God knows, enough women are interested in exercising their wills. . . . So which is it? Is woman aggressive or not? What *is* her nature? This we know next to nothing about. It is this vast area of ignorance that we must explore.

"I think, as far as the future is concerned, that everything depends on where society goes. The counter-culture offers some interesting possibilities, but even those, if you look closely enough, don't get to the heart of the matter as far as women are concerned. For instance, one of the ideas of the counter-culture is that competitiveness is bad. You are a bad *person* if you compete. If this idea should begin to dominate the norm, and women seeking to develop themselves for the first time should then rise to high positions, well they're still in bad shape! Because men define the good. It is what *men* do that determines the values of society, and this no less so in the counter-culture than in the one they left behind.

"But perhaps all these issues—the counter-culture, ecology, liberation from sexual stereotypes—can eventually feed into a new normative world in which women may finally be able to define themselves. I have great hopes."

I walked out into the Cambridge afternoon sun, feeling benign toward every unknown person whose path crossed mine. After all, this campus had given Matina Horner a place to work, a place to continue her search for new answers, and, perhaps more important, a place to examine and discard all those old questions. Here, her gift as a scientist has led her to ask *new* questions about women. And new questions are what Women's Liberation is all about.

THE BLACK FAMILY AND FEMINISM

A Conversation with Eleanor Holmes Norton

CELLESTINE WARE

The anteroom is city government contemporary, all gray metal surfaces. The office of Eleanor Holmes Norton is thickly carpeted and has photographs of Billie Holiday and Charlie Parker on the walls. Ms. Norton is the chairman of the New York City Commission on Human Rights, and holds the additional position of Executive Assistant to Mayor Lindsay. She has become the city government's foremost champion of the rights of minority men and all women.

I was surprised to see a tawny brown-skinned woman, so slight as to seem frail, sitting behind a big desk. Eleanor Norton photographs a lot larger than she is. She talks so rapidly that she often doesn't finish sentences as her minds swoops two thoughts ahead. We were constantly interrupted by phone calls and people, all handled with the Norton dispatch and friendliness.

As she finished persuading a telephone caller to endorse a letter asking women to attend a meeting of the Manhattan Women's Political Caucus, she mused: "This is the first time I've known of black and white women working together in a feminist context. It's encouraging."

We settled down, in spite of phone calls, and began to talk.

Cellestine: You once stated that "the chief effect of

Cellestine Ware, a founder of the New York Radical Feminists, is working on two books, one an interpretation of black art, the other a novel.

racism for black women has been that it has divided them from black men and thus from love." Will you explain what you meant?

Eleanor: Black people have felt very defensive on the family question. There's been a great distortion and lack of honesty in the whole picture of the black family. White people do not understand its strengths, but it's also true that black people don't always come to grips with its weaknesses. Because any woman who has that many children needs to have somebody love her. And if the only way she's found that love is through involvement with a man who leaves her when the child is born, then she'll continue without thinking that ultimately such a man may do her more harm than good. I think that this is the predicament of a large number of urban black women. Until we clear up this weakness among us, we are never going to be a wholly independent and viable people. The big weakness is that, in a hugely disproportionate number of cases, black men are not living with their women and children. That's what has led some black women to think that the first order of business is getting "behind" the black man, though I think the real answer is reconstructing the black family on strongly egalitarian lines, with the understanding that children need both a mother and a father. In New York the number of female-headed families is increasing. A welfare mother who has seven or eight children and no husband has more children than any single person can keep under control. A woman who has child after child by man after man is on a search for love and needs to be involved with a man.

Cellestine: Are you saying that because a woman associates love with involvement with a man that terminates in having a child, she will seek to repeat that experience again and again?

Eleanor: Yes, I think that's the syndrome. More attention needs to be paid to the individual black woman who goes through this cycle, rather than to reforming the welfare system. We who are lawyers have spent the last ten years being great reformers of the welfare system, and I tell you, people on welfare are just as badly off as when we started. It is an illusion that welfare reform will solve the problems of the poor urban black woman.

I think that racism has undermined the role of many black men. All societies are sexist. Therefore, if they are trying to enact an oppressive system, they go after those they consider powerful—the males. They can deal with the women by rape and defamation, as they always have, but American society considers a very special effort necessary to dethrone and castrate the black man. That castration was systematized through slavery. While black women suffered as much through slavery as anybody else, the long-lasting effects on black men, it seems to me, were far more devastating because men were debased from a higher position. They had much farther to fall!

Cellestine: Would you then say that the chief effect of racism has been different for black men than it has for black women? You said that the chief effect of racism on black women has been that it has divided them from men and love. Are you saying that the separation from love and from his woman was not the most important loss that the black man suffered through slavery?

Eleanor: Only because, in a sexist society, men are not brought up, as women are, to rely so completely on love and the need for the person of the opposite sex to be permanently with them. The most important thing for a man is to achieve. The fact that black men were kept from achieving has been their biggest problem. And, of course, we black women have had to bear some of their resentment for being unable to fill the role this society calls "masculine."

Cellestine: It seems to me that some of the solutions you suggest accept the idea of sexism. For instance, you once said, and I think this contradicts other things that you have said, "Our special role in helping the black male is to help regain what was taken from him in greater proportion than from black women by slavery and racism." That seems to accept the idea of sexism and to base your solutions on an acceptance of it.

Eleanor: I think that we black women have a special role with the psychologically bruised man. It's incumbent on a black woman to help him find his way back. She may not have been bruised because she happened to be a little girl and nobody thought it as important to bruise little black girls psychologically. When such a man was growing up in a ghetto, everyone told him he was shit. His mother began by telling him, "You're just like your no-good father who left me when you were three months old."

My husband and his brother, alone among their peers, grew up in a stable, conventional household. His father was a postal clerk and his mother was a seamstress who worked at home. You've never seen a more stable household in the patriarchal style. This stable environment made such a difference that even though Edward was growing up in Harlem during the fifties, when heroin first came to the area, he became a lawyer and his brother John became a doctor, and their father had no money at all.

Cellestine: In fact, the patriarchal household was the experience of most of the black people I grew up with, in the Middle West.

Eleanor: That's true for the great majority of blacks, but the female-headed household occurs with disproportionate frequency in New York and other big cities. About a third of the children in New York grow up in fatherless households.

Cellestine: I'd like to ask you if it's possible for a woman—supposing she is as intelligent and talented as the man, with her own needs to use her abilities—to marry and please the psychologically bruised black man?

Eleanor: You have a point. It was no accident that I was out of law school and practicing law before I got married, because there are not many males, black or white, who wish to get involved with a woman who's committed to her own development in the sense that I am. The number of black men who can accept such women is probably no more than that of white men.

Cellestine: But, white men are so used to having power. If you get into a relationship with one, you have even more conflict over equality. Do you think that the experience of black men has prepared them for sexual equality better than other American men, since black survival had so often depended on strong women? And what do you feel about those black men who are formidably opposed to black women's involvement in feminism?

Eleanor: I don't take their opposition too seriously. There was a Black Power conference about three years

39

ago in Newark, and some of that crap about black men's opposition to feminism came out then. You notice that Black Power has retreated into the woodwork in terms of the media. One of the things they harped on at the Black Power conference was abortion—the idea that abortion is genocide, because we have to expand the black race. Considering the number of sisters who have been hacked to death trying to get rid of an unwanted fetus, you have to say that any black man who speaks against abortion has no moral capital. He's allowing a kind of genocide from butchered abortions. By the time the abortion reform bill went through two years ago, there wasn't a black male voice raised against it. I think the sisters had set some brothers straight.

White people have said, and some black men have agreed with them, that black men resent the strength of black women. I think that a man who has had a good relationship with a strong black woman knows the value of her strength and sees that his development has been enhanced. Many times, she has been the difference between eating and going hungry, between staying in school and dropping out. A man raised by or married to such a woman will not be intimidated by the fact that she was strong enough to persevere. I think that there are more black men like that than the fringe voices would indicate. I've got to believe that, or else we're sicker than I think. Are there that many insecure black men in the world?

Cellestine: Yes. I've met too many high school and college women who say, or feel they have to say, "Get behind your black man." They feel that a black woman has no business joining the Women's Liberation movement.

Eleanor: I know there are those voices, but you have to ask yourself if they are representative voices. Let the white people talk about "matriarchy." Let us recognize what black women have done and had to do in the home, without adding to the myth of matriarchy. Nothing could divide black people more than for us to say, after fighting for equality for our race, that half of it ought to stay back, to be *un*equal.

Cellestine: In my class, we read a textbook that said

black male slaves had suffered more than black female slaves because women are accustomed to submission.

Eleanor: I don't think to admit that is to admit anything except the fact that most societies are sexist. All I can say is that I condemn any society, black or white, in which women wouldn't feel as demeaned as men by slavery.

Cellestine: But I'm saying that, in a sexist society, women *do* feel as demeaned as men. I was born in America where men are more powerful than women, and I say that I have suffered as much from racism as a black man.

Eleanor: Well, I think you have too. But when taking yourself as an example, you are describing a girl who had a sense of herself, her capabilities and her ego. Somehow, you got raised right. Now, think for a moment about the girl who's been raised as a girl. Her brother's going to college. She isn't. That girl has come down so far when she's told at age eighteen, "Go out and have some babies." When you were told that, you couldn't accept it.

Cellestine: I get scared by the fact that these black anti-feminists are at the most impressionable age.

Eleanor: And the explanation that I've given is not their explanation. They really believe that men are more important than women, and that therefore men suffered more.

Cellestine: Then why did you say in your essay "Sadie and Maude" that returning the black male to his historic strength in the family unit is the foremost task of the black struggle today?

Eleanor: Ultimately, the theme of that essay was that black people, having been deprived of the ability to follow the pattern of American family life, have a chance to start anew, to build a different kind of life where men and women are equal. Let's build an entirely new kind of family with the recognition that there may be two people who work, two people who are strong, and nobody has to be dependent. That's the only version of family life I consider viable for black people. Black family life will be a disaster if it copies white family life.

41

WOMEN AND WAR

DANIEL ELLSBERG

The Pentagon Papers have been studied a great deal, but they don't give up their secrets easily. For one thing, they are often examined mainly to find out which official was more or less wrong, more or less guilty of misjudgments —an interesting exercise, but not one that sheds light on why almost *all* our officials made similar misjudgments during the 25 years we have been in Indochina. The second problem is that the Papers themselves don't explain the underlying motive of the decision-makers. Those are buried so deeply that explanations of policy don't include them.

The paradox is this: why did our officials continue to escalate in spite of intelligence estimates that made it clear, before each decision to escalate, that the chosen measure could not bring victory? The Papers clearly disprove the theory that we were deluded into believing victory was just around the corner. Most decisions to increase bombing or troop strength were taken in an atmosphere of desperation and great pessimism. What made so many officials feel desperate? What made so many intelligent men make so many unrealistic decisions for so long?

Daniel Ellsberg is a foreign policy expert, former Pentagon adviser in Washington and State Department official in Vietnam, and the disseminator of the Pentagon Papers. This article was edited from a transcribed conversation between Daniel Ellsberg and the editors of "Ms." The conversation took place while the Vietnam War was in full swing, and peace settlement was nowhere in sight.

In fact, the Pentagon Papers pose more questions than they answer. They offer only rhetorical explanations—the Domino Theory, for instance, which dates back to the Truman Administration. But documentation also makes it clear that this theory was challenged by at least some expert analysts every step of the way, that it was less arrived at inevitably than chosen—chosen as the preferred perception by the officials themselves.

Over the last several years, I have tried to search for data and hypotheses that might explain this paradox. The main thing implicit in the Pentagon Papers is a great and sometimes irrational fear of losing; both the decision-maker's fear of appearing irresolute or "soft," and his perception of the American voter's inability to accept defeat.

At a personal level, the language used—both in writing, as seen in the Pentagon Papers, and in the verbal versions I used to hear in policy discussions—was very dependent on sports analogies, wartime analogies, phrases indicating toughness, guts, and a mastery of people and circumstance. This is truer of group discussions than private ones, and most true of public speeches. In other words, the language itself reflects the officials' perception of their colleagues' need, and of the voters' even greater need, to reject any possibility of defeat.

Their perception is not necessarily related to polls or actual election results at all. The proof of a public need to avoid defeat at any cost is searched for until it is found. The punishment of the Democrats for allegedly losing China to the Communists was often brought up, for instance. But contemporary polls showing that the majority of American voters wanted to get out of Indochina—even felt that being there in the first place was a mistake—those polls were much less present in the official consciousness.

There was an assumption that Government officials knew better than the voters what those voters' reactions would be. They might now *think* they could accept a defeat, but the officials knew that they could not.

In November, 1969, for instance, Nixon explained his decision against withdrawing from Vietnam explicitly in terms of protecting the American nation from the feeling of being "a helpless giant." At first, he said, many people would feel relieved by a withdrawal and would thank him for it. But, as they thought about it—as they woke up the morning after, as I would paraphrase it—they would be filled with remorse, revulsion, and shame.

Nixon, like other Presidents before him, was making a judgment of the American character. His perception of a native inability to accept defeat is one that many would agree with. But was it really true? I began to gather data, based particularly on analyses of polls taken over the past five or six years. If his character judgment was accurate, then it would be a factor distributed among all classes and all kinds of social groups.

The fear of defeat might logically be thought especially strong among blue-collar workers and the less educated, who would demand a powerful country with which they could identify.

In fact, I found startling evidence to the contrary. The lowest-income groups are the most dovish; likewise the least educated. People with a grade school education are more likely to be against the war than those with a high school education, and they, in turn, are more dovish than the college educated. Young people used to be more hawkish than the old. The least hawkish of all were those over 50. Since 1968, older people have become even more dovish, but they have been outstripped in change of attitude by the young, now far more likely to oppose war as a result of Vietnam. The black population has been and continues to be more anti-war in general than the white population.

These results ran counter to expectation in many ways, but I'll just summarize by saying that, as far as hawkishness is concerned, it is closely related to higher social and economic status. In other words, our policy-making officials were from that part of the population most likely to be hawkish: white, male, well educated, high income, with a drive for increased status.

Throughout these data, the most striking exception to official expectations was women. Regardless of race and socioeconomic position, they were statistically less likely than men to support the war—and this held true even if they were married to men of the group most likely to be hawkish. Going back to 1964 and 1965, and including

44

the referendums on the war which have been held in various communities since 1966, this pattern held true. I'm speaking statistically now. There are obviously individual women who are as hawkish or more so than many men. But on the average, the difference was much greater than I would have supposed.

The man who first showed me these polls, Andre Modigliani, is a social psychologist at Harvard. After clearly noting the sex difference in his own analysis, he hypothesized that it might be related to the fact, also confirmed in his studies, that women tend to read less about foreign affairs than men do. The other groups previously noted as dovish also read less. He concluded that anti-war sentiment simply reflected a lower level of awareness about the war.

I argued that this neglected the question of *why* women, and others identified as "out" groups, chose to read less. Might they not share the simple perception that the war had little relevance to their needs and America's needs? Might they not share a skepticism about the information handed down to them by the white-middle- or upper-class men who dominate the media and policy-making?

Checking on women's attitudes during World War II, I discovered a startling difference: women supported that war to about the same degree that men did. With or without reading, women old enough to have lived through World War II seemed to have judged it "necessary," but the same women often changed their minds when confronted with Indochina. To a much greater degree than men of the same age—and this applies to me, as of the mid-sixties—they were capable of seeing a difference between the two wars.

I began to ask some of the men who had worked with me in the Pentagon—men clearly devoted to a military victory, or at least to saving face internationally by not losing—what their wives thought about the war. In virtually every case, I found the wives had been strongly opposed to the war for some time. Occasionally, it had become a problem in the marriage itself. (I remember especially questioning one of my superiors, a man I knew was working fourteen hours a day on the war. "My wife?" he said. "She thinks we're crazy.") But the husbands were more likely to perceive the difference in attitude as a matter of personality, not a feminine cultural or group distinction.

The wives, on the other hand, said very clearly that women just feel differently than men about such issues. There was amazing unanimity on that point. They often cited motherhood as the basis of the difference—even those women who were not themselves mothers. Having borne and cared for a child was supposed to be the reason women didn't want that child sent off to war. When I noted the fact that a son has *two* parents, women accepted the idea that both parents ought to care equally about a son's death, but they still maintained that men were different. Some cited the fact that mothers were more likely than fathers to support their draft-resisting sons. Some were shockingly frank about their feeling that most men would even encourage their sons to go off to war, that the father's manhood was somehow diminished if the son did not go. To say that is to say a man is willing to sacrifice his son for his own personal, psychological needs.

The more I questioned, the more I became aware of a cultural chasm which, as a man, I had ignored, but which women had simply been taking for granted. It seemed true even at the highest levels. It has been widely reported, for instance, that Robert McNamara's wife and children were very critical of the war, even while he was Secretary of Defense, and that they had caused him to question some of the Johnson Administration decisions. President Johnson himself reported that his doubts about the war in 1968 stemmed in part from his daughter's objections to the senselessness of her husband and other young men going off to fight

In fact, I should have become aware of it earlier myself. I had experienced it socially.

The first date I had with my wife, Patricia, for instance, was on a Saturday in the spring of 1965. McNamara had gone to visit the Johnson ranch in Texas, so I had my first Saturday off from the Pentagon in seven months. I decided to call Patricia, whom I'd just met briefly at a party. She said she was covering an anti-Vietnam rally at the Washington Monument for her radio show, and I could come along if I liked.

46

I did, though the last thing I wanted to hear on a day off was more speeches about Vietnam. As it turned out, I had to go back to the Pentagon for an emergency that night. Patricia and her friends, who were totally in sympathy with the rally, couldn't understand how I could work for the Pentagon, an attitude that I found very unfair at the time. After all, I still thought it was possible to bring reason and evidence to bear on our policy decisions. And that's what I was trying to do. Later, when my own opinions had begun to change, my memory of her skepticism helped me to see the war more clearly, to see that I could not change a process that was built on false needs and assumptions, a process that had a life of its own.

It wasn't only Patricia. That whole year, I'd found it difficult to ask women out, both because of the long Pentagon hours and because some atrocity would occur that women I knew opposed. The first time we used tear gas, which I, too, had opposed, I couldn't say hello to women friends without being denounced just for working in the Pentagon. I was made much more aware than my married colleagues of how unacceptable our Vietnam policies were.

Early in 1971, I spoke at a League of Women Voters meeting in Massachusetts. By this time, I had become fascinated with male-female cultural differences and had come to think women's values were a major hope of saving the country from its patterns of machismo and violence. I was heartened, really, to see that a set of values existed among many Americans—in fact, roughly half the population—that were different from those held by the men in power, and that might therefore replace the ruling values. So I asked the women at the League meeting to raise their hands if they believed then, at the beginning of 1971, that the 1969 Goodell Resolution taking the country out of the war should have passed.

Virtually every woman in the audience raised her hand. Then I asked how many had reached that position well before their husbands had. Again, as far as I could see, almost every woman raised her hand. Finally, I asked how many women present had taken some direct action to oppose the war. Almost no hands went up.

I tell this story for two reasons. First, it indicates that

cultural differences between men and women do exist at a very concrete level. Second, it shows that some women don't want to accept that fact, and many more are not fully acting on it. If women *did* accept it and were less afraid of losing the approval of men, would there still be secretaries in the Pentagon? Would there be doves sleeping with hawks? Wouldn't there be more resistance from women at every level?

Some of those objections may sound frivolous or impossible, but I mean them seriously. I remember touring our Pacific bases in 1960 and talking to our Commander in Japan. He brought up the problem of keeping an American base in Japan in spite of deep-seated resentment of the Japanese-American security treaty, and told me that the Japanese could force us out any time they wanted to. How? "Well," he said without a smile, "they could just take away the maids."

It isn't a facetious idea. I would like to see secretaries strike the Pentagon and the State Department, and see women impede the war machine at every level. The consumer boycott is probably women's natural weapon since, whether or not the money is theirs, they make 80 per cent of the purchases. All the companies that depend on the war, particularly those that make anti-personnel weapons, should be boycotted. Maybe some of the women in those companies could run strategic labor strikes. There could be demonstrations and obstruction of bases and military shipments. We haven't seen the kind of militant women who chained themselves to the White House fence since the Suffrage Movement. It's time they came back. We need them.

This may seem to be putting an undue burden on women: to cure the country of a cancer to which women contributed least of all. Other groups must act too: all the young people, working people and minorities who are against the war. In other words, it is those who are really against the war who will have to stop it.

But I think we have to face the fact that the war will be almost endless until this kind of activist coalition stops it. Now, we are waiting for a group of white, middle-aged, highly-educated men to change their minds. Yet they are precisely the group that spawned the war in the first place, and they are the most vulnerable to the Masculine Mystique that allows its continuation. These are the men who have sacrificed thousands of American and Vietnamese soldiers—and millions of Indochinese civilians—to their own cultural inability to admit defeat. I don't believe the country can afford to wait for their change of heart. True, we must not give up pressuring them, but we must take action at the same time.

Our Congressmen and Senators must be forced to obey a popular resistance movement. So far, even the most dovish men in Washington have not been willing to do for peace what Southern Senators have long been willing to do for segregation—to filibuster against the war and against all appropriations for it.

Women who are considering personal resistance should remember that the policy-makers, in and out of Government, see the opposition of their children as less invidious and challenging than the opposition from their wives or female contemporaries. Their children's hostility is explained away with Generation Gap arguments. "If only these kids had been through World War II, they'd understand the danger of expansionist powers." Or, "The kids will change, they'll see the light." But women who have been through exactly the same years and experiences as the men supporting the war—if *they* confronted these men, together with their children, it would be much more threatening.

We must gratefully admit that the young people have had an enormous impact. If you ask some policy-makers why Nixon doesn't feel free to bomb North Vietnam heavily, they'll explain that the kids wouldn't allow it. That means parents are allowing their children to put their careers and bodies on the line, in demonstrations and in draft resistance, to change policies most of us know are destructive and wrong. But the anti-war movement has to be a much broader coalition to work. Women may be the heart and soul of it.

I hope women will put ending the war very high on their list of priorities. After all, women are never going to be considered as Presidential material as long as the President is viewed primarily as the Commander of our Armed Forces. Women don't want to imitate that role, and they shouldn't. They should humanize leadership roles for both men and women.

Perhaps women and their cultural values will save this country from itself. And for all of us.

WELFARE IS A
WOMEN'S ISSUE

JOHNNIE TILLMON

I'm a woman. I'm a black woman. I'm a poor woman. I'm a fat woman. I'm a middle-aged woman. And I'm on welfare.

In this country, if you're any one of those things, you count less as a person. If you're *all* those things, you just don't count, except as a statistic.

I am a statistic.

I am 45 years old and I have raised six children.

I grew up in Arkansas, and I worked there for fifteen years in a laundry, making about $20 or $30 a week, picking cotton on the side for carfare. I moved to California in 1959 and worked in a laundry for nearly four years. In 1963, I got too sick to work anymore. My husband and I had split up. Friends helped me to go on welfare.

They didn't call it welfare. They called it A.F.D.C.— Aid to Families with Dependent Children. Each month I got $363 for my kids and me. I paid $128 a month rent; $30 for utilities, which included gas, electricity, and water; $120 for food and non-edible household essentials; $50 for school lunches for the three children in junior and

---

Johnnie Tillmon organized the nation's first welfare rights group in the Watts area of Los Angeles in 1963 and was first chairwoman of the National Welfare Rights Organization. She is currently N.W.R.O.'s Executive Director. This article is excerpted from conversations with Ms. Tillmon by Nancy Steffen, a former N.W.R.O. staff member.

senior high school who were not eligible for reduced-cost meal programs. This left exactly $5 per person per month for everything else—clothing, shoes, recreation, incidental personal expenses and transportation. This check allowed $1 a month for transportation for me but none for my children. That's how we lived.

There are millions of statistics like me. Some on welfare. Some not. And some, really poor, who don't even know they're entitled to welfare. Not all of them are black. Not at all. In fact, the majority—about two-thirds—of all the poor families in the country are white.

Welfare's like a traffic accident. It can happen to anybody, but especially it happens to women.

And that's why welfare is a women's issue. For a lot of middle-class women in this country, Women's Liberation is a matter of concern. For women on welfare it's a matter of survival.

That's why we had to go on welfare: survival. And that's why we can't get off now.

We've been raised to expect to work, all our lives, for nothing. We're the worst educated, the least-skilled and the lowest-paid people there are. We're the most liable to disease, disability, early death, and unemployment. And we've got to carry alone the whole responsibility for our children. Bit by bit, society has pecked away at our independence and pride, and then, when we're pecked nearly clean, it's blamed us for being "dependent."

That's what a welfare check is: a certificate of blame. And it arrives every month.

Welfare is the most anti-woman institution in this country, even more than marriage, which it tries to imitate. Let me explain that a little.

Forty-four per cent of all poor families are headed by women. That's bad enough. But 99 per cent of all A.F.D.C. families are headed by women. That means there is no man around. In half the states there really can't be men around because A.F.D.C. says if there is an "able-bodied" man around, then you can't be on welfare. If the kids are going to eat, and the man can't get a job, then he's got to go. So his kids can eat.

The truth is that A.F.D.C. is like a super-sexist marriage. You trade in *a* man for *the* man. But you can't divorce him if he treats you bad. He can divorce you, of course, cut you off anytime he wants. But in that case, *he* keeps the kids, not you.

The man runs everything. In traditional marriage, sex is supposed to be for your husband. On A.F.D.C., you're not supposed to have any sex at all. You give up control of your own body. It's a condition of aid. You may even have to agree to get your tubes tied so you can never have more children just to avoid being cut off welfare.

The man, the welfare system, controls your money. He tells you what to buy, what not to buy, where to buy it, and how much things cost. If things—rent, for instance —really cost more than he says they do, it's just too bad for you. He's always right. Everything is budgeted down to the last penny; and you've got to make your money stretch.

The man can break into your house and poke into your things and you've got no right to protest. You've got no right to privacy when you go on welfare.

Like I said, welfare's a supersexist marriage.

In fact, welfare was invented mostly for women. It grew out of something called the Mother's Pension Laws. To be eligible, you had to be female, you had to be a mother, you had to be "worthy." "Worthy" meant were your kids "legitimate," was your home "suitable," were you "proper"?

In 1935, the Mother's Pension Laws became part of the Social Security system. And they changed the name of the program to Aid to Families with Dependent Children.

Of course now there are other welfare programs, other kinds of people on welfare—the blind, the disabled, the aged. (Many of them are women, too, especially the aged.) Those others make up just over a third of all the welfare caseloads. We A.F.D.C.s are two-thirds. But when the politicians talk about the "welfare cancer eating at our vitals," they're not talking about the aged, blind and disabled. Nobody minds them. They're the "deserving poor." Politicians are talking about A.F.D.C., talking about us, talking about women and children as if we were a disease to be cured.

In fact, welfare isn't even for mothers. It's for the children. It's like a bonus for reproducing the race. Some

53

bonus—all of $720 a year or $60 a month for a family of four if you live in Mississippi. It's more in other places —up to $324 a month for a family of four in New Jersey. But nowhere, nohow, is it enough to live on.

In this country, we believe in something called the "work ethic." That means that your work is what gives you human worth. But the work ethic itself is a double standard. It applies to men, and to women on welfare. It doesn't apply to all women. If you're a society lady from Scarsdale and you spend all your time sitting on your prosperity paring your nails, well, that's okay. Women aren't supposed to work. They're supposed to be married.

But if you don't have a man to pay for everything, particularly if you have kids, then everything changes. You've "failed" as a woman, because you've "failed" to attract and keep a man. There's something wrong with you. It can't possibly be the man's fault, his lack of responsibility. It must be yours. That's why Governor Reagan can get away with slandering A.F.D.C. recipients, calling them "lazy parasites," "pigs at the trough," and such. We've been trained to believe that the only reason people are on welfare is because there's something wrong with their character. If people have "motivation," if people only *want* to work, they can, and they will be able to support themselves and their kids in decency.

If this were true, we wouldn't have the working poor. Right now, 66 per cent of the "employable" mothers are already employed—many full time—but at such pitifully low wages that we still need, and are entitled to, public assistance to survive.

The truth is a job doesn't necessarily mean an adequate income. A woman with three kids—not twelve kids, mind you, just three kids—that woman, earning the full Federal wage of $1.80 an hour, is still stuck in poverty. She is below the Government's own official poverty line. There are some ten million jobs that now pay less than the minimum wage, and if you're a woman, you've got the best chance of getting one. Why would a 45-year-old woman work all day in a laundry ironing shirts at 90-some cents an hour? Because she knows there's some place lower she could be. She could be on welfare. Society needs women on welfare as "examples" to let every

54

woman, factory workers and housewife workers alike, know what will happen if she lets up, if she's laid off, if she tries to go it alone without a man. So these ladies stay on their feet or on their knees all their lives instead of asking *why* they're only getting 90-some cents an hour, instead of daring to fight and complain.

And still, 33 per cent of the employable mothers are looking for work.

We are this country's source of cheap labor. And often willing to be. But we can't, many of us, get any jobs.

The President keeps repeating the "dignity of work" idea. What dignity? Wages are the measure of dignity that society puts on a job. Wages and nothing else. There is no dignity in starvation. Nobody denies, least of all poor women, that there is dignity and satisfaction in being able to support your kids through honest labor.

We wish we could do it.

The problem is that our country's economic policies deny the dignity and satisfaction of self-sufficiency to millions of people—the millions who suffer every day in underpaid dirty jobs—and still don't have enough to survive.

People still believe that old lie that A.F.D.C. mothers keep on having kids just to get a bigger welfare check. On the average, another baby means another $35 a month—barely enough for food and clothing. Having babies for profit is a lie that only men could make up, and only men could believe.

There are a lot of other lies that male society tells about welfare mothers: That A.F.D.C. mothers are immoral. That A.F.D.C. mothers are lazy, misuse their welfare checks, spend it all on booze and are stupid and incompetent.

If people are willing to believe these lies, it's partly because they're just special versions of the lies that society tells about *all* women.

For instance, the notion that all A.F.D.C. mothers are lazy: that's just a negative version of the idea that women don't work and don't want to. It's a way of rationalizing the male policy of keeping women as domestic slaves.

The notion that A.F.D.C. mothers are immoral is another way of saying that all women are likely to become whores unless they're kept under control by men and marriage.

A.F.D.C. mothers misuse their welfare checks? That's simply a justification for harassment. It comes from the male theory that women have no head for money, that they're naturally frivolous. In fact, an A.F.D.C. mother's probably got a better head for money than Rockefeller. She has to. She has so little to begin with that she's got to make every penny count, if she and her kids are even going to survive.

A.F.D.C. mothers are stupid, incompetent? That allows welfare officials to feel good about being paternalistic and justifies their policy of preventing A.F.D.C. mothers from making decisions about their own lives. It even explains why people are on welfare in the first place: because they're dumb, because there's something wrong with them.

A.F.D.C. mothers are the cause of slums and high taxes? Well, what's that but a special version of the notion that Eve, and Eve only, brought sin into the world? Welfare isn't the cause of high taxes. War is. Plus a lot of other things that poor women would like to see changed.

Society can continue to believe these lies only so long as women themselves believe them, as long as women sit still for them. Even many of my own sisters on welfare believe these things about themselves. Many women on welfare never get over their shame. But those of us who get beyond it are some of the strongest, most liberated women in this country.

To understand how this can be, you've got to remember that women on welfare are subject to all the same phony "female" ideals as all other women. But at the same time they're denied any opportunity to test out those ideals.

On TV, a woman learns that human worth means beauty and that beauty means being thin, white, young and rich. She learns that her body is really disgusting the way it is, and that she needs all kinds of expensive cosmetics to cover it up. She learns that a "real woman" spends her time worrying about how her bathroom bowl smells; that being important means being middle class, having two cars, a house in the suburbs, and a wardrobe full of clothes. In other words, an A.F.D.C. mother learns

56

being a "real woman" means being all the things she isn't and having all the things she can't have.

Either it breaks you, and you start hating yourself, or you break it.

There's one good thing about welfare. It kills your illusions about yourself, and about where this society is really at. It's laid out for you straight. You have to learn to fight, to be assertive, or you just don't make it. If you can survive being on welfare, you can survive anything. It gives you a kind of freedom, a sense of your own power and togetherness with other women.

Maybe it is we poor welfare women who will really liberate women in this country.

Along with other welfare recipients, we have organized together so we can have some voice. Our group is called the National Welfare Rights Organization (N.W.R.O.). We put together our own welfare plan, called Guaranteed Adequate Income (G.A.I.), which would eliminate sexism from welfare. There would be no "categories"—men, women, children, single, married, kids, no kids—just poor people who need aid. You'd get paid according to need and family size only—$6,500 for a family of four (which is the Department of Labor's estimate of what's adequate), and that would be upped as the cost of living goes up.

Of course, nobody in power—and that means rich, white men—wants anything to do with G.A.I. It's too "radical." So it's still just a plan. For the time being.

President Nixon had a welfare plan, too. During his first term. He called it F.A.P.—the Family Assistance Plan—and said it would solve the "welfare crisis" (and, incidentally, some of his own political problems) by putting an "income floor" under all poor people. That sounded pretty good, and a lot of Welfare Experts bought it. But the real welfare experts, we women who have to make the checks stretch, we were better shoppers. We understood from the first that F.A.P. wasn't a reform at all, but a disguised repression. We understood that "establishing an income floor" really meant chopping the floor out from under A.F.D.C. mothers and children.

So we organized and we fought the F.A.P., fought it in the Congress and in our own states, steadily for years. And we won. The F.A.P. is dead now, and we helped kill

57

it. We were poor and we were women and we were lots of us black, the most powerless single group in the nation. Yet, by united political effort, we prevented the most powerful single man in the nation from having something he wanted, politically, very bad.

The F.A.P. is dead. But there are other sticks to hit us with. President Nixon has stopped talking about welfare bills; he's leaving the "reforming" up to the local authorities. All this means that the states now have a free hand to "economize" their mistakes at the expense of A.F.D.C. mothers and children. Flat grants, forced work requirements, eligibility "scandals" and restrictions —bit by bit the politicians peck away at us, "streamlining" government by scapegoating poor women. Only now, there's no place left in the federal government that we can come to for even token justice and help.

As far as I'm concerned, the women of N.W.R.O. are the front-line fighters for women's freedom, both because we have so few illusions and because our issues are so important to all women:

The right to an adequate wage for work, no matter where that work is done, in the home or in a factory.

The right to adequate child care—if and when a woman wants it, where she wants it, and at a cost that still leaves her with an adequate income.

The right to *choose*, with dignity, when she will have children and how many, whether she will work outside her home, and what kind of work is right for her.

When we have fought for and won all these rights, we will have finally won the basic right we should never have had to fight for: the *right to life*, guaranteed to us by the Constitution.

If I were President, I would solve the so-called welfare crisis in a minute and go a long way toward liberating every woman. I'd just issue a proclamation that women's work is *real* work. In other words, I'd start paying women a living wage for doing the work we are already doing— child-raising and housekeeping. And the welfare crisis would be over, just like that. Housewives would be getting wages, too—a legally determined percentage of their husband's salary—instead of having to ask for and account for money they've already earned.

For me, Women's Liberation is simple. No woman in this country can feel dignified, no woman can be liberated, until all women get off their knees. That's what N.W.R.O. is all about—women standing together, on their feet.

If you agree, there are a lot of things you can do to help.

First, be honest about where your own head is at. Do you put down other women for being on welfare? Is it always "those people"? Well it could be you, and soon.

Stop for a minute and think what would happen to you and your kids if you suddenly had no husband and no savings.

Do you believe the "welfare Cadillac" myth? Inform yourself. Who's on welfare, why—and why can't they get off? N.W.R.O.'s got plenty of information out on the subject, and so do other groups. Write and get it.

How do your friends and your own women's group stand on welfare? Push them a little.

Does your community have people on welfare? Is there a local N.W.R.O. group? Help it.

Do you know your own rights to welfare? Find out.

Could you make it on a welfare budget (say, nineteen cents a meal)? Try it for a while. Just one week. Many women have done this—even wives of Congressmen—and they're shocked to see what even seven days is like. Try it now, when you don't have to.

You *may* have to, sooner or later, live on welfare.

Because you're a woman.

WE ARE THE CRAZY LADY AND OTHER FEISTY FEMINIST FABLES

CYNTHIA OZICK

1: The Crazy Lady Double

A long, long time ago, in another century—1951, in fact —when you, dear young readers, were most likely still in your nuclear-family playpen (where, if female, you cuddled a ragbaby to your potential titties, or, if male, let down virile drool over your plastic bulldozer), the Famous Critic told me never, never to use a parenthesis in the very first sentence. This was in a graduate English seminar at a celebrated university. To get into this seminar, you had to submit to a grilling wherein you renounced all former allegiance to the then-current literary religion, New Criticism, which considered that only the text existed, not the world. I passed the interview by lying—cunningly, and against my real convictions, I said that probably the world *did* exist—and walked triumphantly into the seminar room.

There were four big tables arranged in a square, with everyone's feet sticking out into the open middle of the square. You could tell who was nervous, and how much, by watching the pairs of feet twist around each other. The Great Man presided awesomely from the high bar of the square. His head was a majestic granite-gray, like a

---

Cynthia Ozick is author of "Trust" (New American Library, 1966) and "The Pagan Rabbi and other Stories" (Knopf, 1971). Her work has appeared in numerous periodicals and anthologies. She has received several awards for her writing and was a 1972 nominee for the National Book Award.

centurion in command; he *looked* famous. His clean shoes twitched only slightly, and only when he was angry.

It turned out he was angry at me a lot of the time. He was angry because he thought me a disrupter, a rioter, a provocateur, and a fool; also crazy. And this was twenty years ago, before these things were *de rigueur* in the universities. Everything was very quiet in those days: there were only the Cold War and Korea and Joe McCarthy and the Old Old Nixon, and the only revolutionaries around were in Henry James's *The Princess Casamassima*.

Habit governed the seminar. Where you sat the first day was where you settled forever. So, to avoid the stigmatization of the ghetto, I was careful not to sit next to the other woman in the class: the Crazy Lady.

At first the Crazy Lady appeared to be remarkably intelligent. She was older than the rest of us, somewhere in her thirties (which was why we thought of her as a Lady), with wild tan hair, a noticeably breathing bosom, eccentric gold-rimmed old-pensioner glasses, and a tooth-crowded wild mouth that seemed to get wilder the more she talked. She talked like a motorcycle, fast and urgent. Everything she said was almost brilliant, only not actually on point, and frenetic with hostility. She was tough and negative. She volunteered a lot and she stood up and wobbled with rage, pulling at her hair and mouth. She fought the Great Man point for point, piecemeal and wholesale, mixing up queerly-angled literary insights with all sorts of private and public fury. After the first meetings he was fed up with her. The rest of us accepted that she probably wasn't all there, but in a room where everyone was on the make for recognition—you talked to save your life, and the only way to save your life was to be the smartest one that day—she was a nuisance, a distraction, a pain in the ass. The class became a bunch of Good Germans, determinedly indifferent onlookers to a vindictive match between the Critic and the Crazy Lady, until finally he subdued her by shutting his eyes, and, when that didn't always work, by cutting her dead and lecturing right across the sound of her strong, strange voice.

All this was before R.D. Laing had invented the superiority of madness, of course, and, cowards all, no one liked the thought of being tarred with the Crazy Lady's brush. Ignored by the boss, in the middle of everything she would suddenly begin to mutter to herself. She mentioned certain institutions she'd been in, and said we all belonged there. The people who sat on either side of her shifted chairs. If the Great Man ostracized the Crazy Lady, we had to do it too. But one day the Crazy Lady came in late and sat down in the seat next to mine, and stayed there the rest of the semester.

Then an odd thing happened. There, right next to me, was the noisy Crazy Lady, tall, with that sticky-out sighing chest of hers, orangey curls dripping over her nose, snuffling furiously for attention. And there was I, a brownish runt, a dozen years younger and flatter and shyer than the Crazy Lady, in no way her twin, physically or psychologically. In those days I was bone-skinny, small, sallow and myopic, and so scared I could trigger diarrhea at one glance from the Great Man. All this stress on looks is important: the Crazy Lady and I had our separate bodies, our separate brains. We handed in our separate papers.

But the Great Man never turned toward me, never at all, and if ambition broke feverishly through shyness so that I dared to push an idea audibly out of me, he shut his eyes when I put up my hand. This went on for a long time. I never got to speak, and I began to have the depressing feeling that he hated me. It was no small thing to be hated by the man who had written the most impressive criticism of the century. What in hell was going on? I was in trouble; like everyone else in that demented contest I wanted to excel. Then, one slow afternoon, wearily, the Great Man let his eyes fall on me. He called me by name, but it was not my name—it was the Crazy Lady's. The next week the papers came back—and there, right at the top of mine, in the Great Man's own handwriting, was a rebuke to the Crazy Lady for starting an essay with a parenthesis in the first sentence, a habit he took to be a continuing sign of that unruly and unfocused mentality so often exhibited in class. And then a Singular Revelation crept coldly through me: because the Crazy Lady and I sat side by side, because we were a connected blur of Woman, the Famous Critic, master of ultimate distinctions, couldn't tell us apart. The Crazy Lady and I! He couldn't tell us apart! It didn't matter that the Crazy Lady was crazy! *He couldn't tell us apart!*

Moral 1: *All cats are gray at night,*
              all darkies look alike.

Moral 2: Even among intellectual humanists, every woman has a *Doppelgänger*—every other woman.

II: The Lecture, 1

I was invited by a women's group to be guest speaker at a Book-Author Luncheon. The women themselves had not really chosen me: the speaker had been selected by a male leader and imposed on them. The plan was that I would autograph copies of my book, eat a good meal and then lecture. The woman in charge of the programming telephoned to ask me what my topic would be. This was a matter of some concern, since they had never had a woman author before, and no one knew how the idea would be received. I offered as my subject "The Contemporary Poem."

When the day came, everything went as scheduled—the autographing, the food, the welcoming addresses. Then it was time to go to the lectern. I aimed at the microphone and began to speak of poetry. A peculiar rustling sound flew up from the audience. All the women were lifting their programs to the light, like hundreds of wings. Confused murmurs ran along the walls. Something was awry; I began to feel very uncomfortable. Then I too took up the program. It read: "Topic: The Contemporary Home."

Moral: Even our ears practice the caste system.

III: The Lecture, 2

I was in another country, the only woman at a philosophical seminar lasting three days. On the third day I was to read a paper. I had accepted the invitation with a certain foreknowledge. I knew, for instance, that I could not dare to be the equal of any other speaker. To be an equal would be to be less. I understood that mine had to be the most original and powerful paper of all. I had no choice; I had to toil beyond my most extreme possibilities. This was not ambition, but only fear of disgrace.

For the first two days, I was invisible. When I spoke, people tapped impatiently, waiting for the interruption to end. No one took either my presence or my words seriously. At meals, I sat with my colleagues' wives.

The third day arrived, and I read my paper. It was successful beyond my remotest imaginings. I was interviewed, and my remarks appeared in newspapers in a language I could not understand. The Foreign Minister invited me to his home. I hobnobbed with famous poets.

Now my colleagues noticed me. But they did not notice me as a colleague. They teased and kissed me. I had become their mascot.

Moral: There is no route out of caste which does not instantly lead back into it.

IV: Propaganda

For many years I had noticed that no book of poetry by a woman was ever reviewed without reference to the poet's sex. The curious thing was that, in the two decades of my scrutiny, there were *no* exceptions whatever. It did not matter whether the reviewer was a man or woman: in every case the question of the "feminine sensibility" of the poet was at the center of the reviewer's response. The maleness of male poets, on the other hand, hardly ever seemed to matter.

Determined to ridicule this convention, I wrote a tract, a piece of purely tendentious mockery, in the form of a short story. I called it "Virility."

The plot was, briefly, as follows: A very bad poet, lustful for fame, is despised for his pitiful lucubrations and remains unpublished. But luckily, he comes into possession of a cache of letters written by his elderly spinster aunt, who lives an obscure and secluded working-class life in a remote corner of England. The letters contain a large number of remarkable poems; the aunt, it turns out, is a genius. The bad poet publishes his find under his own name, and instantly attains world-wide adulation. Under the title *Virility*, the poems become immediate classics. They are translated into dozens of languages and are praised and revered for their unmistakably masculine qualities: their strength, passion, wisdom, energy, boldness, brutality, worldliness, robustness, authenticity, sensuality, compassion. A big, handsome, sweating man, the poet swaggers from country to country, courted everywhere, pursued by admirers, yet respected by the most demanding critics.

Meanwhile, the old aunt dies; the supply of genius runs out. Bravely and contritely the poor poet confesses his ruse, and in a burst of honesty publishes the last batch under the real poet's name; the book is entitled *Flowers from Liverpool*. But the poems are at once found negligible and dismissed: "Thin feminine art," say the reviews, "a lovely girlish voice." And: "Limited one-dimensional vision." "Choked with female inwardness." "The fine womanly intuition of a competent poetess." The poems are utterly forgotten.

I included this fable in a collection of short stories. In every review the salvo went unnoticed. Not one reviewer recognized that the story was a sly tract. Not one reviewer saw the smirk or the point. There was one delicious comment, though. "I have some reservations," a man in Washington, D.C., wrote, "about the credibility of some of her male characters when they are chosen as narrators."

Moral: In saying what is obvious, never choose cunning. Yelling works better.

V: Hormones

During a certain period of my life, I was reading all the time, and fairly obsessively. Sometimes, though, sunk in a book of criticism or philosophy, I would be brought up short. Consider: here is a paragraph that excites the intellect; inwardly, one assents passionately to its premises, the writer's idea is an exact diagram of one's own deepest psychology or conviction, one feels oneself seized as for a portrait. Then the disclaimer, the excluding shove: "It is, however, otherwise with the female sex. . . ." A rebuke from the world of Thinking: *I didn't mean you, lady.* In the instant one is in possession of one's humanity most intensely, it is ripped away.

These moments I discounted. What is wrong—intrinsically, psychologically, culturally, morally—can be dismissed.

But to dismiss in this manner is to falsify one's most genuine actuality. A Jew reading of the aesthetic glories of European civilization without taking notice of his victimization during, say, the era of the building of the great cathedrals, is self-forgetful in the most dangerous way. So would be a black who read of King Cotton with an economist's objectivity.

I am not offering any strict analogy between the situation of women and the history of Jews or colonialized blacks, as many politically radical women do (though the analogy with blacks is much the more frequent one). It seems to me to be abusive of language in the extreme when some women speak, in the generation after Auschwitz, of the "oppression" of women. Language makes culture, and we make a rotten culture when we abuse words. We raise up rotten heroines. I use "rotten" with particular attention to its precise meaning: foul, putrid, tainted, stinking. I am thinking now especially of a radical women's publication, *Off Our Backs*, which not long ago presented Leila Khaled, terrorist and foiled murderer, as a model for the political conduct of women.

But if I would not support the extreme analogy (and am never surprised when black women, who have a more historical comprehension of actual, not figurative, oppression, refuse to support the analogy), it is anyhow curious to see what happens to the general culture when any enforced class in any historical or social condition is compelled to doubt its own self-understanding—when identity is externally defined, when individual humanity is called into question as being different from "standard" humanity. What happens is that the general culture, along with the object of its debasement, is also debased. If you laugh at women, you play Beethoven in vain.

If you laugh at women your laboratory will lie.

We can read in Charlotte Perkins Gilman's 1912 essay, "Are Women Human Beings?", an account of two opinions current sixty years ago. Women, said one scientist, are not only "not the human race—they are not even half the human race, but a sub-species set apart for purposes of reproduction merely."

A physician said: "No doctor can ever lose sight of the fact that the mind of woman is always threatened with danger from the reverberations of her physiological emergencies." He concluded this entirely on the basis of his invalid patients.

Though we are accustomed to the idea of "progress"

66

in science and medicine, if not in civilization generally, the fact is that more information has led to something very like regression.

I talked with an intelligent physician—the Commissioner of Health of a middle-sized city in Connecticut, a man who sees medicine not discretely but as part of the social complex—and was treated to a long list of all the objective differences between men and women, including particularly an account of current endocrinal studies relating to female hormones. Aren't all of these facts, he asked, how can you distrust facts? Very good, I said, I'm willing to take your medically-educated word for it, I'm not afraid of facts, I welcome facts—*but a congeries of facts is not equivalent to an idea*. This is the essential fallacy of the so-called "scientific" mind. People who mistake facts for ideas are incomplete thinkers; they are gossips.

You tell me, I said, that my sense of my own humanity as being "standard" humanity—which is, after all, a subjective idea—is refuted by hormonal research. My psychology, you tell me, which in your view is the source of my ideas, is the result of my physiology: it is not I who express myself, it is my hormones which express me. A part is equal to the whole, you say. Worse yet, the whole is simply the issue of the part: my "I" is a flash of chemicals. You are willing to define all my humanity by hormonal investigation under a microscope: this you call "objective irrefutable fact," as if tissue-culture were equivalent to culture. But each scientist can assemble his own (subjective) constellation of "objective irrefutable fact," just as each social thinker can assemble his own (subjective) selection of traits to define "humanity" by. Who can prove what is "standard" humanity, and which sex, class, or race is to be exempted from whole participation in it? On what basis do you regard female hormones as causing a modification from normative humanity? And what better right do you have to define normative humanity by what males have traditionally apperceived than by what females have traditionally apperceived—assuming (as I, lacking presumptuousness, do not) that their apperceptions have not been the same? Only Tiresias—that mythological character who was both man and woman—is in a position to make the comparison and present the proof. And then not even Tiresias, because to be a hermaphrodite is to be a monster, and not human.

"Why are you so emotional about all this?" said the Commissioner of Health. "You see how it is? Those are your female hormones working on you right now."

Moral: Defamation is only applied research.

VI: Ambition

After thirteen years I at last finished a novel. The first seven years were spent in a kind of apprenticeship—the book that came out of that time was abandoned without much regret. A second one was finished in six weeks and buried. It took six years to write the third novel, and this one was finally published.

How I lived through those years is impossible to recount in a short space. I was a recluse, a priest of Art. I read seas of books. I believed in the idea of masterpieces. I was scornful of the world of journalism, jobs, everydayness. I did not live like any woman I knew, though it never occurred to me to reflect on this of my own volition. I lived like some men I had read about—Flaubert, or Proust, or James: the subjects of those literary biographies I endlessly drank in. I did not think of them as men but as writers. I read the diaries of Virginia Woolf, and biographies of George Eliot, but I did not think of them as women. I thought of them as writers. I thought of myself as a writer. I went on reading and writing.

It goes without saying that all this time my relatives regarded me as abnormal. I accepted this. It seemed to me, from what I had read, that most writers were abnormal. Yet on the surface I could easily have passed for normal. The husband goes to work, the wife stays home—that is what is normal. Well, I was married. My husband went to his job every day. His job paid the rent and bought the groceries. I stayed home, reading and writing, and felt myself to be an economic parasite. To cover guilt, I joked that I had been given a grant from a very private, very poor, foundation; I meant my husband.

But my relatives never thought of me as a parasite. The very thing I was doubtful about—my economic dependence—they considered my due as a woman. They saw me not as a failed writer without an income, but as a childless housewife, a failed woman. They did not think me abnormal because I was a writer, but because I was not properly living my life as a woman. In one respect we were in agreement utterly—my life was failing terribly, terribly. For me it was because, already deep into my thirties, I had not yet published a book; for them it was because I had not yet borne a child.

I was a pariah, not only because I was a deviant, but because I was not recognized as the kind of deviant I meant to be. A failed woman is not the same as a failed writer. Even as a pariah I was the wrong kind of pariah.

Still, relations are only relations, and what I aspired to, what I was in thrall to, was Art; was Literature; not familial contentment. I knew how to distinguish the trivial from the sublime. In Literature and in Art, I saw, my notions were not pariah notions: *there* I inhabited the mainstream. So I went on reading and writing; I went on believing in Art, and my intention was to write a masterpiece. Not a saucer of well-polished craft (the sort of thing "women writers" are always accused of being accomplished at), but something huge, contemplative, Tolstoyan. My ambition was a craw.

I called the book *Trust.* I began it in the summer of 1957 and finished it in November of 1963, on the day President John Kennedy was assassinated. In manuscript it was 801 pages divided into four parts: "America," "Europe," "Birth," "Death." The title was meant to be ironic; in reality, it was about distrust. It seemed to me I had touched on distrust in every order or form of civilization. It seemed to me I had left nothing out. It was (though I did not know this then) a very hating book. What it hated above all was the whole—the whole!—of Western Civilization. It told how America had withered into another Europe; it dreamed dark and murderous pagan dreams, and hated what it dreamed.

In style the book was what has come to be called "mandarin": a difficult, aristocratic, unrelenting virtuoso prose. It was, in short, unreadable. I think I knew this; I was sardonic enough to say, echoing Joyce about *Finnegans Wake,* "I expect you to spend your life at this." In any case I had spent a decade-and-a-half of my own life at it, and though I did not imagine the world would fall asunder at its appearance, I thought—at the very least—the ambition, the all-swallowingness, the wild insatiability of the writer would be plain to everyone who read. I had, after all, taken History for my subject; and not merely History as an aggregate of events, but History as a judgment on events. No one could say my theme was flighty. Of all the novelists I read—and in those days I read them all, broiling in the envy of the unpublished, which is like no envy on earth—who else had dared so vastly?

During that period, Françoise Sagan's first novel was published. I held the thin little thing and laughed. Women's pulp!

My own novel, I believed, contained everything—the whole world.

But there was one element I had consciously left out, though on principle I did not like to characterize it or think about it much. The truth is I was thinking about it all the time: it was only a fiction-technicality, but I was considerably afraid of it. It was the question of the narrator's "sensibility." The narrator, as it happened, was a young woman; I had chosen her to be the eye—and the "I"—of the novel because all the other characters in some way focused on her, and she was the one most useful to my scheme. Nevertheless I wanted her not to live. Everything I was reading in reviews of other people's books made me fearful: I would have to be very, very cautious, I would have to drain my narrator of emotive value of any kind. I was afraid to be pegged as having written a "woman's" novel, and nothing was more certain to lead to that than a point-of-view seemingly lodged in a woman; no one takes a woman's novel seriously. I was in terror, above all, of sentiment and feeling, those telltale taints. I kept the fury and the passion for other, safer characters.

So what I left out of my narrator entirely, sweepingly, with exquisite consciousness of what exactly I *was* leaving out, was any shred of "sensibility." I stripped her of everything, even a name. I crafted and carpentered her; she was for me a bloodless device, fulcrum or pivot, a recording voice, a language-machine. She confronted moment or event, took it in, gave it out. And what to me was all

70

the more wonderful about this nameless fiction-machine I had invented was that the machine itself, though never alive, was a character in the story, without ever influencing the story. My machine-narrator was there for efficiency only, for flexibility, for craftiness, for subtlety, but never, never, as a "woman." I wiped the "woman" out of her. And I did it out of fear, out of vicarious vindictive critical imagination, out of the terror of my ambition, out of, maybe, paranoia. I meant my novel to be taken for what it really was. I meant to make it impossible for it to be mistaken for something else.

Publication.

Review in *The New York Times* Sunday Book Review.

Review is accompanied by a picture of a naked woman seen from the back. Her bottom is covered by some sort of drapery.

Title of review: "Daughter's Reprieve."

Excerpts from review: "These events, interesting in themselves, exist to reveal the sensibility of the narrator." "She longs to play some easy feminine role." "She has been unable to define herself as a woman." "Thus the daughter, at the age of twenty-two, is eager for the prerequisites that should have been hers as a woman, but is floundering badly in their pursuit." "Her protagonist insists upon coming to terms with the recalcitrant sexual elements in her life." "The main body of the novel, then, is a revelation of the narrator's inner, turbulent, psychic dream."

O rabid rotten Western Civilization, where are you? O judging History, O foul Trust and fouler Distrust, where?

O Soap Opera, where did you come from?

(Meanwhile the review in *Time* was calling me a "housewife.")

Pause.

All right, let us take up the rebuttals one by one.

Q. Maybe you *did* write a soap opera without knowing it. Maybe you only *thought* you were writing about Western Civilization when you were really only rewriting Stella Dallas.

A. A writer may be unsure of everything—trust the tale not the teller is still a good rule—but not of his obsessions; of these he is certain. If I were rewriting Stella

71

Dallas, I would turn her into the Second Crusade and demobilize her.

Q. Maybe you're like the blind Jew who wants to be a pilot, and when they won't give him the job he says they're anti-Semitic. Look, the book was lousy, you deserved a lousy review.

A. You mistake me, I never said it was a bad review. It was in fact an extremely favorable review, full of gratifying adjectives.

Q. But your novel languished anyhow?

A. Perished. Dead and buried. I sometimes see it exhumed on the shelf in the public library. It's always there. No one ever borrows it.

Q. Dummy! You should've written a soap opera. Women are good at that.

A. Thank you. You almost remind me of another Moral: In conceptual life, junk prevails. Even if you do not produce junk, it will be taken for junk.

Q. What does that have to do with women?

A. The products of women are frequently taken for junk.

Q. And if a woman *does* produce junk . . . ?

A. Glory—they will treat her almost like a man who produces junk. They will say her name on television.

Q. Bitter, bitter!

A. Not at all. Again you misunderstand. You see, I have come round to thinking (I learned it from television commercials, as a matter of fact) that there *is* a Women's Culture—a sort of tribal, separatist, ghettoized thing. And I propose that we cultivate it.

Q. You mean *really* writing Women's Novels? On purpose?

A. Nothing like that. The novel was invented by men. It isn't ours, you see, and to us it is to *assimilate*. I see now where I went wrong! So I propose that we return to our pristine cultural origins, earn the respect of the male race, and regain our self-esteem.

Q. All that? Really? How?

A. *We will revive the Quilting Bee!*

Q. Oh, splendid, splendid! What a genius you are!

A. I always knew it.

II. Dealing with the World

ORGANIZING FROM WITHIN

RATE YOUR EMPLOYER

HOW TO WRITE YOUR OWN
MARRIAGE CONTRACT

HOW TO START A CHILD
CARE CENTER

THE ARTIST AS HOUSEWIFE

ORGANIZING FROM WITHIN

SUSAN DAVIS

It usually happens at lunch. Several women co-workers are sitting at a table, and a very angry colleague joins them. She has suffered one of the routine slights all women are subjected to on the job, but for some reason, this one was the last straw, and she's ready to say so. There is a pause after she speaks, and then the floodgates open. All the loving women—the pleasant women proud of their productivity, the brilliant women proud of their profession —all the loving women begin to speak. Before that historic lunch ends, plans have been made for an employees' meeting to discuss job discrimination. And out of that meeting, another women's caucus will be born, to go forth and do battle with management. For lights are going on in places of work all over the land: in the typing pools and private offices where women are recognizing sexism for the first time, never to be innocent again.

Women's caucuses are known to exist in more than a hundred companies, including Polaroid; Blue Cross; Atlantic Richfield; General Electric; Scott, Foresman; Reader's Digest; Celanese; and AT&T and several of its subsidiaries, as well as in such institutions as Care, Inc., the American Civil Liberties Union, the Museum of Modern Art and the Metropolitan Museum of Art in New

Susan Davis is editor and publisher of "The Spokeswoman," a national monthly feminist newsletter. She is vice-president of Urban Research Corp. in Chicago and coordinator of nationwide conferences for institutions attempting to end discriminatory practices in employment.

York, the New York City Rand Institute, *Newsweek* Magazine, Time Inc., and the Ford and the Russell Sage Foundations. So far, the caucuses have won a few actual gains and have also resulted in several firings. It is clear that for women to organize at all is serious business. But it is equally clear that this is the trend of the future, and that women are not likely to be stopped.

A women's caucus usually starts in a low-key way over a relatively nonexplosive issue, as if women are testing the water before they dare to plunge in. In several cases, caucuses have been prompted by a feeling that workers were laid off unfairly, or by a rap session about small grievances—a lack of consideration or respect from male bosses. Usually the meeting consists of a small number of women, and is held, innocently enough, on company property.

Most caucuses go through a relatively long period of consciousness-raising in order to solidify the initial, exuberant sense of solidarity.

A pattern for one kind of model caucus exists at a Southern bank. Eight women met about sex discrimination and decided to begin by making a conscious effort to involve more women. Over the next few weeks, each of them was to talk to and invite five women to that week's meeting. One woman served as a lightning rod by displaying Women's Liberation posters in her office, and talking freely about women's work issues. The fact that nothing terrible happened to her encouraged the others to continue their efforts. Several women reported lingering in the ladies room, rapping with employees as they came in. "Those who didn't want to get involved just walked out," one woman said, "but those interested stayed." These women are getting powerfully organized and will identify their group to management after they are sure an effective number of women employees will definitely support communal or individual demands.

The most important characteristic of the groups is their crossing of status lines. When women start rapping about salary, they find the low salary of secretarial jobs is caused by the same sexism as the lower-than-average salary of the professional women's jobs. When women start rapping about promotion, they find that being stuck in the secretarial pool is caused by the same sexism as being stuck at first-level management. When women start rapping about disrespect, they find they are asked to take notes and fetch coffee whether they are first-level secretaries or a Secretary of the Corporation. And when a woman gets pregnant, she is often refused paid maternity leave, regardless of her status.

Another important characteristic critical to the success of a caucus is its racial composition. Caucuses with both white and minority women have been more successful than those that are all white. The reason is clear. Management responds to an all-white group with divide-and-conquer tactics.

"Delores and I realized from the beginning that we had to work out demands in the context of black demands or we could be pitted against each other," explained one white caucus leader from a Midwest company. "Delores is black, and we discussed everything carefully before speaking to management so that we could present a united front. Also, we went to a black man who is influential in promoting blacks within the company and talked with him about our concerns. We said that, while blacks are primarily concerned with getting hired in the first place, the additional problem that women of all races have is being underemployed. Once women establish career ladders to carry them up from dead-end jobs, this will be an important staircase for black men—for everyone starting at the bottom. We told him that, as we organized and developed power, we would be sure to combine our demands with black demands. It was clear that he respected our efforts and would hang loose to see what we developed. Really, all we could expect was that he be aware of our plans."

The issue of women vis-à-vis blacks is made even more complicated within the administration of the equal-opportunity employment programs. When the Federal Government announced that companies had to set goals and timetables for hiring women just as they did for blacks, companies rarely made an extra effort, either in personnel or in budget. They just gave their equal-opportunity employment officials a double responsibility. Thus, people who had previously worked full-time on behalf of minorities now divided their time between minorities and women or neglected the programs for women. This has created some antagonism on the part of blacks toward women, and vice versa, a serious problem that may grow worse until blacks and women are able to band together to demand greatly increased resources for the equal-opportunity offices of their companies. The same divide-and-conquer problem exists between black and Spanish-speaking groups, with the latter made to feel resentment for the earlier organization and the greater force of the former.

There is no one successful model for the structure of leadership of a women's caucus. Most operate via "steering committee," which usually means a small number of women doing the most work. But their success depends on the support of their constituency. Once, a small group of women presented themselves to management as the voice of women workers without having enlisted the women's support; they were disowned by the other women. Those antagonistic to the Movement had a field day.

One of the fastest growing women's caucuses has taken the opposite tack. In a New York corporate headquarters that employs several hundred women, weekly consciousness-raising meetings are held in an effort to reach virtually all the women. The caucus leaders are insistent, however, that no public meeting will be held until they have things so together that it will be a guaranteed success.

Such tactical decisions must fit the real situation. Sometimes a few women are effective, and their success draws others. Sometimes a larger number is necessary to make a company listen at all.

At this point, many caucuses feel they need the protection of company policy in pursuing their own ends. Said a woman active in a Midwest insurance company, "We plan to go through channels every step of the way. We think there would be just too much resistance otherwise. Every time we ask them [management] something, it's going to be so reasonable and rational that they'll have to say yes."

Caucuses may have to exercise caution on company ground, but outside women's groups have a role to play in "upping the ante." In the last year, Women's Liberation groups have picketed various companies for sexist practices, and subsequently entered negotiations about policy changes. In several instances, women's caucuses within the companies have quietly contacted the feminist groups and supplied them with information about the company's sexist policies. This cooperation is effective, and can be expected to increase.

Particularly when there is outside feminist pressure on a company, women's caucuses are vulnerable to name-calling as being that "Women's Lib," as if Women's Lib were some kind of subversive plot. When this occurs, a caucus may sometimes de-emphasize a connection with outside groups and emphasize specific sexist job policies. "But it's very important to keep the links in mind and to lay the groundwork for further identification," said a New York woman. "We have to respond to name-calling by saying, 'Look, what we're talking about is equal pay for equal work, being treated with respect and uniting with other employees around common concerns so that we have some *real* power. If that's Women's Liberation, we're for it.' No matter what people call us to break us up, we have to unify, and understand why we are organizing."

After initial consciousness-raising comes the hardest work for the caucuses—gathering information about the employment rights of women. The groups investigate four pertinent laws: 1) Equal Pay Act of 1963, 2) Title VII of the Civil Rights Act of 1964, 3) Revised Order 4 issued December, 1971, by the Department of Labor, and 4) legislation that has strengthened the authority of the Equal Employment Opportunity Commission (EEOC).

Because of the court waiting lists and financial cost of taking companies to court, a caucus's best remedy is probably Revised Order 4, which requires companies doing business with the Federal Government to form written "affirmative action" programs for minorities and women. The Order is administered by the Office of Federal Contract Compliance (OFCC, Dept. of Labor, Washington, D.C.). Doris Wooten, the woman responsible for enforcement of Revised Order 4, has earned the respect of feminists for her hard work under fire.

Revised Order 4 applies to those companies having at least 50 employees and doing at least $50,000 in Federal

Government business a year. Simply stated, the Order requires each company to set goals and timetables for moving women into job categories where they are under-represented—blue-collar jobs as well as management positions. In preparation for setting goals and timetables, companies must survey the status of women in their companies: how many women are employed? at what levels? with what pay? in what job categories?

Goals and timetables must relate to the number of women potentially available to fill the positions in question. Usually, the corporation's equal-opportunity office will ask managers in all divisions to submit projections of the number of jobs they expect to have available in the future, and the number of women they plan to recruit for these jobs. The "timetable" can run anywhere from one year to twenty. The corporate office, after evaluating these projections, seeks adjustments where deemed appropriate.

Although goals and timetables are its most important feature, Revised Order 4 extends far beyond this requirement. It attempts to explain what "affirmative action" really is: Companies must be in contact with feminist groups; they must go out to recruit women—from the home to the classroom; they must offer women their jobs back after maternity leave (recent EEOC guidelines require companies to pay women while on maternity leave, as they would for any other temporary disability); and they must consider "management awareness' programs to counteract sexism in company managers.

The pressures of EEOC, OFCC, and feminist groups to give back pay to female employees who have suffered their personnel policies and procedures. More and more organizations have been taken into the courts and required to give back to female employees who have suffered pay and promotion losses due to discrimination. The corporate manager is becoming (although slowly) greatly bothered about the economic pressure on the firm.

The problem with Revised Order 4 has been that companies did not need to make their affirmative action programs, or "aaps," public. The explanation was that by doing this, too much information would be revealed to competing companies. The effect, of course, was to

make the women's caucuses work in the dark. A recent
and they must consider "management awareness" pro-
be made public.

Nevertheless, women in a major publishing company
have been pressuring hard for a role in developing their
company's affirmative action plan. They point out that
Revised Order 4 says companies must let women know
how they can avail themselves of the benefits of the company's "aap." In spite of this requirement, the publishing
company has been balking at recognizing the women's
caucus in any way. The women have countered by making
a series of individual appointments with the president of
the company. They plan to continue this nuisance action
until management cooperates.

One tactic commonly used by women's caucuses is the
questionnaire. It usually asks probing questions such as,
"What has been your experience in trying to get pro-
motions?" and "Do you feel you are paid fairly?" Doing
a survey that can be answered anonymously serves not
only as a consciousness-raiser among women workers
but develops a good profile of one's constituency. In one
company, the equal-employment opportunity officer agreed
to such a questionnaire but insisted it must be administered
to men and women alike. That was fine with the women's
caucus; first, because the women's questionnaire could
always be analyzed separately; second, because, in the long
run, all workers' grievances must be dealt with.

Some women in Chicago used the questionnaire in a
novel way. Deciding there was a need for a group of
"Women in Publishing," they sat down with the Yellow
Pages and called every entry under publishing, from *Teen
Magazine* to *Florists' Review*. They asked for the copy
editor, usually a woman, and told her about their questionnaire on the status of women in publishing. They then
asked for information about the number of women employed by the company, and asked permission to send
that many questionnaires. In this way, hundreds of questionnaires were distributed, and a stunning 70 percent
were returned. The success of the questionnaire prompted
a large city-wide meeting last spring, when Women in
Publishing was formally launched, complete with four
subcommittees: 1) membership and program (including

newsletter and placement service), 2) a work group to follow up on the questionnaire, 3) a work group to investigate unionizing, and 4) a legal and research work group.

The demands of women's caucuses are commonly for 1) a grievance procedure, 2) clearly stated personnel policies regarding hiring, firing, and promotional opportunities, 3) an open discussion of the company's affirmative action program, 4) apprenticeship and management training programs that include women, 5) career ladders for all jobs, particularly such dead-end jobs as that of secretary, 6) a reexamination of the credentials of women already employed, 7) paid maternity leave, and 8) an investigation of the feasibility of child care. *Without exception, a principal demand of the women's caucuses is for respect.*

A number of women's groups are asking their companies to give sensitivity sessions to dispel the myths about women workers (that women tend to be absent, late, weak, or emotional, for instance). Scott, Foresman & Co., a Chicago publishing house, has a thriving women's caucus with some four or five work groups. One, called the professional advancement work group, has suggested to management a three-session training program. The session is for those workers who are already managers and supervisors; it focuses on relating to subordinates on an individual basis, rather than characterizing all women as second-class workers. The second session is for nonsupervisory personnel; it focuses on dispelling socialized hostility—a woman feeling she can't work for a woman boss, for instance. This session also provides information about the company structure, higher-level jobs, and the possibility of career ladders. The third session is for those aspiring to be supervisors or trainers. This includes training in interviewing, promotion, cost-control, and budgeting procedures. (At issue now is whether or not the sensitivity sessions should be compulsory.)

Women at Scott, Foresman have also taken the lead in raising the question of work content. Believing that some children's books published by the compnay are sexist, one subcommittee took on the job of educating editors about sexist attitudes. The women presented a slide show illustrating methods of revising sexist literature. The subcommittee hopes that sexist passages can be eliminated from books about to be published and revised in books already published.

Increasingly, women's caucuses can be expected to concern themselves with the social implications of the company's policies and products, as well as with its internal practices.

In some cases, women's caucuses have demonstrated to stress their point. At a major company based in Denver, women en masse celebrated St. Valentine's Day by paying a visit to the office of the new personnel director. They welcomed him, expressed their interest in the company, cited their high aspirations and their strong belief in their own abilities to perform on behalf of the company. They said they were interested in the company's affirmative action program, and wished to help in its development. The new personnel manager's hostility toward the women was so great that numerous women were radicalized by the incident. This is not uncommon. Various women's caucuses report that sexist reactions by management to women's reasonable demands tended to turn the women on to each other, and to the need to act collectively.

When the women of the New York City Rand Institute presented a memo asking for grievance procedures when they felt they were being treated disrespectfully—for clarification of hiring, firing, and promotion policies; and for clear distinctions between merit and cost-of-living raises —management at first seemed to respond well. In a session with the women's group, the president, vice-president, and treasurer voiced strong concern that women were being treated poorly. The president asked for a sample charter to institute a possible grievance procedure, and the personnel manager gave the women a summary of personnel policies. However, several weeks after this meeting, Linda Stetson, a leader of the group, was told that she was the only employee not being given a pay increase, and that she should begin to look for another job. This incident dampened the enthusiasm of the other women, and the group's progress has been stalemated. Fired early this year, Ms. Stetson has filed a suit of sex discrimination— as well as discrimination on the basis of race and national origin (on behalf of other employees)—against Rand of New York. (Rand has denied the charges.)

Where women attempt to bargain with management without the protection of a union, the firings that often result intimidate and undermine the women's caucus. In fact, there has been considerable discussion within the groups about whether they should attempt to unionize.

Those in favor argue that the few successes women workers have won to date have been won through organizing. For example, in a much-heralded article in the Winter 1971 issue of *Up from Under,* "Taking Care of Business," Margie Albert describes how women office workers organized at Rabinowitz, Boudin and Standard, a New York law firm. Initial discussions with management were getting the women nowhere, so they contacted District 65 of the National Council of Distributive Workers— a union which has been extremely supportive of women's efforts to organize. When the lawyers learned the women were circulating union cards, they agreed to formal negotiations without holding an election. The women won guaranteed annual wage increments (plus cost-of-living increases), 15 days sick/personal leave, three-weeks' paid vacation, 12 legal holidays (plus four religious or other holidays), and complete medical coverage through a 5-per cent wage deduction.

At the National Bureau of Economic Research, women started meeting in June, 1970, and organized the National Bureau Employees Association. (NBEA) in September. Throughout the fall, they attempted to negotiate with management. Their efforts proved futile, however, so they decided to vote in NBEA as an independent union. Many women had been radicalized, and when the union cards were tabulated, 70 of the 83 cards circulated had been signed. What is noteworthy is that the NBEA organized across status lines. It had signed up research assistants and analysts, editors, computer workers, clerks, secretaries, and custodians. The NBEA recently signed a contract that included a cost-of-living increase and a formal grievance procedure. The women say the main issue was commanding respect, and that they won that only by demanding it.

Despite the members in favor of unionizing, women's

caucuses may express an anti-union bias, particularly in their early stages. Many women office workers believe that unions have not represented women's interests, and thus are not desirable structures. Moreover, women are aware that employers react violently to the idea of unionization. An argument can be made that anti-union bias is the expression of the same biases that have kept women apart. Some women fear exercising power. Other women are afraid of seeming too militant or too organized. However, women are coming to see that they have been kept subservient partly because the tools of real power have been denied them. From this perspective, the truth seems to be that unions are not bad per se, but that it is bad that women do not have their own unions, or are not strong enough as a group to influence the male-dominated unions that now exist.

The very existence of women's caucuses has generated an infectious excitement among growing numbers of women. Excluded from many union structures, and from the decision-making process within them, women are only now gaining the sense of widening vistas and the strength that comes from identifying with one another across race and status lines. Few bargaining units have existed among white-collar women workers at all, and this prospect is also new and exciting. Finally, women see in collective action the possibility of redirecting the products of their work in socially relevant ways.

If we look to the future, it is hard to overestimate the potential power of women's caucuses. With women doing so much of the work of so many institutions, with women being a majority "minority," with women wielding institutionalized consumer power, clearly we only lack organization to change the order of the day. Women's caucuses, acting not with uniformity but with unity, may institute flexible working schedules for men and women, career paths which offer hope to all workers, compensation directly related to work load, achievement based on cooperation rather than competition, a relevant mix between school and work, and employee awareness of the social impact of the products we produce and the jobs we perform.

ARTICLES ON SEX DISCRIMINATION AND EMPLOYMENT

1. "The Business and Industry Discrimination Kit." About sex discrimination laws and how to file individual and pattern-of-practice suits against employers. Available from National Organization for Women, 1957 E. 73rd St., Chicago, Ill. 60649; $3 to NOW members, $5 to others. Also available from NOW; "And Justice for All." Information-packed description of NOW's effort to get government compliance agencies to enforce federal laws on sex discrimination. Available for $1 for NOW members, $2 for others.

2. "Sex Discrimination in Employment: What To Know About It, What To Do About It," by the Equal Opportunity Task Force of the Eastern Massachusetts National Organization for Women, March 1972. Up-to-date, and does just what it says it will do. Available for $1.50 from NOW, 45 Newbury St., Boston, Mass. 02116.

3. "Job Discrimination Handbook." Sex discrimination on the job and what the workingwoman can do about it. Available for $1.00 from Human Rights for Women, Inc., 1128 National Press Building, Washington, D.C. 20004.

4. "Developments in the Law: Employment Discrimination and Title VII of the Civil Rights Act of 1964," Harvard Law Review, Vol. 84, No. 5, March 1971. Available for $3.30 from Gannett House, Cambridge, Mass. 02138.

5. "Series on Revised Order 4," by Helen Fogel, Detroit Free Press, March-April 1972.

6. "Equal Pay in the United States," by Morag Simchak, International Labor Review, June 1971. Good wrap-up article by one of the best administrators of the Equal Pay Act. Reprints of article available from Director of Information, Employment Standards Administration, U.S. Department of Labor, Washington, D.C. 20210. No charge for single copies.

7. "Heaven Won't Protect the Working Girl," by Louise Bernikow, Ms., Preview issue, 1972. An introduction to troublemaking on the job.

8. "Day Care Services: Industry's Involvement." The Wom-

en's Bureau, U.S. Department of Labor, Washington, D.C. Free.

9. "Job Discrimination and the Black Woman," by Sonia Pressman, The Crisis (NAACP Journal), March 1970. Fact-filled essay on the double burden of black women that puts them on the bottom of the job market. Available from NAACP, 1790 Broadway, New York, N.Y. 10019. 35 cents.

10. Revised Order 4. Available from Office of Federal Contract Compliance, U.S. Department of Labor, Washington, D.C. 20210. Single copies free.

In addition, two newsletters provide continuing coverage of women's efforts to win employment rights:

1. The Spokeswoman, 5464 South Shore Drive, Chicago, Ill. 60615, $7 per year to individuals, $12 by institutional check.

2. Womanpower, Betsy Hogan Associates, 222 Rawson Rd., Brookline, Mass. 02146. $37 per year.

Another resource is provided by two Chicago women who have experience in organizing women. Day Creamer and Heather Booth have formed Midwest Academy, specializing in training women to organize working women. Contact Ms. Booth, 817 West George Street, Chicago, Illinois.

The best source by far about sex discrimination is the EEOC's study of the American Telephone and Telegraph Company (AT&T) called, satirically, "A Unique Competence." This summary report of the hearings on AT&T is available from David Copus, EEOC, 1800 G St., N.W., Washington, D.C. 20506.

RATE YOUR EMPLOYER

A Sex Discrimination Checklist

JENNIFER MACLEOD

IT'S GETTING HARDER AND HARDER FOR EMPLOYERS TO GET AWAY WITH BOTH THE BLATANT AND MORE SUBTLE WAYS OF DISCRIMINATING AGAINST WOMEN ON THE JOB. HOW DOES YOUR EMPLOYER STACK UP? HAS YOUR FIRM GOT THE MESSAGE? ANSWER THESE QUESTIONS AND SEE.

In your company (or other place of employment), is the top executive group and/or board of directors all male?

Looking at the distribution of female employees in the company, is the proportion successively lower as you move up the hierarchy?

Are there any job categories or training programs in your company that include only women, or only men? Or are there any departments in which the employees are all female up to a certain level, and all male thereafter?

Does your company have separate personnel offices, interviewers, or files for female and male job applicants?

Does your company place help-wanted advertisements in ad columns that are separated by sex? If not, do they place ads that suggest in any way that one sex is preferred over another? (For example, "salesman wanted.")

Dr. Macleod is a research psychologist and consultant to corporations and universities on sex discrimination in employment.

In job interviews, are questions asked of women applicants that probably would not be asked of men—such as intention to marry or have children (or more children), number and age of children, whether (and what kind of) birth control is used, spouse's occupation, income, or likelihood of transfer?

If a job applicant were clearly a "little bit pregnant," would she be turned away?

Are youth and/or good looks and/or white race considered qualifications for a secretarial job?

If a well-qualified man applied for a secretarial job, would he be turned away?

Do salaries paid to recent *male* college (or high school) graduates in your company tend to be higher than those paid to recent *female* graduates?

When there are female and male employees holding essentially the same jobs, are there any differences in their titles, salaries or kinds of work assigned to them?

Are there any differences in work rules for females and male employees? (For instance, work breaks, limits on weightlifting, limits on overtime.)

Are a higher proportion of the female employees in "dead-end" (little or no likelihood of advancement) positions than is the case with male employees?

Are there any differences in seniority procedures, retirement ages, pensions and/or group life- and health-insurance plans for female and male employees?

Are the employee's spouse and children treated any differently in group life or health insurance depending on whether the employee is female or male?

Does the health-insurance plan exclude coverage for abortions or cover abortions only for married women?

Does your company fail to pay maternity benefits or do the benefits cover only *married* women employees?

If a woman leaves to give birth, does she have to take her chances on getting the same or a similar job back?

Is a pregnant employee required to leave at some arbitrary point in pregnancy, such as the fifth month?

Are leave policies for childbirth in any way inferior to those granted for other temporary disabilities, such as a heart attack or a hernia operation?

Are secretarial salaries based mainly on the status of bosses rather than on the secretaries' own merits?

If there are women executives or professionals in your company, do they tend to receive less favorable allocations of secretarial help, office space, or expense-accounts?

Does your company have a restrictive dress code for women? (For instance, no pants for office wear.)

Are secretaries in your company asked to do personal chores for executives, such as fetching coffee, writing checks, polishing furniture, watering plants, or running errands outside the office?

Do executives refer to their secretaries as "my girl" or "my gal"?

Does your company frown on the use of "Ms." or send routine business letters to "Dear Sir" or "Gentlemen" even when the recipient might be a woman?

Are women employees referred to by their husbands' names? (For instance, "Mrs. Robert Brown.")

Do any of the male executives or supervisors mock or make sarcastic remarks about the Women's Liberation Movement or about the abilities or performances of women employees as a group?

If a female and a male employee engaged in an "illicit affair," would the woman be more likely than the man to be fired or otherwise punished?

Is an executive's wife screened when her husband is hired or promoted? Are wives expected to play any company role, such as entertaining clients?

Would a woman employee have to expect reprisals if she filed sex discrimination charges or complained of discrimination to company management?

If a local chapter of the National Organization for Women or some other women's rights organization asked for a meeting to discuss equal opportunity programs for women, would your company refuse the request?

Does your company discriminate against black women more than white women?

Has your company failed so far to officially inform all its employees of a policy of nondiscrimination against women?

Has your company failed to prepare and put into effect a written affirmative action plan to eliminate all sex discrimination policies and practices, and to compensate for the effects of past discrimination?

EVERY "YES" ANSWER INDICATES A "PROBLEM AREA" FOR YOUR COMPANY IN ITS TREATMENT OF WOMEN. FEDERAL, STATE AND LOCAL LAWS, STATUTES, GUIDELINES AND EXECUTIVE ORDERS VARY ACCORDING TO GEOGRAPHIC AREA AND TYPE AND SIZE OF BUSINESS. BUT "YES" ANSWERS, PARTICULARLY THOSE INDICATING DISCRIMINATION AGAINST WOMEN IN HIRING, PROMOTION, SALARIES AND BENEFITS, LEAVE YOUR COMPANY OPEN TO POSSIBLE LEGAL ACTION, COMPLAINTS TO GOVERNMENT AGENCIES AND DENIAL OR WITHDRAWAL OF PUBLIC MONIES OR CONTRACTS.

HOW TO WRITE YOUR OWN
MARRIAGE CONTRACT

SUSAN EDMISTON

First we thought marriage was when Prince Charming came and took you away with him. Then we thought that marriage was orange blossoms and Alençon lace and silver patterns. Then we thought that marriage—at least—was when you couldn't face signing the lease on the new apartment in two different names.

But most of us never even suspected the truth. Nobody ever so much as mentioned that what marriage is, at its very heart and essence, is a contract. When you say "I do," what you are doing is not, as you thought, vowing your eternal love, but rather subscribing to a whole system of rights, obligations and responsibilities that may very well be anathema to your most cherished beliefs.

Worst of all, you never even get to read the contract—to say nothing of the fine print. If you did, you probably wouldn't agree to it. Marriage, as it exists today, is a peculiarly vague, and yet inflexible, arrangement of institutionalized inequality which goes only one step beyond the English common-law concept of husband and wife as one, and, as the saying goes, "that 'one' is the husband." We have progressed from the notion of wife as legal nonentity to the notion of wife as dependent and inferior.

In recent years, many people have taken to writing their own marriage ceremonies in a desperate attempt to make the institution more relevant to their own lives. But cere-

Susan Edmiston is a writer, editor, columnist and contributor to many national magazines. She is now at work on a book, "A Literary Guide to New York."

monies, they are finding, do not reach the heart of the matter. So some couples are now taking the logical next step of drawing up their own contracts. These agreements may delineate any of the financial or personal aspects of the marriage relationship—from who pays which bills to who uses what birth control. Though many of their provisions may not be legally binding, at the very least they can help us to examine the often inchoate assumptions underlying our relationships, help us come to honest and equitable terms with one another, and provide guidelines for making our marriages what we truly want them to be.

Before their first child was born, Alix Kates Shulman and her husband had an egalitarian, partnership marriage. Alix worked full time as an editor in New York, and both shared the chores involved in maintaining their small household. After two children, however, the couple found that they had automatically fallen into the traditional sex roles: he went out and worked all day to support his family; she stayed home and worked from 6 a.m. to 9 p.m. taking care of children and housework. Unthinkingly, they had agreed not only to the legalities of marriage but to the social contract as well.

After six years at home—six years of chronic dissatisfaction—Alix became involved in the Women's Liberation movement and realized that it might be possible to change the contract under which she and her husband lived. The arrangement they worked out, basically a division of household duties and child care, rejected "the notion that the work which brings in more money is more valuable. The ability to earn . . . money is a privilege which must not be compounded by enabling the larger earner to buy out of his/her duties."

Sitting down and writing out a contract may seem a cold and formal way of working out an intimate relationship, but often it is the only way of coping with the ghosts of 2,000 years of tradition lurking in our definitions of marriage. After three years, Alix had written six books, and both Shulmans found their agreement a way of life rather than a document to be followed legalistically.

No less an antagonist than Norman Mailer has attacked the Shulmans' contract. After describing it in *The Prisoner of Sex,* he writes (in his characteristic third person): "No, he would not be married to such a woman. If he were obliged to have a roommate he would pick a man. . . . He could love a woman and she might even sprain her back before a hundred sinks of dishes in a month, but he would not be happy to help her if his work should suffer, no, not unless her work were as valuable as his own." Mailer's comment makes the issues clear: under the old contract the work of child-rearing and housekeeping is assumed to be less important than the work a man does—specifically, here, the career of self-aggrandizement Mailer has cut out for himself—and a wife, unless able to prove otherwise, must do the housework.

The Shulmans' contract renegotiates husband's and wife's roles as far as the care of children and home are concerned. Psychologists Barbara and Myron Koltuv took their agreement one step further.

"We agreed in the beginning that since I didn't care a bit about the house, he would do a lot of cleaning and I would do a lot of cooking," says Barbara. "He does a lot of the shopping, too, because he likes to buy things and I don't. Whenever either of us feels 'I'm doing all the drudge work and you're not doing anything,' we switch jobs. Gradually we've eliminated a lot of stuff neither of us wanted to do. In the early days, we'd cook dinner for people because we didn't feel it was hospitable to ask them to go out, but now we often go out instead.

"In the beginning we literally opened up separate bank accounts. We split our savings and checking accounts. At the time he made a third more money than I did. I deferred to him all the time, even though it was only a third. I felt that if he didn't spend so much money on the eight dozen book clubs he belongs to, I would only have to work about two hours a day. He said I wasn't realistic, that I didn't know how much we had and was being tight.

"Each of us paid the bills alternate months. I thought this was the only way to prove to him I could handle money. After six months, when I figured out how much I was spending and how much of his money I was using, I decided to take on more patients to expand my practice. I found I was spending as much on cabs as he was on book clubs. Since that time we haven't had a single argument about money."

When the Koltuvs' child was born, they reopened negotiations. "We decided to split the care of our daughter between us equally. We knew there were certain hours we'd both be working so we found a woman to take care of her during these hours. Then I had the mornings and he had the evenings. The person whose time it was had to make all the decisions—whether she could have Pepsi-Cola, whether she could visit a friend, and so forth.

"The hardest thing was being willing to give up control. What we call responsibility is often control, power, being the boss. When I was really able to recognize that my husband's relationship with Hannah is his and mine is mine, everything was all right. He's going to do it differently but he's going to do it all right. We've been teaching her all along that different people are different."

Agreements to disagree with the common marriage mores are nothing new. They have their roots in a fine old tradition that probably began with Mary Wollstonecraft, that first feminist of us all, who in 1792 wrote *A Vindication of the Rights of Women*. Though Mary and her husband, English essayist and political theorist William Godwin, submitted to marriage, it was on their own terms. Godwin took an apartment about twenty doors from the couple's house to which he "repaired" every morning. A letter of the time describes this arrangement: "In order to give the connection as little as possible the appearance of such a vulgar and debasing tie as matrimony, the parties have established separate establishments, and the husband only visits his mistress like a lover when each is dressed, rooms in order, etc." The couple agreed that it was wrong for husband and wife to have to be together whenever they went out into "mixed society" and therefore, as Godwin writes, "rather sought occasions of deviating from, than of complying with, this rule."

The principle of separate quarters, which recently cropped up again in reports of a contract between Jacqueline Kennedy and Aristotle Onassis, also appears in the agreement birth-control pioneer Margaret Sanger signed with her husband, J. Noah H. Slee. Their contract stated that they would have separate homes and, later, separate quarters within the same house. Neither was to have the slightest influence over the business affairs of the

94

other, and, when both were busy, communications were to be exchanged through their secretaries. They also agreed that Margaret Sanger would continue to use her own name. (Sanger, in fact, was the name of her first husband, but she had already made it a famous one.)

The ultimate feminist contract, however, was the one Lucy Stone and Henry Blackwell wrote when they married in 1855. Their agreement is a concise catalogue of the legal inequities of marriage in America at that time:

"While we acknowledge our mutual affection by publicly assuming the relationship of husband and wife," they wrote, "we deem it a duty to declare that this act on our part implies no sanction of, nor promise of voluntary obedience to, such of the present laws of marriage as refuse to recognize the wife as an independent, rational being, while they confer upon the husband an injurious and unnatural superiority." The contract went on to protest especially against the laws which gave the husband custody of the wife's person, the sole ownership of her personal property and the use of her real estate, the absolute right to the product of her industry and the exclusive control and guardianship of the couple's children. Finally, they protested against "the whole system by which 'the legal existence of the wife is suspended during marriage' so that, in most States, she neither has a legal part in the choice of her residence, nor can she make a will, nor sue or be sued in her own name, nor inherit property."

While it is obvious that we have made some progress since Lucy Stone's day, in many ways we are still living under the heritage of the kind of laws she deplored. The American institution of marriage derives from English common law, which developed a peculiar concept, unknown on the Continent, called the "unity of spouses." As Blackstone put it, "By marriage, the husband and wife are one person in law; that is, the very being or legal existence of the woman is suspended during marriage, or at least is incorporated or consolidated into that of the husband."

Beginning in 1839, one version or another of what was called the Married Women's Property Act was passed in each state of the Union, correcting some of the gross injustices of marriage. Most of these laws granted married women the right to contract, to sue and be sued without joining their husbands, to manage and control the property they brought with them to marriage, to engage in gainful employment and retain the earnings derived from it. Like a case of bad genes, however, the fiction of the unity of the spouses has never quite gone away. Husband and wife today are like Siamese twins: although largely separate persons under the law, they are still joined together in one spot or another. In one state, the wife's ability to contract may still be impaired; in another, she may not have full freedom to use her maiden name; in a third, she may not be considered capable of conspiracy with her husband.

These vestiges of the unity of spouses, however, are not the only ways in which marriage treats man and woman unequally, for we have evolved a different—but still unequal—concept of marriage. Today we regard husband as head of household and wife as housewife; husband as supporter and wife as dependent; husband as authority and wife as faithful helpmeet. This concept of marriage has not been *created* by the law but is an expression of culturally shared values which are *reflected* in the law. It is the conventional notion of marriage consciously embraced or unthinkingly held by many, if not most, Americans.

What's wrong with it? The responsibility of support is commonly thought to favor women at the expense of men; I leave it for men to document how this notion injures them and will only deal here with the disabilities from a woman's point of view. Like all commonly held notions, the idea of marriage as a relationship between supporter and dependent is so much a part of our very atmosphere that it is hard to see it objectively. (To counter this difficulty, many women's groups are suggesting that people wishing to get a marriage license should have to take a test on the laws, as they do to get a driver's license.) Basically, the bargain in today's unwritten marriage contract is that the husband gets the right to the wife's services in return for supporting her. Whereas under common law the husband had "the absolute right to the product of the wife's industry," today the husband has only the absolute right to the product of the wife's industry *within the home.* "The wife's services and society are so essential a part of what the law considers the husband entitled to as part of the marriage," says Harriet Pilpel in *Your Marriage and the Law*, "that it will not recognize any agreement between the spouses which provides that the husband is to pay for such services or society."

The concept of the husband as supporter and wife as dependent underlies all the current legal inequalities of married women. To cite some specific examples:

Property. In common-law property states—like New York—husband and wife each exercise full control of what they own before, or acquire during, the marriage. But the woman who works only inside the home never has a chance to acquire property of her own, and therefore may never have any legitimate interest in, or control of, the family assets. (The only way she can acquire property is by gift, which makes her subject to her husband's patronage.) As John Gay said in *The Beggar's Opera*, "The comfortable estate of widowhood is the only hope that keeps up a wife's spirits." Her situation is improved by her husband's death; in every common-law property state, each spouse has a non-barrable interest in the estate of the other. However, this sometimes adds up to very little. For instance, in New Jersey, a wife only has "dower rights"; if her husband dies, she is entitled to one-third of the income from his real property. If the couple lived in an apartment and didn't own any real estate, the law guarantees her nothing.

Even in six of the eight community-property states where the spouses share equally in the property acquired during the marriage, the husband is given management control. Thus a woman may earn as much as her husband and have no say in how her money is spent. In the two exceptions, Washington and Texas, husband and wife have separate control of the property each acquires. Even this arrangement leaves the non-earning spouse without any control of the purse strings.

Name. In many states the law deprives the wife of full freedom to use her own name: in Illinois in 1965 when a woman sought the right to vote although she had not registered under her married name, the Appellate Court said she couldn't. In a recent case, a three-judge

97

Federal court upheld the Alabama law requiring a woman to assume her husband's surname upon marriage by ruling that a married woman does not have a right to have her driver's license issued in her maiden name. In Michigan, if a man changes his last name his wife must also change hers; she may not contest the change, although the couple's minor children over the age of sixteen may do so.

Domicile. Domicile is a technical term sometimes defined as a "place where a person has a settled connection for certain legal purposes." (You can live in one place and be domiciled in another.) Domicile affects various legal rights and obligations, including where a person may vote, hold public office, serve on juries, receive welfare, qualify for tuition advantages at state educational institutions, be liable for taxes, have his or her estate administered, and file for divorce. In general, a wife's domicile automatically follows that of her husband and she has no choice in the matter. (NOW members have been challenging this law in North Carolina.)

The Onassis Marriage Contract

According to Christian Kafarakis, former chief steward on Aristotle Onassis' yacht, the marriage contract between Onassis and Jacqueline Bouvier Kennedy contains 170 clauses, covering every possible detail of their marital life.

There have been charges and countercharges, proofs and refutations flying ever since the contract was printed in *The People,* a Sunday newspaper in England. Does the contract exist? Was it created by an ex-steward with great legal imagination? Was Christian Kafarakis even a steward?

Truth or hoax, the document works more to support the current system of wife-as-prostitute than to equalize men and women. But it does spur our imaginations to greater possibilities of contract-making.

Separate bedrooms are stipulated, according to Mr. Kafarakis, for instance. He feels this may explain why Jackie O. has her own house on the island of Skorpios and stays in her Fifth Avenue apart-

---

The husband, generally, also has had the right to decide where he and his wife live, although recently he has been required to make a reasonable decision taking her wishes into account. The burden of proving she is reasonable, however, still rests with the wife.

To some women the loss of these rights may seem a small price to pay for support. In fact, the arrangement works out differently depending on economic class. The higher up the ladder her husband is, the better a woman is supported and the fewer services she gives in return. For the many millions of women who work outside the home, on the other hand, the bargain is not a terribly good one: in reality all they earn for the services they give their husbands is the responsibility of working outside the home as well as in it to help their families survive. These women learn another price they pay for the illusion of support— the low salaries they receive compared with men's are ironically justified by the argument that the "men have families to feed." This is not the fault of husbands but of

---

ment rather than in Onassis' floor-through at the Hotel Pierre.

So that Mrs. Onassis may be "sheltered from want," the Greek millionaire is supposed to have contracted for $600,000 a year in maintenance.

More, according to Mr. Kafarakis:

"If Onassis should ever part from Jackie, he will have to give her a sum of nearly £4.2 million [$9.6 million] for every year of their marriage.

"If she leaves him, her payoff will be a lump sum in the neighborhood of £7.5 million [$18 million], which is a highly desirable neighborhood. That is, if the parting comes before five years.

"If she sticks it out longer, she will receive, in addition to the £7.5 million, an alimony of £75,000 a year for ten years.

"If Onassis dies while they are still married, she will inherit the staggering sum of £42 million [$100 million]."

an economy structured on the unpaid services of women.

But the heaviest price those women who accept the role of dependent pay is a psychological one. Economic dependency is in itself corrupting, as can be seen in rawest form in country-and-Western songs of the "I-know-he's-being-untrue-but-I-never-confront-him-with-it-because-if-he-left-me-who-would-support-the-children" variety. And economic dependency breeds other kinds of dependency. The woman who has no established legal right in the family income fares better or worse depending on how well she pleases the head of the household. In the attempt to please she may surrender her own tastes, her own opinions, her own thoughts. If she habitually defers to or depends on her husband's decisions she will eventually find herself incapable of making her own.

The solution is not that wives should never work in the home or that husbands should not share their incomes with them. The solution is that we must begin to recognize that the work wives do belongs to them, not their husbands, and should be accorded a legitimate value. If wives make the contribution of full partners in their marriages, they should receive the rights of partners—not only, like slaves, the right to be housed, clothed and fed, or in other words, supported. This is hardly a new idea: in 1963 the Report of the President's Commission on the Status of Women recommended that "during marriage each spouse should have a legally defined right in the earnings of the other, in the real personal property acquired through these earnings, and in their management."

There is, however, hope of progress. Although the Uniform Marriage and Divorce Act drafted by the National Conference of Commissioners on Uniform State Laws has not yet been adopted anywhere (Colorado has adopted the divorce portion of the law), it embraces some of the principles of marriage as partnership. It would make irremediable breakdown of the marriage the only ground for divorce, institute a division of property based on the assumption that husband and wife have contributed equally to the marriage, and determine custody according to the best interests of the child without the traditional bias in favor of the mother.

Should the Equal Rights Amendment be passed, it may require that most of the inequalities in the marriage relationship be abolished. According to an analysis published in *The Yale Law Journal*, the amendment would give women the freedom to use any name they wish, give them the same independent choice of domicile that married men have now, invalidate laws vesting management of community property in the husband alone, and prohibit enforcement of sex-based definitions of conjugal function. "Courts would not be able to assume for any purpose that women had a legal obligation to do housework, or provide affection and companionship, or to be available for sexual relations, unless men owed their wives exactly the same duties. Similarly, men could not be assigned the duty to provide financial support simply because of their sex." Even should the amendment pass, however, it would take years of action in the courts to implement it. Meanwhile, perhaps the best we can do is to say with Lucy Stone and Henry Blackwell that while we wish to acknowledge our mutual affection by publicly assuming the relationship of husband and wife, we do not promise obedience to laws that discriminate against us. And perhaps, by writing our own contracts we can modify the effect of those laws.

The problem with a husband and wife sitting down together and drafting a legal contract incorporating their beliefs concerning marriage is that the state immediately horns its way into the act. Marriage, contrary to popular belief, is more *ménage à trois* than *folie à deux*. It is a contract to which the state is a third party, and though you and your spouse may be in perfect accord, there are certain things the state will not tolerate. Most of these things are against what is known as public policy. Under public policy, according to Harriet Pilpel, "the courts, in many states, will not enforce any agreement which attempts to free the husband from the duty of support to the wife. . . . Nor will the courts uphold any agreement which attempts to limit or eliminate the personal or conjugal rights of marriage as distinguished from property rights. An agreement that the parties will not live together after marriage is void. So is an agreement not to engage in sexual intercourse or not to have children. One court has even held that it is against public policy for an engaged

101

couple to agree that they will live in whatever place the wife chooses. Under the law, said the court, that is the "husband's prerogative and he cannot relinquish it." Public policy also forbids contracts which anticipate divorce in any way. Agreements defining what will happen if a couple divorces or the conditions under which they will divorce are seen as facilitating the dissolution of marriages.

There are certain contracts, called ante-nuptial agreements, that the state clearly permits us to make. These contracts, according to Judith Boies, a matrimonial and estate lawyer with the New York law firm Paul, Weiss, Rifkind, Wharton & Garrison, may concern property owned before marriage, property acquired after marriage by gift or inheritance, and property right in each other's estates. A

THE UTOPIAN MARRIAGE CONTRACT

1. The wife's right to use her maiden name or any other name she chooses.

2. What surname the children will have: husband's, wife's, a hyphenated combination, a neutral name or the name the children choose when they reach a certain age.

3. Birth control: Whether or not, what kind and who uses it. (One couple—the wife can't use the Pill—splits the responsibility 50-50. Half the time she uses a diaphragm, half he uses a condom.)

4. Whether or not to have children, or to adopt them, and if so how many.

5. How the children will be brought up.

6. Where the couple will live: Will the husband be willing to move if the wife gets a job offer she wants to take? Separate bedrooms? Separate apartments?

7. How child care and housework will be divided: The spouse who earns less should not be penalized for the inequities of the economic world by having to do a larger share.

8. What financial arrangement will the couple embrace? If husband and wife are both wage-earners, there are three basic possibilities:

   a) Husband and wife pool their income, pay ex-wife cannot waive support, but she can waive interest in her husband's estate.

Some lawyers believe that people should be able to make whatever marriage contracts they like with one another. "Why should marriage be any different from any other contract?" asks constitutional lawyer Kristin Booth Glen, who teaches a course in women's rights at New York University Law School. She believes that the state's intervention in people's marriages may be in violation of Article I, Section 10, of the United States Constitution, which says that the states are forbidden to pass laws "impairing the obligation of contracts." Other lawyers feel that we don't really know which of the contracts we might wish to make concerning marriage would

penses and divide any surplus. (This was Leonard and Virginia Woolf's arrangement. At the end of the year, after payment of expenses, they divided the surplus between them equally so each had what they called a personal "hoard.")

b) Husband and wife pay shares of expenses proportional to their incomes. Each keeps whatever he or she has left.

c) Husband and wife each pays 50 per cent of expenses. Each keeps what he or she has left.

If husband earns significantly more than wife, the couple might consider a) that the disparity is a result of sexist discrimination in employment and there should perhaps be some kind of "home reparations program" to offset this inequity, and b) whether the couple really has an equal partnership if one has greater economic strength, and therefore possibly greater power psychologically, in the relationship.

9. Sexual rights and freedoms. Although any arrangement other than monogamy would clearly be against public policy, in practice some people make arrangements such as having Tuesdays off from one another.

10. The husband might give his consent to abortion in advance.   —S.E.

be enforceable. "There will have to be some litigation first," says Kathleen Carlsson, a lawyer for the Lucy Stone League. "In the light of the new feminist atmosphere, the decisions rendered today might not be the same as those rendered twenty years ago."

Judith Boies concurs with this view and feels that couples should begin right now to make whatever contracts suit their needs. If both spouses are wage-earners, they should contract how money and expenses will be divided. If they decide to have any joint bank accounts, they should sign a written agreement defining in what proportions the money in the account belongs to them. Then if one party cleans out the account—a frequent if unfortunate prelude to divorce—the contract would establish how they had intended to share the property.

Wives often assume—erroneously—that everything their husbands own belongs to them. In the common-law property states, property belongs to the person whose name it is in. When property is jointly owned, half presumably belongs to each spouse. However, this presumption is rebuttable. The husband can claim, for instance, that he and his wife only have a joint account so she can buy groceries.

The second kind of agreement couples might make is one in which the husband agrees to pay the wife a certain amount for domestic services. If there is no money to pay her, the debt accrues from year to year. When money becomes available, the wife would have first claim on it.

A third kind of financial contract could be made between husband and wife when one spouse puts the other through medical school or any other kind of education or training. The wife could agree to provide the husband with so much money per year to be paid back at a certain rate in subsequent years. This contract has a good chance of being enforceable, since even the tax laws recognize that spouses make loans to one another.

"All these financial contracts have a reasonably good chance of standing up in court," says Judith Boies. The one with the least chance is the one providing payment for household services. Since the financial contracts are more likely to be valid than those affecting personal aspects of the marriage, they should be made separately.

Judith Boies believes that, ideally, the personal contracts should also be valid. "The state shouldn't even marry people; it should just favor every contract that makes adequate provision for wife and children." The areas that might be covered in a comprehensive, total, utopian contract might include the wife's right to use the name she chooses, the children's names, division of housework and child care, finances, birth control, whether or not to have children and how many, the upbringing of the children, living arrangements, sexual rights and freedoms, and anything else of importance to the individual couple.

Since the marriage relationship is not a static one, any contract should permit the couple to solve their problems on a continuing basis. It should be amendable, revisable or renewable. One possibility is to draw up the first contract for a short period of time, and renegotiate later.

Although current policy clearly makes any agreement concerning it invalid, our utopian contract might also cover divorce. After all, the court in California's Contra Costa County now permits couples to write their own divorce agreements and receive their decrees by mail.

At this point, many readers are probably thinking, "Why get married at all, why not just draw up a contract that covers all contingencies?" Again, the state got there first. Such an agreement would be considered a contract for the purpose of "meretricious relations," or in other words an illicit sexual relationship, and therefore would be invalid.

Other readers are probably thinking, "But we love each other, so why should we have a contract?" As Barbara Koltuv says, "Part of the reason for thinking out a contract is to find out what your problems are; it forces you to take charge of your life. Once you have the contract, you don't have to refer back to it. The process is what's important."

Whether these contracts are legally enforceable or not, just drawing them up may be of great service to many couples. What we are really doing in thrashing out a contract is finding out where we stand on issues, clearing up all the murky, unexamined areas of conflict, and unflinchingly facing up to our differences.

105

THE SHULMANS' MARRIAGE AGREEMENT

I. Principles.

We reject the notion that the work which brings in more money is more valuable. The ability to earn money is a privilege which must not be compounded by enabling the larger earner to buy out of his/her duties and put the burden on the partner who earns less or on another person hired from outside.

We believe that each partner has an equal right to his/her own time, work, values, choices. As long as all duties are performed, each of us may use his/her extra time any way he/she chooses. If he/she wants to use it making money, fine. If he/she wants to spend it with spouse, fine.

As parents we believe we must share all responsibility for taking care of our children and home—and not only the work but also the responsibility. At least during the first year of this agreement, *sharing responsibility* shall mean dividing the *jobs* and dividing the *time*.

II. Job Breakdown and Schedule

(A) Children

1. Mornings: Waking children; getting their clothes out; making their lunches; seeing that they have notes, homework, money, bus passes, books; brushing their hair; giving them breakfast (making coffee for us). Every other week each parent does all.

2. Transportation: Getting children to and from lessons, doctors, dentists (including making appointments), friends' houses, etc. Parts occurring between 3 and 6 p.m. fall to wife. She must be compensated by extra work from husband. Husband does weekend transportation and pickups after 6.

3. Help: Helping with homework, personal questions; explaining things. Parts occurring between 3 and 6 p.m. fall to wife. After 6 p.m. husband does Tuesday, Thursday and Sunday; wife does Monday, Wednesday and Saturday. Friday is free for whoever has done extra work during the week.

4. Nighttime (after 6 p.m.): Getting children to take baths, brush their teeth, put away their toys and

clothes, go to bed; reading with them; tucking them in and having nighttime talks; handling if they wake at night. Husband does Tuesday, Thursday and Sunday. Wife does Monday, Wednesday and Saturday. Friday split according to who has done extra work.

5. Baby sitters: Baby sitters must be called by the parent the sitter is to replace. If no sitter turns up, that parent must stay home.

6. Sick care: Calling docors; checking symptoms; getting prescriptions filled; remembering to give medicine; taking days off to stay home with sick child, providing special activities. This must still be worked out equally, since now wife seems to do it all. In any case, wife must be compensated (see 10 below).

7. Weekends: All usual child care, plus special activities (beach, park, zoo). Split equally. Husband is free all Saturday, wife is free all Sunday.

(B) Housework

8. Cooking: Breakfasts during the week are divided equally; husband does all weekend breakfasts (including shopping for them and dishes). Wife does all dinners except Sunday nights. Husband does Sunday dinner and any other dinners on his nights of responsibility if wife isn't home. Whoever invites guests does shopping, cooking and dishes; if both invite them, split work.

9. Shopping: Food for all meals, housewares, clothing and supplies for children. Divide by convenience. Generally, wife does daily food shopping; husband does special shopping.

10. Cleaning: Husband does dishes Tuesday, Thursday and Sunday. Wife does Monday, Wednesday and Saturday. Friday is split according to who has done extra work during week. Husband does all the housecleaning in exchange for wife's extra child care (3to 6 daily) and sick care.

11. Laundry: Home laundry, making beds, dry cleaning (take and pick up). Wife does home laundry. Husband does dry-cleaning delivery and pick-up. Wife strips beds, husband remakes them.

HOW TO START A
CHILD CARE CENTER

LINDA FRANCKE and
DOROTHY PITMAN HUGHES

We almost got a Child Development Bill. Fought through the Senate and the House, hacked up, watered down, kicked around in Committee, it still *almost* became the first comprehensive attempt to deal intelligently with the needs of our children. Then President Nixon, calling the bill "family-weakening," wielded his Almighty Veto. Why? Because it was going to cost too much. At least, too much to fit into his priorities. Now, more than ever, parents must go ahead on their own. Here are ten basic guidelines for setting up child care centers in your community.

1) Canvass the neighborhood to attract children who reflect the diversity of your community's racial, ethnic and economic groups. Because word-of-mouth rarely travels much beyond your own circle of friends, ring doorbells and post notices in supermarkets, churches, local banks, club rooms, employment offices and laundromats in order to reach all strata of the community.

2) Find out how many parents need care for infants, toddlers, pre-schoolers; how much need there is for after-school play hours, night or weekend coverage for parents on off-hour work shifts.

3) Keep parents fully involved in the planning stages. Avoid elitist structures, "executive councils" or closed meetings. The most committed, hardworking parent is

---

Linda Francke is associate editor of "Newsweek." Dorothy Pitman Hughes is founder of the West 80th Street Community Child Care Center in New York.

one with a stake in the action and a voice in the policy-making.

4) Check into rules and procedures for day care licensing in the state and municipality in which you live. In most states, the Department of Welfare will dispense the red tape. If not, then try the Department of Public Health or Education. Don't be dismayed by the maze of regulations. Licensing rules were formulated as a common denominator for purely "custodial" care. They should be challenged and improved upon, rather than taken as gospel.

5) Your local Sanitation Department, Fire Department, Zoning Commission and building inspectors also publish requirements for group care facilities. In many cases the rulings are so antiquated that they are waived as a matter of routine. To avoid harassment, make sure that they have been waived before you sign a lease, rather than chance litigation later.

6) To locate a site for the center, a group of parents can fan out across the community to check the possibility of free or low-rent space. Churches, temples, civic centers, meeting rooms in housing projects, public schools and hospitals are often good bets. Check local industries and factories for unused space (and possible financial support). If a benefactor doesn't materialize, turn to local real estate agents and contractors to save time. Failing that, you'll have to patrol the area block-by-block looking for storefronts, unused garages, vacant buildings, and the like. There's no such thing as defeat. Neighborhood living rooms will do until the center outgrows them.

7) Financing is the biggest hurdle. If your center provides care for children of welfare mothers, Federal funding can be obtained under Title IV-A of the Social Security Act. Help with kitchen and food expenses is available through the National School Lunch Act. Foundations around the country offer money to child care programs, as do local service institutions such as the Community Chest. Neighborhood businessmen sometimes donate money or equipment. Finally, a small but steady income is generated by weekly fees charged to each family. The fee might be from $5 to $35, depending on how much outside financing is available.

8) Enlist the services of a local doctor and lawyer (preferably free). Incidentally, female doctors and lawyers are often the most sympathetic to the needs of a child care center. In the early stages of founding your center, it is especially helpful to have a lawyer on call for the inevitable problems with forms and bureaucractic procedure. Ask the lawyer to incorporate your center as a non-profit organization as soon as possible. Fund raising is a lot easier when the donor knows that contributions are tax deductible.

9) When hiring staff, don't get hung up on degrees and credentials. Look at the applicant's human qualities and be sure that she or he shares your goals and values for your children. If possible hire as many men as women; hire old people, young people, whites, blacks and other minorities to offer the children a wide range of cultural, intellectual and emotional viewpoints. With careful staffing, your child care center can be the "extended family" that most modern children have been denied.

10) Realize your strength and build upon it. When people work together in their mutual interest, social barriers break down and a sense of true community develops. As your group gains expertise it can help other neighborhoods to launch their own child care programs. Together, you can pressure for new legislation. In coalition you become an interest group, a force to reckon with on all issues affecting children, families, and the community at large.

Psychologically, it's a big leap for a parent to go from the playground to the public sphere. But once you make that leap, your private frustrations are replaced by activism

THE ARTIST AS HOUSEWIFE

The Housewife as Artist

ERICA JONG

God knows it's hard enough to be an artist at all, so why make a fetish about sex? The future's a mouth. Death's got no sex. The artist propelled by her horror of death and some frantic energy which feels half like hunger, half like hot pants, races forward (she hopes) in a futile effort to outrun time, knowing all the while that the race is rigged, doomed, and ridiculous. The odds are with the house.

Being an artist of any sex is such a difficult business that it seems almost ungenerous and naïve to speak of the special problems of the woman artist. The problems of becoming an artist are the problems of selfhood. The reason a woman has greater problems becoming an artist is because she has greater problems becoming a self. She can't believe in her existence past 30. She can't believe her own voice. She can't see herself as a grown-up. She can't leave the room without a big wooden *pass*.

This is crucial in life but even more crucial in art. A woman can go on thinking of herself as a dependent little girl and still get by, if she sticks to the stereotyped roles a woman is supposed to play in our society. Frau Doktor. Frau Architect. Mrs. George Blank. Mrs. Harry Blank.

Erica Jong's first book of poems, "Fruits & Vegetables," was published in 1971. Her second collection, "Half Lives," appeared in 1973; and her novel, "Fear of Flying," is scheduled for Fall, 1973 (all Holt, Rinehart & Winston). Her poems have been awarded numerous prizes including "Poetry" magazine's Bess Hokin Prize.

Harold's mother. Mother of charge plates, blank checks, bankbooks; insurance beneficiary, fund raiser, den mother, graduate student, researcher, secretary. . . . As long as she goes on taking orders, as long as she doesn't have to tell herself what to do, and be accountable to herself for finishing things. . . . But an artist takes orders only from her inner voice and is accountable only to herself for finishing things. Well, what if you have no inner voice, or none you can distinguish? Or what if you have three inner voices and all three of them are saying conflicting things? Or what if the only inner voice which you can conjure up is male because you can't really conceive of authority as soprano?

Just about the most common complaint of talented women, artists manqué, women who aspire to be artists, is that they *can't finish things*. Partly because finishing implies being judged—but also because finishing things means being grown up. More important, it means possibly succeeding at something. And success, for women, is always partly failure.

Don't get a doctorate or you'll never find a husband.

Don't be too successful or men will be scared of you.

The implication is always that if you're a success with your brain (or talent or whatever), you'll be a failure with your cunt (or womb or whatever). Success at one end brings failure at the other (Edna St. Vincent Millay's candle notwithstanding). No wonder women are ambivalent about success. Most of them are so ambivalent, in fact, that when success seems imminent they go through the most complex machinations to ward it off. Very often they succeed, too.

The main problem of a poet is to raise a voice. We can suffer all kinds of kinks and flaws in a poet's work except lack of authenticity. Authenticity is a difficult thing to define, but roughly it has to do with our sense of the poet as a *mensch*, a human being, an *author* (with the accent on authority). Poets arrive at authenticity in very different ways. Each poet finds her own road by walking it— sometimes backward, sometimes at a trot. To achieve authenticity you have to know who you are and approximately why. You have to know yourself not only as defined by the roles you play but also as a creature with an inner life, a creature built around an inner darkness.

Because women are always encouraged to see themselves as role players and helpers ("helpmate" as a synonym for "wife" is illuminating here,) rather than as separate beings, they find it hard to grasp this authentic sense of self. They have too many easy cop-outs.

Probably men are just as lazy and would cop out if they could. Surely men have similar and very crushing problems of selfhood and identity. The only difference is that men haven't got the built-in escape from identity that women have. They can't take refuge in being Arnold's father or Mr. Betty Jones. Women not only can, but are encouraged to, are often forbidden not to, are browbeaten into believing that independence is "castrating," "phallic," or "dikey."

It's not that women lack the inner darkness—one might almost argue that women are ideally suited to be artists because of their built-in darkness, and the mysteries they are privy to—but women don't explore that darkness as men do. And in art, the exploration is all. Everyone has talent. What is rare is the courage to follow the talent to the dark place where it leads.

Of course, it's also a question of trust. Katherine Anne Porter said that becoming a writer was all a question of learning to trust yourself, to trust your own voice. And that's just what most women can't do. That's why they are always seeking someone to dictate to them, someone to be their perennial graduate student adviser, someone to give them gold stars for being good girls.

Naming is the crucial activity of the poet; and naming is a form of self-creation. In theory, there's nothing wrong with a woman's changing names for each new husband, except that often she will come to feel that she has no name at all. (All men are mirrors. Which one will she look into today?) So her first name, her little girl name is the only one which winds up sounding real to her.

Erica.

Erica X.

My father (death) has come to get me.

May I please leave the room?

I have a sleep-over date.

If women artists often elect to use their maiden (or even maternal) names, it's in a sort of last-ditch attempt to

113

assert an unchanging identity in the face of the constant shifts of identity which are thought in our society to constitute femininity. Changing names all the time is only symbolic of this. It's only disturbing because it mirrors the inner uncertainty.

To have ten identities (wife, mother, mistress, cook, maid, chauffeur, tutor, governess, banker, poet?) is really to have none—or at least none you can believe in. You always feel like a dilettante. You always feel fragmented. You always feel like a little girl. Characteristically, women think of themselves as first names (children): men think of themselves as last names (grown-ups).

And what about "writing like a man" and the word "poetess" (which has come to be used like the word "nigrah")? I know of no woman writer who hasn't confessed the occasional temptation to send her work out under a masculine nom de plume, or under initials, or under the "protection" of some male friend or lover. I know women who can never finish a novel because they insist on making their narrators men, and women poets who are hung up on "androgynous poems" in an attempt to fool the first readers (often self-hating women like themselves).

But sex—it seems so obvious one shouldn't even have to say it—is a part of identity, and if a writer's problem is to find her human identity, only more so, then how can she manage this while concealing her sex?

She can't.

I knew I wanted to be a writer from the time I was 10 or 11 and, starting then, I attempted to write stories. The most notable thing about these otherwise not very memorable stories was that the main character was always male. I never tried to write about women and I never thought anyone would be interested in a woman's point of view. I assumed that what people wanted to hear was how men thought women were, not what women themselves thought they were. None of this was quite conscious, though. I wrote about boys in the same way a black child draws blond hair (like mine) on the faces in her sketchbook.

Yet I did not think of myself as self-hating, and it was only years later (when I was in my late twenties) that I realized how my self-hatred had always paralyzed me as

114

a writer. In high school, I thought I loved myself and I was full of dreams of glory. At 14, I declared myself a feminist, read bits and pieces of *The Second Sex*, and ostentatiously carried the book around. I talked about never wanting to marry—or at the very least not until I was 30 (which then must have seemed like old age to me). But for all my bravado, whenever I sat down to write, I wrote about men. Why? I never asked myself why.

It may also be relevant to point out that until I was 20 or so, all the characters I invented had WASP names— names like Mitch Mitchell, Robert Robertson, Elizabeth Anderson, Bob Briggs, Duane Blaine. Names like the ones you saw in school readers. Names like the ones you heard on radio soap operas. None of the kids I grew up with had such names. They were all Weinbergers and Hamburgers and Blotniks and Briskins and Friskins. There were even some Singhs and Tsangs and Wongs and Fongs. There were even some McGraths and Kennedys and Mc-Cabes. The Mitchells in my high school class could be counted on the digits of one severely frostbitten foot, or one leprous hand. But they were in all my stories.

This only proves that one's own experience is less convincing than the cultural norm. In fact, one has to be strong indeed to *trust* one's own experience. Children characteristically lack this strength. And most women, in our culture, are encouraged to remain children. I know two little girls whose mother is a full-time practicing physician who works a very long day and works at home. The children see the patients come and go. They know their mother is a doctor, and yet one of them returned from nursery school with the news that men were doctors and women had to be nurses. All her mother's reasoning and all the child's own experience could not dissuade her.

So, too, with my feelings about writers. I spent my whole bookish life identifying with writers and nearly all the writers who mattered were men. Even though there were women writers, and even though I read them and loved them, they did not seem to *matter*. If they were good, they were good *in spite of* being women. If they were bad, it was *because* they were women. I had, in short, internalized all the dominant cultural stereotypes. And the result was that I could scarcely even imagine a woman as an author. Even when I read Boswell, it was with him that I identified and not with the women he knew. Their lives seemed so constricted and dull compared with his dashing around London. I, too, loved wordplay and clever conversation. I, too, was a clown. I, too, was clever and a bit ridiculous. I was Boswell. The differences in our sexes honestly never occurred to me.

So, naturally, when I sat down to write, I chose a male narrator. Not because I was deluded that I was a man—but because I was very much a woman, and being a woman means, unfortunately, believing a lot of male definitions (even when they cause you to give up significant parts of your own identity).

Of course there were women writers, too, but that didn't seem to change anything. There was Dorothy Parker, whose stories I had by heart and whose bittersweet verses I'd recite whenever I could find a baffled adolescent boy who'd listen. There was Edna St. Vincent Millay, whose sonnets I had memorized from my mother's old, leather-bound, gold-tooled, tear-stained editions (with the crushed violets between the pages). There was Simone de Beauvoir, who seemed so remotely intellectual and French. There was Colette, who wrote of a baffling theatrical world of lesbian love whose significance eluded me then. And there was Virginia Woolf, whose style, at that point in my life, was too rich for my blood.

Except for Parker and Millay (whom I mythicized as much as read), it was to the male writers that I had to go. I even learned about women from them—trusting what they said, even when it implied my own inferiority.

I had learned what an orgasm was from D. H. Lawrence, disguised as Lady Chatterley. I learned from him that all women worship "the Phallos"—as he so quaintly spelled it. (For years I measured my orgasms against Lady Chatterley's and wondered what was *wrong* with me. It honestly never occurred to me that Lady Chatterley's creator was a man, and perhaps not the best judge of female orgasms. It honestly never occurred to me to trust myself or other women.) I learned from Shaw that women can be artists. I learned from Dostoevski that they have no religious feeling. I learned from Swift and Pope that they have too much religious feeling (and therefore can never

116

be quite rational). I learned from Faulkner that they are earth-mothers and at one with the moon and the tide and the crops. I learned from Freud that they have deficient superegos and are ever "incomplete" because they lack the one thing in this world worth having: a penis.

I didn't really become an avid reader of poetry until college. The modern poets I loved best then were Yeats and Eliot, Auden and Dylan Thomas. Diverse as they were, they had in common the assumption of a male viewpoint and a masculine voice, and when I imitated them, I tried to sound either male or neuter. Despite Emily Dickinson, poetry, for me, was a masculine noun. It came as a revelation to discover contemporary women poets like Anne Sexton, Sylvia Plath, Muriel Rukeyser, Carolyn Kizer, Adrienne Rich, and Denise Levertov, and to realize that strong poetry could be written out of the self that I had systematically (though perhaps unconsciously) repressed. And it was not until I allowed the femaleness of my personality to surface in my work that I began to write anything halfway honest.

I remember the year when I began to write seriously, when I threw out all my college poems and began again. What I noticed most persistently about my earliest poems was the fact that they did not engage my individuality very deeply. I had written clever poems about Italian ruins and villas, nightingales and the graves of poets—but I had tried always to avoid revealing myself in any way. I had assumed a stock poetic voice and a public manner. It was as though I disdained myself, felt I had no *right* to have a self. Obviously an impossible situation for a poet.

How did this change? It's hard to chronicle in detail because the change was gradual and I can't retrace each step. I was living in Europe in a kind of cultural and intellectual isolation. I was part of no consciousness-raising group. I was part of no writing seminar. Yet gradually I managed to raise my own consciousness as a poet. The main steps were these: first I owned up to being Jewish, urban, and American; then I owned up to my femaleness.

It was in Germany that I first set myself the task of writing as if my life depended on it (and of writing every day). For an atheistic New York Jew who had been raised to feel as indifferent to religion as possible, Germany

117

was an overwhelming experience. Suddenly I felt as paranoid as a Jew in hiding during the Nazi period. For the first time I began to confess to my primal terror, to my sense of being a victim. I began to delve into my own tears and fantasies, and finally I began to write about these things. Little by little, I was able to strip away the disguises. I was able to stop disdaining myself. I was able to stop feeling that what I was (and therefore what I had to write about) must, of necessity, be unimportant.

From persecuted Jew to persecuted woman is not a very long step. When you begin to open up your own sense of vulnerability and make poetry of it, you are on your way to understanding your femaleness as well. That was the progression for me. First I confessed to being a victim. Then I identified with victims. Finally, I was able to cast off the mask of the WASP male oppressor which I (and my writing) had worn for so long.

From then on, it was just a question of burrowing deeper and deeper. I no longer had anything to hide. Once I confessed to my vulnerability, I was able to explore it, and from that everything followed. I stopped writing about ruins and nightingales. I was able to make poetry out of the everyday activities of my life: peeling onions, a trip to the gynecologist, a student demonstration, my own midnight terrors and dreams—all the things I would have previously dismissed as trivial.

Because of my own history, I think women poets have to insist on their right to write like women. Where their experience of the world is different, women writers ought to reflect that difference. They ought to feel a complete freedom about subject matter. But most important, our definition of femininity has to change. As long as femininity is associated with ruffles and flourishes and a lack of directness and honesty, women artists will feel a deep sense of ambivalence about their own femaleness. In a culture where *woman* is a synonym for *second-rate,* there's no mystery about why women want to "write like men."

In cultural life, as elsewhere, women are damned if they do and damned if they don't. They are often paralyzed and afraid to write because they feel their experience is trivial, yet if they write outside of their experience, they are condemned as inauthentic. No matter how great their achievement, they are always called *women* artists rather than artists. No wonder they are so afraid to write, and having written are so afraid to submit their work for display or judgment. Even their greatest successes are tinged with failure. They are never praised without being patronized. Their jacket photographs are reviewed instead of their books.

When I was in college, I remember listening (and growing increasingly depressed) as a visiting writer went on and on about how women couldn't possibly be authors. Their experience was too limited, he said. They didn't know blood and guts and fucking whores and puking in the streets, he growled. At the time this silly cliché made me miserable. How could a girl hope to be a writer unless she had a history more lurid than that of Moll Flanders? (It never occurred to me then that this let out most men, too.) It was the old Hemingway-Miller-Mailer routine. The writer as tough guy. The writer as Tarzan crossed with King Kong. Naturally, if you believed that *machismo* garbage, you had to believe that (most) women couldn't be authors. And certainly men who had empathy with women (or indeed with anyone) were excluded, too.

A few years later, when I got to know Neruda's elemental odes about lemons and artichokes, and Ponge's prose poems about soap and seashells and oysters, and William Carlos Williams's red wheelbarrow, and Gary Snyder's essay about the poet as tender of the earth household, I was able to reconsider the relation between the poet and the housewife and find it far more congenial than any growling male writer of the Tarzan-King Kong school would want to believe. The trouble with the phallic-warmongering-whoring image of the damned, doomed artist was not only that it so often backfired (literally in Hemingway's case, figuratively in the case of others), but that it was essentially so destructive and so false. It came out of a sensibility which can only be called imperialist: man against nature and man against woman. What was needed was a different concept of potency (and *poetency*) and a different concept of the artist. Perhaps all artists were, in a sense, housewives: tenders of the earth household. Perhaps a nurturing sensibility had never been more needed. Besides, it was the inner experience, not the outer one, which was crucial. One of the things which makes a poet a poet is the ability to see the world in a grain of sand or eternity in a wild flower (or in an onion). As Valéry says, "It is with our own substance that we imagine and create a stone, a plant, a movement, an *object*: any object is perhaps only the beginning of ourselves."

Like blacks, women will have to learn first to love their own bodies; and women poets will have to learn to write about their bodies. Their breasts: those two blind animals with painted eyes. Their cunts: those furry deaf-mutes speaking a red tongue. The astounding royal purple of their blood. It will not do to continue to confuse the pen with the penis. Despite all the cultural stereotypes which equate femininity with second-rateness, women artists will have to learn to explore their own femininity and to define its true nature. Just as male artists will have to confront their envy of women (which often takes the form of asserting that women can't be artists), women artists will have to confront their own bodies and the symbolic implications of their bodies. It seems to me not accidental that two of the most prolific and courageous contemporary women poets (Anne Sexton and Denise Levertov) long ago attempted to write about their bodies and never attempted to conceal that they were women.

Nor does it seem accidental that one of the few female artists to fully explore her own anger at being a woman (Sylvia Plath) could never return from that exploration. Plath's extraordinary burst of creativity after childbirth bears witness to the kind of power hidden in women if only it could be tapped. We can no longer doubt its existence. Our problem is how to tap it without going mad.

The pseudocompliment ("you write like a man"), and the contempt in which the term "poetess" is held both attest to the fact that all of us (even feminists) continue to regard masculinity as a standard of excellence. We still use the word "feminine" as if it were synonymous with foolish, frivolous, and silly. In his sniggeringly sexist introduction to *Ariel*, Robert Lowell "compliments" Sylvia Plath (who is too dead to hear) by saying that she is "hardly a person at all, or a woman, certainly not another 'poetess'. . . ." No wonder Lady Lazarus rises out of the ash with her red hair—"And I eat men like air."

Note also the Kirkus-Service blurb on the back of Marge Piercy's second book of poems: "Angry, alive, loving, real poetry: not feminine, but powerfully female." As if "feminine" and "real poetry" were opposites.

Since authenticity is the key to everything, it seems particularly fatal for a woman artist to become a surrogate male. Nearly all the women poets of our time who have succeeded in becoming individual voices know this. They explore the fact of being female and go beyond it, but they never deny it. Of course, they pay dearly for this in condescending reviews (which seldom fail to disparage their sex in some way or other), and their reputations are somehow never taken as seriously as those of male poets of the same (or lesser) quality. But at least they go on writing and publishing; they go on working. Yet they are so pitifully few in number! For the handful of Levertovs, Plaths, Richs, Piercys, Swensons, Wakoskis, Sextons—there must be thousands of talented women, sitting on unfinished books, wondering how to make themselves sound unfeminine.

I think that as we become more aware of the deep relationship between poetry and ecology, we will begin to revalue the female sensibility in poetry (and in all the arts). We will begin to value the exploration of femaleness (as many ancient civilizations did) rather than to reject it.

But if there's too much male chauvinism in literature and in the literary world, the answer to it is not female chauvinism. Beyond the initial freedom women writers need (of allowing themselves to write like women), there's the greater goal of the mature artist: to become artistically bisexual.

Virginia Woolf points out that the process of developing as an artist means at some point transcending gender. It means having empathy for both sexes, partaking of both halves of humanity and reconciling them in one's work.

At just about this point I anticipate a howl of outrage about my use of the words "male" and "female" and my assumption that there is such a thing as "female sensibility" in poetry or elsewhere. Unfortunately, the terms male and female have become so loaded and politicized, so laden with old prejudices, that they are almost useless for purposes of communication. We don't know what masculine really means, nor what feminine really means. We assume them to be opposites and we may not even be right about that. Yet we are stuck with these words. They are deeply embedded in language and in our minds (which language in part helped to shape). What shall we do with masculine and feminine? Does it do anyone any good just to pretend that they don't exist?

Gradually, we will redefine them. Gradually, society will change its false notions of male and female, and perhaps they will cease to be antitheses. Gradually, male experience and female experience will cease to be so disparate, and then maybe we will not have to worry about women understanding their own self-hatred as a prerequisite to authentic creative work. But what are we to do in the meantime? In our society, men and women still *do* have different life patterns and different experiences. Shouldn't each sex be permitted an authentic expression of its own experience?

Luckily, the artist has an answer. The artist is not finally male or female, but both at once. It is as though the artist were one of those African votive figurines which have breasts, a pregnant belly, and a penis. I think of Leopold Bloom giving birth, of Orlando changing sexes with the centuries. I think of the artist as a mental hermaphrodite, or as a shaman who exploits sexuality in order to get beyond sexuality. The artist starts by exploring her/his particular sexual identity, but this is only the beginning. It is only a necessary way inward. Once women writers are able to write freely about being women, they will be able to write freely about being human. They will be able to explore the world with the confidence that it really belongs to them—just as male writers have done.

Women artists cannot escape exploring their own sexuality because the connection between sex and inspiration is intimate. They are both forms of intense energy. They connect and correspond. The relationship between the artist and the Muse is a sexual relationship in which it is impossible to tell who is fucking and who is being fucked. If sex and creativity are often seen by dictators as subversive activities, it's because they lead to the knowledge that you own your own body (and with it your own voice), and that's the most revolutionary insight of all.

III. In Search of Sexual Freedom

THE SEXUAL REVOLUTION
  WASN'T OUR WAR

THE SATURDAY MORNING
  NAP-CONVERSION

LESBIAN LOVE
  AND SEXUALITY

BODY HAIR:
  THE LAST FRONTIER

THE SEXUAL REVOLUTION WASN'T OUR WAR

ANSELMA DELL'OLIO

The Women's Liberation Movement caught men off guard. They thought women had *already* been liberated by the Sexual Revolution.

According to most men, a liberated woman was one who put out sexually at the drop of a suggestive comment, who didn't demand marriage, and who "took care of herself" in terms of contraceptives. As far as men were concerned, that's all the liberation any woman needed. The bonus of bra-lessness and economically independent women simply fueled the misconception that the Women's Liberation Movement was in some way a continuation of the Sexual Revolution, also known as the More-Free-Sex-For-Us Revolution.

In truth, women had been liberated only from the right to say "no" to sexual intercourse with men. Kinsey in the fifties, and Masters and Johnson in the sixties, contributed scientific ammunition for the Sexual Revolution which freed women from Victorian morality. This gift relieved us of centuries of moral and social pressure which had dictated that no *nice* woman would ever "go all the way" with a man until marriage.

But it destroyed the sanctuary of maidenhood, pressuring us to give our bodies without respite from late adolescence to old age, or until our desirability as sex ob-

---

Anselma Dell'Olio is a writer, lecturer, TV producer and actress, and founder and director of the New Feminist Theater.

124

jects waned. For the first time, we were shorn of all protection (patronizing as it may have been, and selective in terms of class privilege) and openly exhorted to prostitute ourselves in the name of the New Morality.

We have come to see that the so-called Sexual Revolution is merely a link in the chain of abuse laid on women throughout patriarchal history. While purporting to restructure the unequal basis for sexual relationships between men and women, our munificent male liberators were in fact continuing their control of female sexuality.

With the advent of the new feminism, women finally began to ask, "What's in it for us?" And the answer is simple. We've been sold out. The Sexual Revolution was a battle fought by men for the great good of mankind. Womankind was left holding the double standard. We're supposed to give but what do we get? Kinsey's *Sexual Behavior in the Human Female* offered a priceless handbook for the Revolution in its findings that 1) women could and did enjoy sex after all, 2) there is no such thing as a frigid woman, only inept men, 3) virginity in women was no longer considered important or particularly desirable by most men, and 4) women and men were now equals in bed and equally free to screw their bottoms off for the sheer fun of it.

What the popularizers of Kinsey's findings neglected to emphasize would have provided the seeds for a *real* revolution in the bedroom. We still remained ignorant about the difference between orgasm and ejaculation, about the speed-of-response differential between male and female orgasm, about the fallacy of the vaginal-clitoral orgasm dichotomy, about women's multi-orgasmic nature, and so on. Because of this deliberate or unconscious *excising* of Kinsey, and later Masters and Johnson, we have managed to survive into the seventies with the double standard intact, alive and well in the minds of average American males. And many females as well.

The new freedom of the Sexual Revolution was at best a failure, at worst a hoax—because it never caused significant changes in the social attitudes and behavior of men to correspond with this New Morality being forced upon women. There has been no real revolution in the bedroom.

For this crucial reason, the Sexual Revolution and the Women's Movement are polar opposites in philosophy, goals and spirit.

The real point is that there are not many women—liberated, unliberated, feminist or otherwise—who are sleeping around for the sheer pleasure of it. The Achilles' heel of the Sexual Revolution is persistent male ignorance of the female orgasm.

Now, if there was anything that a Sexual Revolution should have been able to accomplish, especially with the data made available by Kinsey as early as 1953, it should have been more pleasure for women during intercourse. Yet 19 years later, the majority of women have to put up with relatively infrequent orgasms during sexual—at least heterosexual—encounters.

Of course, before Freud, the question of orgasm was moot, because women weren't supposed to enjoy sex at all. Decent women submitted to it with clenched teeth. With Freud, female orgasm was rediscovered, and the high incidence of female frigidity was declared to be an emotional and psychological problem of "sexually immature" women. Vexed by the fact that women could reach orgasm freely and quickly through masturbation, but less frequently during standard intercourse, Freud thought there must be two kinds of female orgasm: clitoral and vaginal. The clitoral orgasm, which worked for most women, but was difficult in the standard male-gratifying positions, was defined as "adolescent." The vaginal orgasm was declared to be the only true, mature, womanly orgasm. It could only be achieved during intercourse through vaginal penetration by the penis. Since overwhelming numbers of women weren't experiencing the "mature" orgasm, Freud concluded that women, recognizing their inferiority to men, were loath to accept their femininity. For this dreadful condition he prescribed psychiatric assistance.

Over the decades psychiatrists have treated scores of us with little success, trying to get us to surrender to our destinies by transferring our orgasms from clitoris to vagina. Generations of women, including the present one, grew up masturbating in secret (men talked about masturbating long before women did), and faking orgasm during intercourse.

126

Kinsey and Masters and Johnson should have changed all that. Neither study produced a shred of evidence in defense of the double-orgasm theory. As a result of their extensive experiments, Masters and Johnson advanced four important conclusions:

1) The dichotomy of vaginal and clitoral orgasm is entirely false. Anatomically, all orgasms are centered in the clitoris, whether they result from direct manual pressure applied to the clitoris, indirect pressure resulting from the thrusting of the penis during intercourse, or generalized sexual stimulation of other erogenous zones, such as the breasts.

2) Women are naturally multiorgasmic. That is, if a woman is immediately stimulated following orgasm, she is likely to experience several orgasms in rapid succession. This is not an exceptional occurrence, but one of which most women are capable. In all of their students, Masters and Johnson found no incidence of a totally or clinically frigid woman.

3) While women's orgasms do not vary in kind, they vary in intensity. The most intense orgasms experienced by the research subjects were by masturbatory manual stimulation by the partner. The least intense orgasms were experienced during intercourse.

These findings were surely cataclysmic and should have been liberating, at least to the degree that they served to destroy established myths. Yet five years after publication they still have had little or no impact on men's minds or women's lives.

Many women are still not having orgasms and still, as noted earlier, not sleeping around for pleasure—an unchanging fact despite the Sexual Revolution. In the meantime, men *are* pursuing sex for just that reason.

If pleasure is rarely the reward, women's continued willingness to have intercourse doesn't make sense. Why, then, are we doing it?

The truth is we are often pressured into it, and not only by the litany of the Sexual Revolution. It may be the need for affection and attention. Or the desire to please; the need for approval. It's no news to any of us that men can have intercourse with women they are totally disinterested in as human beings. For many women sex fails to bring physical satisfaction, and depersonalized sex denies women even the side benefits of communication and approval.

What the Sexual Revolution should have taught us is that *need* shouldn't be confused with *love*; that men and women can neither give nor receive love until we stop confusing it with a need for security and approval. The Women's Movement is trying to teach that lesson. Love is not getting high on fantasies of romance, the perfect lover, absolute happiness and sexual ecstasy. Love is based on two-way communication and respect, and that only exists between equals.

When feminists are critical of romance, there is often a panicked reaction: "But you can't possibly want to get rid of love?"

No, we don't want to negate the emotion. We want a better definition. We want to get rid of the sick and hoary old illusions which women have pursued relentlessly at the price of our humanity. What is called love now is so clearly exploitative and unsatisfactory that it should make us suspicious that men want to preserve it at all costs. What is called love now is vital to the oppression of women.

Men have poured their creative energies into work; we have poured ours into love, and an unequal social and sexual relationship was the inevitable result. And because this was the situation the Sexual Revolution failed to correct, feminists are moving into an area they have won by default.

The problems are enormous. Whenever we manage to combat our sense of insecurity long enough to get out and actually do something, our attitude is betrayed by our conditioned belief that women's work is dispensable, our contributions secondary. When the man in our life complains about our absorption in work, we are apologetic. We turn somersaults to accomplish it at odd hours rather than claim our time as our own and risk his disapproval, anger or complete rejection. Often, we apologize for our work even before a man has time to object—so thorough is our conditioning. And men most often accept our sacrifice as their due. The *droit du seigneur* of the Sexual Revolution.

Therefore, a sexually liberated woman without a feminist consciousness is nothing more than a new variety of prostitute for the Sexual Revolution. If we don't sell ourselves for money in the street or security in the suburbs, we sell ourselves in exchange for some measure of approval and (we hope) lasting affection.

Feminism was reborn in part to protest and correct the fact that, although women are no longer burdened by an old-fashioned morality (which is good), we are now saddled with the entire range of emotional and physical consequences of sexual availability (which is bad).

That old form of censure—every woman a virgin or else —was simply one side of the coin. The ancient epithet of "promiscuous" was always the other, and the coin has now been turned over. Promiscuity has lost none of its old sting. It has only acquired a whole new negative connotation with the aid and comfort of psychology, psychoanalysis and psychiatry. Practitioners in these fields have taken to accusing the sexually active woman of "emotional" frigidity, inability to relate, nymphomania, etc. So even the apparent gain for women is illusory. If we are no longer expected to be virgins physically, we are still expected to be "practicing" virgins—mentally pure and only "in love" with one man.

There are many women who have decided to challenge the hypocrisy of the Sexual Revolution by refusing to tolerate this double-standard nonsense and becoming at least as sexually liberated as men are. They soon find out that, emotional problems aside (and they are not insignificant), the physical obstacles are close to insurmountable. The physical price a woman stands to pay for sexual nonchalance is staggering. A woman's chances of getting pregnant are still good (meaning bad), and those chances get better (meaning worse) as the frequency of, and number of partners for, intercourse increases.

The Pill is hazardous, and other forms of contraception are a drag, a distraction and a nuisance, not to mention being failure-prone. Tampering with women's vastly more complex reproductive system is all right with men, but vasectomy, still the most practical, inexpensive method of birth control which can be performed in minutes in a doctor's office, is not; at least, not with most men. The virility-fertility connection is sacrosanct. And there you have the clearest evidence of why feminists view the Sexual Revolution as one more male ego-trip. What kind of Sexual Revolution is it when, in the year 1971, the possibility of a practical male contraceptive still goes largely unresearched and unpublished?

It's now clear that the dice are loaded and the Women's Movement is the one force that can make the game honest. The rising chorus of laments about a growing incidence of male impotence probably means that our feeble attempts to correct the situation are going in the right direction. It can't hurt for men to begin to experience a small dose of the medicine women have had to swallow for a century.

The sexual politics imbedded in the culture shows itself clearly through the language bias. When men don't function sexually, they are called "impotent," *without power*. When women don't, they called "frigid," *icy cold*. The active-passive dichotomy is apparent. Men know a good thing when they have it, and they go to whatever lengths are necessary to protect their potency. If a woman is a threat to that potency, then her ego must be crushed. Notice that we never hear about females being "castrated" when our egos are destroyed and our potency denied. Such melodramatic symbolism is reserved for men. In fact, a woman's loss—her frigidity, her inability to derive pleasure from sex—is frequently described by men as "castrating." Frigidity is our fault, and male impotency is our fault too!

Perhaps the best evidence of the phoniness of the Sexual Revolution is the prevailing eighteenth-century attitude toward masturbation. For men, it is a fact of life. Locker rooms and little boys' habits have made it so. But for women, auto-eroticism is a newly discovered secret. In view of the fact that there are women who still fake orgasm, women who feel embarrassed to request their own satisfaction in intercourse, or women who flatly tell a partner, "I don't come, so don't wait for me," it's about time we perfected the art of masturbation. Not as a substitute for intercourse, but as one means to pleasure and to the understanding of our own bodies.

These subjects remain difficult to discuss in plain language, and so the Women's Movement has rushed in where the Sexual Revolution feared to tread. And none too soon. As Susan Lydon says in *Sisterhood Is Powerful,* "Appearances notwithstanding, the age-old taboos against conversation about personal sexual experience haven't yet been broken down." This reluctance on the part of most people to discuss the issues openly and honestly has allowed the creation of many myths about sexual supermen and superwomen. Men who are inadequate lovers squirm out of their plight by claiming that a previous girlfriend was a real sexpot who had fourteen vaginal orgasms in five minutes, so what's wrong with *you* anyway? Men strangle us with our sisters' lies. The next time you're tempted to fake orgasm, just think of the harm you may be doing to the next woman, if not to yourself.

A man with some respect for himself and you will not be turned off by your honesty. You may be the first woman who ever talked to him straight, and he may welcome the opportunity to clear up doubts of his own. And if he is turned off, you are well rid of him. As long as you allow yourself to be victimized, rest assured you *will* be—again and again. If female sexuality has been such a mystery to women for so long, think how mysterious it must be to men.

Men are severely troubled by women picking lovers with an awareness of self-interest. We are still ridiculed for wanting, after all this time, to reclaim our true sexuality. We are accused of *demanding* orgasms like spoiled children demanding sweets before dinner. Men are never accused of the same. For them, orgasms are regarded as necessary to health.

As often as we repeat the following story, it never seems to be enough: According to Ovid, Tiresias, the blind prophet of Thebes who had been both a man and a woman, was asked to mediate in a dispute between Jove and Juno as to which sex got more pleasure from lovemaking. Tiresias unhesitatingly answered that women did. Two thousand years and several Sexual Revolutions later, we still believe the opposite to be true.

Ideally, of course, we shouldn't have to *demand,* but we are going to have to start becoming more vocal and insisting on a sexual bill of rights if the situation is ever to

131

change. Otherwise we will end up abandoning the idea of men as sexual partners or accepting our own mutilated sexuality. It's a radical truism that power is never relinquished, it must be taken—and potency is a synonym of power.

THE SATURDAY MORNING NAP-CONVERSION

MARGARET EDMONSON SLOAN

How could you ever really believe you were beautiful, sister? Do you remember all those painful Saturdays you spent in the little storefront beauty shop sometimes waiting three or four hours cause Mrs. Jones had scheduled two or three other people at the same time and of course she had to "squeeze in" the woman who had to get her head done to speak at her church supper that night, and you sat there rather anxious reading *Seventeen* and *Ingenue* and wondered in passing how come you didn't have "good" hair and the smoke from the burning hair and the hot grease would rival any neighborhood rib joint finally she called you and as you sat there with your head in braids under the dryer (Mrs. Jones said it dried quicker that way) you looked at the nine or ten other women at their various stages on the road to beauty and all the chatter and conversation came together somehow because this was the only place in the neighborhood that black women could Talk and not be uptight about The Man or their men and hell yes you know that Ruby would never leave Al but she sure as hell had us convinced she was going to every week and Mrs. Jones gave you the mirror and you gave her the three-fifty you had rolled up in your hand all this time and you emerged with hotdog

Margaret Sloan, one of the editors and writers on the "Ms." staff, is an activist and lecturer in the Black and Women's Liberation Movements, and is currently at work on a book about black feminism.

bangs or Shirley Temple black curls and you walked home carrying that proudness tight inside you tighter than a Mary Jane stuck in your cavity and the new holes in your ears tasted the round gold rings that had just replaced the tiny broom straws and the few places that Mrs Jones accidentally burned you with that hot comb didn't hurt so bad now cause your head wasn't nappy no more at least for about two weeks or until it rained but for right now your head was looking good and you saw Bobby Lee coming toward you and you just knew he would notice cause last time he saw you your head was nappy but now your ends were straight and you quick wiped the grease from the edges of your forehead and flashed a big grin at that handsome dude and he half smiled and said hey what's happnin' and went right on past and you tried to hide your hurt feelings by skipping home cause running wouldn't be cool and you stopped at Mr. Johnny's and got you a greasy 10¢ no 25¢ bag of potato chips and told him to pour lots of hot sauce on it you were hungry now he surely must have noticed your head maybe he was just being cool you walked upstairs and no one was home checked the mirror once or twice hoping the reflection wouldn't catch you and you turned on the set and there was Maureen O'Hara in "Sentimental Journey" and you saw all that long hair hanging down and how that man took that white woman and ran his fingers through her hair she lay sick in that bed with all that long hair on that pillow and you wondered if Bobby Lee had seen that woman too she sure was pretty and you caught yourself again in that mirror trying to shake your hair back and it's two weeks later and naps don't shake anyway and you walked back to the beauty shop with a newspaper in case it's still raining when you get out you weren't gonna go but your momma had said this morning before she left for work girl get your hair done cause it really looks bad you hope you don't see Bobby Lee until after you get out and maybe this time he'll notice cause you gonna get a permanent.

LESBIAN LOVE AND SEXUALITY

DEL MARTIN AND PHYLLIS LYON

So little is known about lesbians that even we ourselves are caught up in the myths and stereotypes so prevalent in our society. These stereotypes are based upon the false assumption that the lesbian is first and foremost sexual in all her thoughts, desires, and actions. What people fail to realize is that being a lesbian is not merely indulging in physical acts of lovemaking. For the woman involved, it is a way of life, encompassing her whole personality, one fact of which is, of course, her sexuality. For her it is the expression of a way of feeling, of loving, of responding to other human beings.

A lesbian is a woman whose primary erotic, psychological, emotional, and social interest is in a member of her own sex, even though that interest may not be overtly expressed. At a time when women, the forgotten sex, are voicing their rage and demanding their personhood, it is fitting that we emerge from the shadows. Like her heterosexual sister, the lesbian has been downtrodden,

Ms. Martin and Ms. Lyon are founders of the Daughters of Bilitis, Inc. Both have served on the board of the Council of Religion and the Homosexual. Ms. Martin was the chairperson of Citizens Alert, a group involved in police-community relations, and Ms. Lyon is Associate Director of the National Sex Forum of the Glide Foundation.

From "Lesbian/Woman" by Del Martin and Phyllis Lyon, published by Bantam Books, Inc. and Glide Publications, San Francisco. Copyright © 1972 by Del Martin and Phyllis Lyon. By permission of Bantam Books, Inc. All rights reserved.

135

but doubly so: first, because she is a woman, and second, because she is a lesbian.

We are lesbians. We have lived together as lovers for 19 years. We also helped to found the Daughters of Bilitis in 1955. Over the years in which we have been deeply involved in the homophile movement, we have talked to, counseled, socialized with, and been friends with thousands of lesbians. We have lived the experiences that we are writing about.

When we first started living together as a couple, we knew practically nothing about female homosexuality. We only knew that we loved each other and wanted to be together.

Del had read a few books. She had been to a number of gay bars, which was always a twitchy experience, since police raids were commonplace then. She had met a few lesbians and had had one previous affair.

Phyllis had been vaguely aware of homosexuality, but the possibility that she and her roommate had been thrown out of their college dorm due to implied homosexuality had never occurred to her until years later. Although she liked men, dated them, and even once went so far as to become engaged, Phyllis still had reservations about taking that final step down the aisle. She had always maintained several close friendships with women.

That's about where we were. Hardly the ideal background from which to launch a lesbian "marriage," which is the way we thought of our relationship. The only model we knew, a pattern that also seemed to hold true for those few lesbians we had met, was that of the mom-and-dad, or heterosexual, marriage. So Del assumed the role of "butch," while Phyllis, being completely brainwashed in society's role of woman anyway, decided she must be the "femme."

In the course of our 19 years together, we have learned that many lesbians in our age group (late forties) went through the same kind of role-playing. While a few became trapped in this butch-femme pattern, most come in time, as we did, to the realization that they are both women and that's why they are together.

Although she is most often seen solely as a sexual person by straight society, the lesbian has as many sexual

136

problems as her heterosexual sisters. For she is caught in the same morass of sexual suppression as other women. By and large, she is raised to prepare herself to become wife and mother and helpmeet to her male mate. She is still taught that woman must save herself sexually for her husband—the nice girl doesn't play around. She is taught that woman is not aggressive—at least not obviously— but rather uses devious (feminine) means to achieve her ends. She is taught, more often than we would like to think, that sex is something evil or dirty and not, heaven forbid, something which is pleasurable and joyous.

It is not at all strange, then, that the lesbian often grows to adulthood denying her sexuality, afraid of her sexual feelings, and in many instances unaware and un-knowledgeable of what they mean and how to cope with them. You can imagine the chaotic state of mind that a young lesbian may suffer: not only is she, like every woman, basically ignorant about the real meaning of sex-uality, but she is also faced with the horrifying fact that the sexual feelings surfacing in her are directed toward another woman. It is little wonder, then, that a percentage of lesbians find themselves frigid (or nearly so), that many lesbians are completely passive and cannot bring themselves to reciprocate and make love to their partners, and that a number of lesbians never have any sex at all.

To understand the lesbian as a sexual being, one must understand woman as a sexual being. Until about the end of World War I in America, a woman was considered nonsexual by men and by herself. It seems incredible now, but prior to that time it was considered totally "unlady-like" for a woman to enjoy sex. So heavy was this pressure that some women had operations for clitoris re-moval, so that they would not act in such an unseemly manner. From this background, women started the long and still not completed fight to regain control of their own bodies, the fight to be considered full sexual beings.

Imagine a young woman 18 years old finally sorting out her feelings, her emotions, her sexual responses only to find that they all point toward the fact that she is a lesbian. At the same time she will find that she is con-sidered illegal, immoral, and sick; a man-hater, a wom-an-seducer, masculine, and hard.

Further, considering that most young women of 18 in this country are very naïve about sex, either theirs or anyone else's, it follows that our young woman probably hasn't the foggiest notion of how to go about making love to another woman. In fact, she probably hasn't any idea of how to go about meeting another woman of like persuasion. Depending on her background, she either feels that sex is a good thing, a bad thing, or just a thing. These values will be with her as a lesbian, just as they would have been with her had she been heterosexually oriented. Fate will have something to do with the outcome. Her first sexual contact may be with an experienced lesbian, in which case at least she will have some idea of what goes on; it may be with someone as inexperienced as she. If this is the case, much will depend on the attitudes of both women toward sex.

A third possibility for our 18-year-old is that she may have had her first introduction to sex with a man. According to a study on "Sexual Behavior of the Female Homosexual" done by Drs. Marcel T. Saghir and Eli Robins, more than three-fourths of the lesbians interviewed had experienced heterosexual intercourse. For the majority, this occurred between the ages of 20 and 29 and was primarily done in a spirit of experimentation rather than because of strong sexual arousal.

We mentioned earlier that many lesbians are frigid, a concept that blows the minds of most straight persons who have always thought of lesbians only as sexual beings. It shows, too, that heterosexual women do not have a corner on the frigidity market.

There is nothing mysterious or magical about lesbian lovemaking (except, perhaps, for the two people involved). The body goes through certain physiological changes during the sexual cycle whether the initiator of the cycle is you, a partner, or an inanimate object. The mystery and the magic come from the person with whom you are making love. Everything that one woman does to another can be done also by a man, but for a lesbian that would change everything. It isn't the actions or the act: it is the woman involved who makes it more than just "physiological changes."

What do lesbians do sexually? We do very much the

138

same thing a man and a woman (or a man and a man) do, with the exception that there is no penis present. There are many ways that two women can seek and find sexual gratification together, ways limited only by the imaginations of the persons involved.

The three most common techniques used in lesbian lovemaking are: mutual masturbation, cunnilingus, and tribadism. Mutual masturbation consists of manipulation of the clitoris, caressing the labia, and/or penetration of the vagina by the fingers until sexual excitation or orgasm occurs. This can be done simultaneously by the partners or in turn. Cunnilingus is the stimulation of the clitoris, the labia, and sometimes penetration of the vagina by the tongue of the partner. Again, this can be done by one to the other or, in the "69" position, by both at the same time. Tribadism, on the other hand, involves one woman lying atop the other, followed by up-and-down rhythmic movements to stimulate the clitoris of each. It is a technique which takes time to master but which may fulfill the butch-femme fantasies of male-and-female sexual role-playing. Whatever the variations of position, satisfaction comes from stimulation of the clitoris by the friction of movement against the body of the partner.

Two other methods by which two women may achieve sexual gratification seem to be relatively rare in practice. One is the use of penis substitutes or dildos (usually a rubber apparatus shaped and colored to look like a penis). While this idea tickles the fancy of most men who cannot imagine women enjoying or being satisfied sexually without a penis, the dildo's most prevalent use is by heterosexual women in masturbation. But the truth is that the great majority of women, whether lesbian or heterosexual, have never seen a dildo. Women who feel the need for inserting a penis substitute in the vagina to fulfill their heterosexual fantasies are more apt to improvise and use a candle, a banana or a cucumber. However creative these intercourse devices may be, it is important to emphasize that a penis (or penis substitute) is not necessary for a woman's sexual gratification.

In all studies (and there haven't been that many) about lesbian sexual practices, one unanimous finding has

139

been that the use of penis substitutes is relatively rare. We are sure that most lesbians have tried something at one time or another, but for continuing satisfaction in sex there is nothing like a living, breathing, responding person. As one lesbian declared during a discussion one evening, "If I wanted a penis for sex, I'd go find a live one, not a fake."

The remaining technique is anilingus, use of the tongue in and around the anus. The finger of one partner may also be used to stimulate the anal region, which is an erogenous zone.

As in the case of any sexual communication between two people, full knowledge and prowess come only by practice. Further, there are a number of possible variations on these basic techniques. Foreplay (embracing, kissing on the mouth and other parts of the body, breast fondling and sucking, nibbling at the ear, and touching and stroking various erogenous zones of the body) is important in lovemaking.

These, then, are the techniques, open to much variation by individual women. They have been listed in books before, primarily in those of a scientific or pseudo-scientific nature. This has been helpful to many a young lesbian. Not so long ago, about the only way she could educate herself was to go to a gay bar and pick up (or be picked up by) someone more experienced than she was.

Although the great majority of lesbians make love to one another, there are some who either refuse to make love to their partners or who refuse to be made love to. The former is usually a woman with one (or all) of three problems. She has been brainwashed into thinking that women are passive in sex; she is new at the game and afraid she won't perform correctly; or she really feels sex is dirty and can't bring herself to action. Given half a chance, with the right partner, she can overcome all three of her blocks.

But the woman who won't let anyone make love to her, who can only be the aggressor, has a much deeper problem. Mac, very much the sophisticated business-woman during the day, metamorphosed into very much the "male" and "husband" when she was at home. Her "wife," who didn't work, literally brought Mac her slippers and pipe. "I can't let Jan touch me sexually," she explained. "It would destroy the illusion. Besides, the man should be the aggressive one." It was unfortunate she hadn't discussed the matter with Jan, for Jan didn't have any illusions that Mac was a man. She loved *her* and would much have preferred a woman-to-woman relationship. Jan had tried discussing the matter with Mac early in their relationship, but had run into a mammoth wall of stubbornness and had given up.

The gay terminology for a couple like Mac and Jan is butch and femme. Why did the butch-femme idea arise, and why has it lasted? For one thing, it isn't difficult for women, regardless of their age, to look around and see that it is an advantage to be a man. It seems fairly logical, also, that if you are sexually attracted to a woman, you should play the "masculine" role. Especially if what you have in mind is getting yourself a wife. Two women setting up housekeeping have only the model of the heterosexual marriage: the division of labor along strictly sex-role lines.

The stereotype of the dyke is an extreme of the butch. A young woman who has decided she is a lesbian may know only this stereotype: a masculine-looking woman *à la* Stephen Gordon in *The Well of Loneliness*. So she dresses and acts the part she thinks she must as she makes her first tentative forays into homosexual society. In some lesbian circles, she is likely to find herself pressured into declaring herself either butch or femme, and she is then expected to conform in matters of dress, speech, and action to the prevailing mode of the group she hopes to join.

There are also lesbians who truly believe they are more "masculine" than "feminine" and that they were born so. One assumes that they equate the masculine role with aggression, power, and superiority, while they feel that the feminine means passivity, inferiority, and softness.

Those women who feel that they are "born butch" tend to ape all the least desirable characteristics of men. In this case, one may say to these butches, "Up against the wall, male chauvinist pigs!" For to consider oneself a heterosexual, to stress that male and female are opposites which presumably attract, is to accept the entire male-imposed doctrine that woman's place is indeed in the home serving the male. Much of the polarity between men and women has centered around procreation. But the sex act itself is neither male nor female: it is a human being reaching out for the ultimate in communication with another human being. The roles men and women (or butch and femme) play in our country are only acting, not honest and equal relationships between two human beings.

We can't stress too strongly that the great majority of lesbians think of themselves as women and are looking for (or have found) another woman with whom to share their lives. Many go through the butch stage for the identification factor. If you look like any other woman on the street, how in the world are you going to find other lesbians, or, more to the point, how are you going to find you? So stereotyping yourself may be a plus factor at the beginning of one's gay career. Thankfully, the vast majority of those now proudly fighting their "butchhood" in gay bars and meeting places around the country will shift to their true identity as women as they become older, wiser, and more sure of their identity as people.

We have found some interesting anomalies in the butch-femme pattern over the years. One which crops up rather consistently is women—usually divorced and, we suspect, not lesbian at all—who pair up with butch lesbians. In these partnerships the entire male-female dichotomy is acted out to the nth degree. The femmes insist that their butches wear only male clothing and that they appear and act as nearly like the stereotyped male as possible.

Most of these femmes have been divorced more than once. Their only knowledge of a relationship is that of man to woman, so they fashion their own "man" out of the woman they can relate to. It does not make for a happy situation for either party, and usually the two-some doesn't last very long. Most lesbians, whatever their life-style, are striving today for more egalitarian relationships.

We have watched the gradual decline of the butch-femme concept of a relationship for 16 years, though the stereotype has not yet vanished. As a life-style it has

142

many disadvantages. One is the jealousy which invariably creeps in. Jealousy of one's partner, especially obsessive jealousy, indicates an uncertainty of the relationship and bears witness to the fact that the two partners feel possessed like chattel, by one another. If you are sure of your partner's love, if your partner is a person and not a thing, then jealousy either doesn't exist or is extremely minimal.

While there is a certain amount of jealousy among lesbian couples, as much as there is between heterosexual couples, the Saghir-Robins study previously mentioned indicates that jealousy ranks last as a reason for relationships breaking up. Further, many women who break up their relationship as lovers remain fast friends. This wouldn't be possible if the split had come over jealousy rather than a change in, or loss of, emotional attachment— the reason given for most "divorces."

Much change has taken place in the way all women (straight or gay) in this country think about sex roles and personal relationships. There appear to be three strong influuences: 1) a questioning of religious dogma, exposing myths and reexamining taboos, thereby developing a new code of sexual and social ethics; 2) research on human sexuality, opening up avenues to more widespread sex education, and discovery of the Pill; and 3) the various liberation movements, which all decry the use of labels to separate people and which raise the question of what it really means to be human.

The homophile thrust for freedom and equality has forced some clergymen at least to recognize that love and sex between two persons of the same sex can be, and is, equal to and as valid as that between two persons of the opposite sex. Such a realization leads inevitably to a reevaluation of the sacred institution of marriage. If the church recognizes love between two homosexuals, it cannot very well continue to condemn love between two heterosexuals who have not bothered to "sanctify" their love through wedding vows. Theologians are presently wrestling with these problems.

Those naturalists who have condemned homosexuals not only point to Adam and Eve, but to lower animals as proof that our true nature is to be heterosexual. Biologists, however, have observed homosexual contacts in widely varied species of mammals, and anthropologists have found homosexual activity in creatures as diverse as hamsters and horses or porcupines and pigs.

More recently, Dr. Albert Ellis, sexologist and executive director of the Institute for Rational Living in New York City, has stated that those persons who are either exclusively heterosexual or exclusively homosexual are neurotic. The Kinsey studies verify that American men and women are not necessarily as exclusive in their private sexual behavior as they pretend publicly.

As Dr. C.A. Tripp, psychologist, pointed out, most human sexual behavior is *learned*. It is only in the lower animals that it is totally instinctive. The higher on the evolutionary scale you are, the less instinctive are your sexual relations. So our life experiences "teach" us our sexuality, which may turn out to be hetero, homo, or bi. The Kinsey staff, in *Sexual Behavior in the Human Female*, pondered the fact that, given the physiology of human sexual response plus our mammalian background of behavior, "it is not so difficuult to explain why a human animal does a particular thing sexually. It is more difficult to explain why each and every individual is not involved in every type of sexual activity." At least three-fourths of the lesbians we have known have had heterosexual intercourse more than once. For the majority of these women, the experience was good erotically; that is, orgasm was achieved, and there was a pleasurable feeling. But there was not the emotional involvement which was present in a lesbian sexual relationship.

And that is what makes the difference.

BODY HAIR: THE LAST FRONTIER

HARRIET LYONS and
REBECCA W. ROSENBLATT

Actress Faye Dunaway boldly reveals her unshaven arm-pits for a photograph in a national magazine, and says that that's the way she will appear in all future film roles.

Eunice Lipton, an art historian in her thirties, strokes the growth on her legs and says, "It may seem ugly, but it's *me*."

Graduate student Grace Boynton, 23, explains that she has thrown away her razor because, "I got insulted that my natural body processes were considered disgusting by society."

And social worker Peg Brennan, 47, has decided "not to add anything that isn't me—and not to remove anything that is me."

While cosmetics imply the real woman is not enough, shaving says the real woman is too much. There is probably nothing more tedious, messy, or hazardous in the feminine beauty regimen than the removal of hair from underarms, legs, eyebrows, lips, chin, and breasts.

Ah, the pain . . . a splash of cologne or, heaven forbid, a dip in the ocean after shaving could produce a strong desire for Darvon. Several moments of teeth-gnashing usually follow a dab of deodorant to a newly depilated armpit. And who among us has not hacked ankles, shins,

---

Harriett Lyons is a member of the "Ms." editorial staff and a free-lance writer. Rebecca W. Rosenblatt, a free-lance writer, hosted "The Urbanites," which appeared on WCBS-TV in New York during 1971-72.

and knees in hurried preparation for a date, and then tried desperately to stop the bleeding with dainty dots of toilet paper when a tourniquet would have been more appropriate?

Because anything that destroys hair is likely to have a similar effect on skin, depilation can also be dangerous —particularly if it's electrical or chemical.

Electrolysis, the use of short-wave electric current to remove hair permanently, must be done expertly if permanent scarring is to be avoided. If the follicle is not thoroughly destroyed, those cursed hairs, for whose eternal removal you suffered and paid dearly, will resurface. Home electrolysis devices are downright unsafe and rarely successful.

Cream depilatories smell awful and, if the explicit label instructions are not carefully followed, can cause irritation, allergic reactions, and eye injuries. Waxing, one of the oldest methods of hair removal, can be a masochistic trip. After the wax preparation is applied and allowed to harden, it is pulled off, taking both your hair and your breath away.

An emerging feminist consciousness tells us that all this punishing depilation reflects the depth of our socialized distaste for our bodies. We slavishly remove body hair and substitute artificial scents for natural body odors because we dare not expect approval if we look or smell as we really are.

Despite the all too familiar bother and pain—as well as the new feminist mandate to let it all hang out—the custom of depilating is still alive and well. Those who do vastly outnumber those who don't, but discussions of female body hair reveal disquieting associations.

In psychoanalytic parlance, hair is the accepted symbol of the genitals, so sexual behavior and hair-removal rituals are closely associated. Hairiness, in this lexicon, is translated as unrestrained animal sexuality. Conversely, extremes of haircutting and shaving are symbolic of castration or the repudiation of the very existence of sex. Anthropological evidence linking shaving customs to celibacy and ceremonial mutilation rites (such as cutting off of finger joints) supports this symbology.

With hairiness equated to animal sexuality, the unchecked or uncovered appearance of hair in the armpits and on the legs of women collides with the culture's premise of female sexuality as passive. The implication that a woman's underarm and leg hair are superfluous, and therefore unwanted, is but one embodiment of our culture's preoccupation with keeping women in a kind of state of innocence, and denying their visceral selves. Some women will even shave pubic hair, thereby emulating the infantile sexlessness of a little girl. And only within the last two years has the men's magazine, *Playboy,* conceded that adult women have pubic hair at all.

The acceptance of hairiness in men, like its suppression in women, is connected to animality, but, ironically, the association is misguided. Man/woman is the only animal sexually active beyond the need to reproduce; the only animal that can experience orgasm at times when conception is impossible. We are both the most sex-driven and the least hairy of the animal kingdom, yet we persist in equating sexuality with furriness. The bald or non-hairy-chested man suffers a minor discrimination all his own.

While our puritanical attitude makes the hairless female body the quintessence of femininity, our obsession with cleanliness works to modify the acceptance of hairiness even in men. Long hair and beards are for dirty hippies. The clean-shaven and the crew cuts satisfy the American ideal.

Hair shares with feces, urine, semen, menstrual blood, spittle, and sweat a centuries-old association with impurity. As a result, fastidious women throughout history have felt obliged to remove hair that appeared anywhere but on the head or pubis. In the 1850s, women were so devoted to their hygienic images that they inflicted skin ulcers upon themselves by reckless use of depilatories made from lime, arsenic, and potash.

Biologists have given shaving yet another crude rationale. In their belief, hair is a surplus human product; its original function—to provide protection from the elements, extremes in temperature, insect bites, and the sun's rays—has been supplanted by clothing and technology. Hair growth is becoming a vestigial process, which will eventually disappear. Therefore its removal by shaving

147

is, in the biologists' view, as natural a way for human beings to get rid of it as shedding is for animals.

Race and class, with their attendant prejudices, determine special cultural attitudes toward body hair. The connotation of dirty foreigner *vs.* clean American has always been evident in our national thoughts on hair. A young woman involved in a bicycle accident was asked by a New York policeman examining her injured, unshaven leg, "You're not Puerto Rican, are you?"

It's true that, in Puerto Rico, women do not remove body hair unless they are upwardly mobile or mainland-oriented. In France, only lower class or provincial women remain hairy. Even the supposedly earthy Italian women have begun shaving underarms to conform with standards of chic-ness. In Spain, a moustache on a woman is considered sexy, but not necessarily well bred.

Hair underscores the various myths and mysteries which have arisen from our different skin colors. Intimidated racial groups try to lose their identity by adopting the hair texture and styles of the majority or ruling class. The kinky hair of American-born blacks has been obscured for generations by straighteners, pomades, and pageboy wigs. In Sweden, where most women are fair enough to make shaving a non-issue, dark-complexioned women shave to be less conspicuous.

The Afro-coifed black and the unshaven woman, regardless of her color, nationality, and class, make of their personal grooming a political statement. They reject an image of beauty and acceptability imposed by the society, and risk the censure reserved for the rebel.

In America in the 'seventies, the hirsute woman is not yet an idea whose time has come. The shaving of body hair by women stubbornly defies extinction. Given the convoluted symbolism of the ritual and the repellent stares directed at the unshaven woman, we are not surprised to discover that even the most liberated women backslide when beach weather arrives.

But more and more individual women are risking those stares to affirm their natural femaleness. Eventually, this small but intimate tyranny will be resisted, so that one more oppressive hangup can be retired forever and the hirsute will live happily with the hairless.

148

IV. Biology vs. Destiny

THE HOLE/BIRTH CATALOG

*DOWN WITH
    SEXIST UPBRINGING*

THE HOLE/BIRTH CATALOG

CYNTHIA OZICK

(1) The Logic of the Hole

It may be that almost everything separating women from
men is a social fabrication—clothing, occupations, thinking habits, temperament. It may be that when we say
"woman" we are invoking a heritage of thought, a myth,
a learned construct: an *idea*. But childbirth is not any of
these.

"Woman" can be an imagining, a convenient dream
of law or economics or religion. But childbirth is an event,
the event of the race, and only half the race undergoes it.
Is it, for that half, an illimitable experience, endlessly
influencing, both before and afterward, an event that domi-
nates until death?

Everyone is born, everyone dies, and though styles of
death are subject to invention and misfortune—getting
a bullet through your skull feels different, presumably,
from the slow, drugged death of the terminal cancer victim—we all struggle out of the birth canal with the same
gestures and responses. What happens immediately afterward—who cares for the infant, and how, and where—
is all at once the expression of the culture. If anatomy is

*Cynthia Ozick is author of "Trust" (New American Library,
1966) and "The Pagan Rabbi and Other Stories" (Knopf,
1971). Her work has appeared in numerous periodicals and
anthologies. She has received several awards for her writing
and was a 1972 nominee for the National Book Award.*

destiny, technology is also a kind of destiny, and the baby bottle, no less than the jet plane, can alter a civilization. Beds, stirrups, hospitals, doctors, nurses, stitches, bandages, pills, pillows, all the debris of folklore that flies out after every birth with the certainty of the expulsion of the placenta—these are the social impedimenta that clutter the event. They seem almost to be the event itself.

But the person in childbirth can be alone in a forest, and still the baby's head will be driven through the hole at the bottom of her torso. It is sensible for the hole not to be covered. The baby is born entirely exposed, either with a hole of its own or with an inseminatory rod. It is attached by a string of flesh. When the string is cut, that is the end of the event.

Is it the end of the event?

How long is the event of childbirth? Several hours; it varies with the individual. How long is a human life? Here the variation is greater. It is possible to die at birth, to be run over by a truck at 30, to be bombed at 40, to live to be old. But "woman" is concretely—not mythologically—woman only for the sake of the few hours of childbirth. All the rest of the time, her life and body are subject to more ordinary interruptions, by which she is distinguished very little from anyone else. Childbirth is an appointment (menstruation is the appointment calendar, listing only cancellations; like any negative calendar it requires small attention)—an appointment undertaken nine months before, which, unless nullified by abortion, volitional or not, must inevitably be kept.

But imagine a lucky and healthful land where a human being is likely to live peaceably until 80. Imagine one who has experienced childbirth only twice, with the event lasting each time about six hours. For the sake of 12 hours out of a life 700,800 hours long, this person is called "woman." For the sake of 12 hours out of a life 700,800 hours long, this person is thrust into an ethos which enjoins rigid duties on her, almost none of them rationally related to the two six-hour events of childbirth.

Or imagine, in this lucky and healthful land, a person 60 years old. She is widowed and lives alone in a dark little flat. Consider her. Thirty years ago she spent six hours expelling an infant out of her hole via powerful involuntary muscular contractions. She did it in a special room in a big building. It was a rod-bearing infant, which affterward grew to be somewhat under six feet in height, dressed itself in two cloth tubes cut off at the ankles, and by now has spurted semen up a number of human holes; having settled down in a house in California, it has inseminated one hole three times. The person in the dark little flat thinks of herself as the grandmother of Linda, Michael, and Karen. Which is to say: she thinks of herself as a hole; the *Ur*-hole, or call it the primordial cavity; and that is very interesting.

It is also very interesting to look closely at this person who thinks of herself as a hole. She is covered up by a cloth tube cut off at the knees. Why is she covered up by one cloth tube cut off at the knees, instead of two cloth tubes cut off at the ankles? Thiry years ago she expelled an infant out of her hole; that is the reason. Anatomy is destiny, and it is her destiny, because of her hole, to wear one cloth tube cut off at the knees instead of two cloth tubes cut off at the ankles.

Now look at the hair that grows on her head. Do not look for the hair in her armpits; she has clipped that. The reason she has clipped the hair in her armpits is that 30 years ago she expelled an infant out of her hole. But her head hair: look at that. It is of a certain length and is artificially curled. The reason her head hair is of that length, artificially curled, is that 30 years ago, she expelled an infant out of her hole.

Watch her. She is sitting at the kitchen table sewing another cloth tube. Once in a while she rises and stirs something in a pot. The reason she is sitting at the kitchen table sewing a cloth tube (the kind cut off at the knees), the reason she gets up now and then to stir her pot, is not that she is hungry or is in need of another cloth tube. No: the reason is that 30 years ago she expelled an infant out of her hole, and ever since then she has conscientiously performed the duties that do not flow from the event.

And if the event had not taken place? She would still conscientiously perform those duties that do not flow from the event that did not happen. The hole in her body dictates her tasks, preoccupations, proprieties, tastes, character. Wondrous hole! Magical hole! Dazzlingly influential hole! Noble and effulgent hole! From this hole everything follows logically: first the baby, then the placenta, then, for years and years and years until death, a way of life. It is all logic, and she who lives by the hole will live also by its logic.

It is, appropriately, logic with a hole in it.

(2) Destiny, Birth, Life, Death

"Anatomy is destiny." These are Freud's words, and they have become almost as famous as his name itself. But ah, fame is not truth; and destiny is precisely what anatomy is *not*. A hole is not destiny. A protuberance is not destiny. Even two protuberances—a pair of legs, nearly half the human body—are not destiny. If anatomy were destiny, the wheel could not have been invented; we would have been limited by legs.

Destiny is what is implicit in the very area we cannot speak of because it is not known—the sense of things beyond and apart from shape or dimension or hole or protuberance. There is an armless painter who holds the brush between his toes. Cut off two more limbs and he will use his teeth. The engineering is secondary to the vision. Aantomy is only a form of technology—nature's engineering. Destiny means, at the lowest, a modification of anatomy, and, at the highest, a soaring beyond anatomy. A person—and "person" is above all an idea—escapes anatomy. To reduce the person altogether to her anatomy is to wish the person into a nullity.

There is, first of all, the nullity of the servant.

In *Civilization and Its Discontents*, Freud posits a remarkable anatomical theory for the secondary and dependent condition of woman. The argument begins with the assertion that since fire represents the power of civilization, whoever can control fire can be dominant over civilization. By the "control" of fire, Freud explains, he means the ability to put it out at will. A man can pee on a fire from a little distance. Prevented by her anatomy, a woman cannot. Therefore man is in charge of civilization and woman cannot be.

Later in the same essay Freud identifies woman as

having a "retarding and restraining influence" on civilization. This is because the tasks of civilization require "instinctual sublimations of which women are little capable."

But all this is the later Freud. *Civilization and Its Discontents* was composed after cancer had already begun to ravage Freud's face, and when Hitlerism had already begun to corrode German civilization. If he was writing, under such circumstances, with a kind of melancholy truculence, it might be instructive to see what Freud's views were at an earlier and happier time. Consider, then, Freud in love.

In love with Martha Bernays, Freud translated John Stuart Mill's essay "On the Subjection of Women" into German. He did not notice its relevance to his fiancée's position—she had committed herself to a long and chaste engagement, during which she was to idle years away in waiting for the marriage. As for the essay itself, he did not like it. For one thing, he complained of its "lifeless style." (In a footnote, Freud's biographer, Ernest Jones, a Freudian disciple, explains: "In exculpation of Mill one should mention that his wife is supposed to have been the main author of the book in question." It is axiomatic that a wife's style is inferior.) Freud's letter about Mill, written to his fiancée, is long; but worth, one supposes, the attention due genius:

He [Mill] was perhaps the man of the century who best managed to free himself from the domination of customary prejudices. On the other hand—and that always goes together with it—he lacked in many matters the sense of the absurd; for example, in that of female emancipation and in the woman's question altogether. I recollect that in the essay I translated a prominent argument was that a married woman could earn as much as her husband. We surely agree that the management of a house, the care and bringing up of children, demand the whole of a human being and almost exclude any earning, even if a simplified household relieve her of dusting, cleaning, cooking, etc. He had simply forgotten all that, like everything else concerning the relationship between the sexes. That is altogether a point with Mill where one simply cannot find him human. His autobiography is so prudish

154

or so ethereal that one could never gather from it that human beings consist of men and women and that this distinction is the most significant one that exists. In his whole presentation it never emerges that women are different beings—we will not say lesser, rather the opposite—from men. He finds the suppression of women an analogy to that of Negroes. Any girl, even without a suffrage or legal competence, whose hand a man kissses and for whose love he is prepared to dare all, could have set him right. It is really a stillborn thought to send women into the struggle for existence exactly as men. If, for instance, I imagined my sweet gentle girl as a competitor it would only end in my telling her . . . that I am fond of her and that I implore her to withdraw from the strife into the calm uncompetitive activity of my home. It is possible that changes in upbringing may suppress all a woman's tender attributes, needful of protection and yet so victorious, and that she can then earn a livelihood like men. It is also possible that in such an event one would not be justified in mourning the passing away of the most delightful thing the world can offer us—our ideal of womanhood. I believe that all reforming action in law and education would break down in front of the fact that, long before the age at which a man can earn a position in society, Nature has determined woman's destiny through beauty, charm, and sweetness. Law and custom have much to give women that has been withheld from them, but the position of women will surely be what it is: in youth an adored darling and in mature years a loved wife.

"Nature has determined woman's destiny." It is, to borrow from Jones, no exculpation of Freud to note that he was a man of his class and era, and that this letter was written before 1890. Mill's essay is dated 1869; if Freud was, at his own valuation, a judge of human affairs, he was a retrogressive judge. And if he is, at the valuation of his posterity, a genius, his is the genius of retrogression.

But also of something worse. We come now to the nullity of death.

Mill, all lucidity and sanity, is called "prudish" and

"ethereal"—words meaning precisely the opposite of what Mill's essay exhibits to everyone who has ever read it attentively, with the exception of its German translator. Who is the prude—the man who sees the distinction between men and women as "the most significant one that exists," significant chiefly for reducing women to pet-like dependency in "my home," or the man who refuses to turn distinctions into liabilities? Who is the ethereal thinker—the man who poeticizes about tender attributes and adored darlings and miracle-working kisses, or the man who draws up a solid catalog of palpable discriminations against women? In inventing anatomy-is-destiny, Freud justified his having a household servant all the days of his life. The letter to his fiancée (who appears to have swallowed it all) is not only prudish and ethereal, but also bleatingly sentimental—because that is what sentimentality *is*: justification, exculpation, a covering-over, a retreat from clarity—prudishness and etherealism concealing real conditions.

Still, running a household, after all, is not tantamount to death, anguish, or even waste. Decent and fulfilling lives have gone down that road, if fulfillment is counted in pies and sock-washings. And why not? Bureaucrats and dentists are equal drudges and fiddlers, jobs are cells of domesticated emotion, offices are repetitious and restrictive boxes. Both men and women practice housewifery, wherever they are. Hemingway's early tales are cookbooks. If only "the management of a house" were the whole story! But no: once invoke Nature and Destiny and you are inviting an intensified preoccupation with death. Death becomes the whole story.

This is simply because all the truth any philosophy can really tell us about human life is that each new birth supplies another corpse. Philosophy tells only that; it is true; and if the woman is seen only as childbearer, she is seen only as disgorger of corpses. What is a baby-machine if not also a corpse-maker? Philosophy—Freud is a philosopher—leads only to the inexorable cadaver, and never to the glorious So What: the life-cry.

To say anatomy-is-destiny is to misunderstand the So What, that insatiable in-between which separates the fresh birth from the cadaver it turns out to be. To say anatomy-

156

is-destiny is to reverse the life-instinct—to reverse not only the findings of Darwin, but civilization in general. If the fish had stuck to its gills there would have been no movement up to the land. Lungs came because a creature of the sea wanted to take a walk, not vice versa. When a previous abundance of water began to evaporate during the breakup of the Ice Age, the unlucky fish had either to adapt to its destiny—air—or die. Air preceded lungs. In the history of evolution, destiny always precedes anatomy, and anatomy conforms by thinking up a convenient modification. In the history of civilization, dream precedes engineering. Imagine walking on the moon, and the artifact to take you there will follow the conception.

Freud, a retrograde thinker, had it backward. Celebrated for theorizing on evanescent and gossamer dream-life, he nevertheless limited humanity to the grossest designs of the flesh. In postulating anatomy-is-destiny, he stopped at the flesh; and the flesh dies. It is no surprise that Freud came finally to "discover" what he called the "death-instinct." He divided the mind between Eros and destructiveness, making death as central to his scheme as sexuality. And in choosing the centrality of death, he re-invented as instinct what the priests of the Pharaohs took to be ontology. By putting birth first, he put death before life.

This is no paradox. The life-instinct, insofar as we can define it (and we cannot), is the struggle to dare higher and higher, beyond the overtly possible, and in spite of knowing we will die. "The force that through the green fuse drives the flower/Drives my green age."

In the light of Freud's assertion of the death-instinct, it is absolutely no wonder that he distorted, misunderstood, and hated religion—which is to say holiness: which is to say the struggle to dare higher and higher, beyond the overtly possible. Freud's *Selbsthass** was of a piece with his hatred for his inherited faith. He despised Judaism because it had in the earliest moment of history re-

---

* Freud was joyous when Jung became a disciple—until then, he wrote, psychoanalysis had seemed like a "Jewish national affair," but now, with a Gentile attached to it, it would gain in value.

jected the Egyptian preoccupation with a literal anatomy of death and instead hallowed, for its own sake, the time between birth and dying. Judaism has no dying god, no embalming of dead bodies, above all no slightest version of death-instinct—"Choose life." In revenge against Judaism's declared life-principle, and to satisfy the urgencies and priorities of the death-instinct, Freud—this was the theme of *Moses and Monotheism*—turned Moses into an Egyptian. It meant he was turning himself into an Egyptian. It is no joke to notice that for mummies anatomy is all the destiny they will ever own.

(3) Death (continued), A letter from a Madman, and a Prudish and Ethereal Conclusion.

The being-born belongs to all of us, yet we remember nothing. In the forgetting itself lies the life-principle, the glorious So What—you are here, get started, live, see, do, dream, figure a destiny and make its mold for your little time. This is the meaning of the forgetting. And just as the being-born belongs to all of us, so the giving-birth belongs to no one. It is not a property or a lasting act. The making of the child gets done, and thereafter the child is a person, not a consequence or an ornament, and must be seen to with the diligence and generosity due all persons.

To make of the giving-birth a lifelong progression of consequences is to make a shrine of an act. It is a species of idolatry. A moment is mummified and consecrated— that very moment which the whole human race cannot remember. We are told that the capacity for childbirth makes a "woman." Woman, then, becomes the amnesia of the race. She is nullified into an absence.

But now there is a contradiction. She is not an absence; she represents, above all, the protoplasmic *thereness* of the human animal. She represents precisely what decays. She stands for dust, being dust-bringer. I took note earlier of that stupendously simple point: whoever creates the babies creates the corpses. Whoever signifies Birth signifies Death. Anatomy—in the case of woman, parturition —is destiny, the uterus is a grave, the childbearer carries death.

Freud saw woman wholly as childbearer. Seemingly apart from this perception, he came upon the notion of the death-instinct. This he related to the killing of the "primal father" by the sons banded together (a curious unprovable fiction on which a great part of Freud's work rests). He, the great connector, did not connect his perception of the destructiveness and aggressiveness in human nature with the act of parturition. Logic makes the connection. Whoever destroys, whoever is aggressive, has first to be born; the childbearer becomes Shiva the Destroyer. It is the logical product of anatomy-is-destiny. The uterus destines the woman to spew destruction.

How can this terrible logic, this ultimate *reductio* which places the whole burden of humankind's failings on the woman's uterus, be contravened?

With great simplicity. Do not define woman solely by the act of parturition, and the demonic structure dissolves. Then the woman bears the baby, but her entry into parenthood—parenthood, that brevity—does not tie off the world. Parenthood becomes a rich episode in a life struck full with diverse and multiform episodes. She is a mother, a worker, a reader, a sailor. She is a judge, a peddler, a druggist, a polisher of shoes, a pilot, a publisher, an engineer. She is any combination of anything. She chooses life. She is not mythologized by a definition: one-who-gives-birth-and-therefore-spreads-destruction-and-creates-graveyards.

Now it is time to tell about my letter. It is from a madman. The usefulness of madmen is famous: they demonstrate society's logic flagrantly carried out down to its last scrimshaw scrap.

My madman's letter is typed on four long sheets of law-sized paper, and all in carbon. Many copies of this letter have been broadcast by the diligent fellow, typing day and night on his machine. Here and there, at some especially passionate point, he has underlined with a heavy pencil. I pity him so much labor.

The reason he has sent the letter to me is clear. I have published some pieces on women and society. He must somehow have worked up a list (he is a master of lists, as we shall see)—a list of writers on the Woman Question, and we are his targets. He begins:

159

"Friend: women will soon be the most hated and despised of all living things. It is your fanaticism for fecundity that is over-populating the earth and ruining our ecology."

Good: my madman is not so crazy after all. He wants to save the environment. And he calls me friend. Already I like him a little.

But already I notice the Freudian turn in him. He, too, thinks of woman solely as childbearer. He continues:

"Years ago the fist was man's weapon to slay other men. Then the rock and the club were used. Spears and swords followed, with long lances. The bow and arrow preceded the rifle and six-shooter. Machine guns, artillery pieces, tanks, and aerial bombs followed.

"Finally, the A-bomb."

Another Freudian turn. My madman has discovered the death-instinct. But, though mad, he is logical (and here he has underlined with a furious blackness):

"The progress of weaponry corresponded with the output of women's wombs. That sums it up!"

But apparently the summing-up is insufficient. There is more, much more:

"Anyone who has a money-interest in population growth is apt to be against birth control and abortion."

He means us to understand that it is women who are preeminently against birth control and abortions. It follows that women represent the money-interests. But now begin my madman's lists, and here is a little lapse: his catalog of money-interests is curiously devoid of women. He lists doctors, diaper manufacturers, morticians, sellers of graveyard space, tombstones, funeral flowers, caskets, chauffeurs who drive hearses and funeral limousines, publishers of schoolbooks, auto firms that sell cars, trucks, and school buses, oil firms, tire manufacturers, road-builders, realtors, contractors. "Lawyers, judges, cops, and jailers get their cut, too." He finishes kindly:

"I don't mean to be harsh, but you women will have to assess your priorities a bit better! You women, with your mania to procreate to keep the Pentagons of the world up all through the small hours night after night scheming ways to kill and maim the product of your overworked wombs. Great will be the animosity toward your overwhelming womb-output! Toward your selfish spawning! Soon" [now he begins to underline again, and this makes his saliva flow nastily]—"soon pregnant women will be spat on, assaulted, and even killed!"

So much for Freud's adored darlings. The death-instinct, having given up on the primal father, is ganging up on pregnant women, who always used to be sure of at least a seat on the bus.

Reductio ad absurdum. My madman is after all a madman. But he is also, observe, a *practical* logician. Further, he owns the courage of connection which Freud lacked. He celebrates the Logic of the Hole measurelessly extended. Reduce woman to her anatomy—to Womb—and it is death, death, death, all the way; death and death and death, always, endlessly, gluttonously death. The destiny of anatomy is death.

DOWN WITH SEXIST UPBRINGING

LETTY COTTIN POGREBIN

Our twin daughters aren't into Women's Liberation. For all they know, a male chauvinist pig is the fourth little porker on the big bad wolf's menu. They've never suffered job discrimination, never been treated as sex objects and can't be characterized as bra-burners since they're still in undershirts.

But living with Abigail and Robin, age six, is an ongoing consciousness-raising session for my husband and me. In them, and in their three-year-old brother David, we see ourselves. They mirror our attitudes and mimic our relationship. They are constant reminders that lifestyles and sex roles are passed from parents to children as inexorably as blue eyes or small feet.

From empirical evidence our children have concluded that women's work is writing books and articles, having meetings, making dinner, doing puzzles with the kids, and fixing the electrical wiring. Man's work, on the other hand, is writing legal briefs, arguing cases, having meetings, making breakfast, reading stories with the kids and fixing the plumbing.

In our household, whoever can, does. Call it convenience plus ability. I make dinner because I like to and because I cook better. My husband makes breakfast because I simply cannot get up that early in the morning and the children love his pancakes.

Letty Cottin Pogrebin, author of "How To Make It in a Man's World," is a "Ms." editor. She writes "The Working Woman" column in "The Ladies Home Journal."

In homes where male and female roles are rigidly defined, children would tune in a wholly different picture. If the father restricts himself to the television room, the evening paper and the "masculine" chores in the backyard, his son is not likely to feel that folding laundry is a man's lot in life. If the mother is exclusively engaged in domestic activities, her daughter may question whether women were meant to have other interests.

Home environments tend to set the stage for sex-role stereotypes. We've all seen little girls' rooms that are so organdied, pink and pippy-poo one would never dream of besmirching them with Play-Doh or cartwheels. We've seen little boys living in nautical decors or in cell-like rooms heavy on athletic equipment but lacking a cozy place to read a book. We've seen boys scolded for parading in their sisters' ballet tutus; girls enjoined from getting soiled; boys forbidden to play with dolls; girls forbidden to wrestle.

Why are parents so alert to sex-typed behavior? Why do they monitor the "masculine" or "feminine" connotations of children's clothes, games, toys, reading material and physical activity? What's the big worry?

Homosexuality is the big worry. The specter of having a son turn out gay haunts nearly every father. Mothers seem to join in the obsession—not because they have the same investment in the boys' masculinization, but because they've been made to feel women are responsible for producing Mama's boys who fall prey to homosexual temptation.

The prospect of having a Lesbian daughter doesn't seem quite as threatening. Keeping girls feminine is largely a matter of keeping them attractive, alluring and marriageable. The tomboy is said to be "going through a phase." It can be cured with a lace petticoat and a new hair ribbon. It can even be turned into an advantage: "My daughter throws a ball like a boy," or "I swear, she thinks like a man." While some find it enviable to have a daughter who knows what a gridiron is, a son who likes to iron is another dish of neuroses. Somehow, sissy is what tomboy isn't; a grave threat to the future of the child and to the stability and social status of the entire family.

163

Although male homosexuals are often truck-driver-tough and many heterosexuals are gentle poets, the assumption remains that superficial masculine and feminine identities and activities will prevent sexual confusion.

"There is absolutely no scientific validity to this assumption," says Dr. Robert E. Gould, Director of Adolescent Psychiatry at the Bellevue Hospital Center. "Boys become homosexual because of disturbed family relationships, not because their parents allowed them to do so-called feminine things.

"Kids must be allowed all available opportunity to develop and achieve their full potential. They should have free access to *human* toys, books, games and emotions—all of them free from sex-stereotyping."

Dr. Sirgay Sanger, a New York child psychiatrist, puts it this way: "In the child's earliest years, masculine or feminine differences are a fake issue. Until three or four years of age children have the same needs. Beyond that age, what they require most is individual differentiation, not gender differentiation. To highlight differences only denies one sex the advantages permitted to the other.

"Such gender differences can be alarming and threatening to children. Unisex clothes and relaxed dating rituals among the young indicate that there's a natural tendency to minimize sex differences and to find comfortable common areas of human communication."

Maybe the next generation of parents will be uncoerced and uncoercive. Meanwhile, those of us raising children now must face our own prejudices and society's pervasive sexism.

How do you telegraph your prejudices and preconceptions? Blue and pink is the first label. The way you handle and coo to the infant differs. Girls get cuddled and purred over. Boys get hoisted and roughhoused. The choice of toys also tells a child something without words. Do-it-yourself crib games for boys. Delicate mobiles for girls. And later—he gets baseballs, model ships, Erector sets, chemistry kits. She gets Barbie dolls, tea sets, nurse kits, mini-mops. And still later—he goes skiing, camping, skin-diving and plays football with Dad. She goes to ballet class, piano lessons, art exhibits and bakes brownies with Mom.

And they both get the signal. That they are expected to be very different from one another. That he can experiment, solve problems, compete and take risks. That she is passive, domestic, cultured and cautious.

If the profile sounds familiar, your children may need a strong dose of non-sexist upbringing. Open the options. Let your boy know the challenge of tackling a recipe; let your girl know the challenge of tackling another kid. And beware of outside pollutants. Well-meaning friends can muddy feminist waters. The following tales are typical.

During a visit to their father's office, our three children were introduced to one of his associates. The man told David that when he grew up he could be a lawyer in Daddy's firm. Turning to the twins the man said: "And we can use some new legal secretaries, too."

On a recent plane trip, a stewardess asked my husband how many and "what kind" of children he had. Then she brought back three gold pins: one Junior Pilot wings and two Junior Stewardess wings. (My husband told the kids that all the wings were pilot's.)

When David started howling after a bad fall I overheard our babysitter tell him: "Come on now, boys don't cry." ("Crying is the ultimate human reaction to pain and sadness," says Dr. Gould. "In Egypt men were wailing in the streets when Nasser died. But Americans are trapped in the mystique of the ideal man—someone like John Wayne striding emotionless through a war movie. It's unreal.")

While individual sexist acts or statements can be counteracted by sensitive parents, for most of us the problem becomes overwhelming when we examine the educational system and the media. Here's where doctrinaire "experts" legitimize sex roles. And here's where cultural brainwashing techniques are most entrenched and hardest to fight.

In opposition to censorship, Mayor Jimmy Walker once said, "No girl was ever ruined by a book." Well, maybe not by one book. But a cumulative library of negative, stultifying stories, books and poems can go a long way toward ruination of the female spirit.

We didn't really notice them coming at us. The fairy tales that show girls sleeping away their lives until the prince hacks through the underbrush to rescue them. The nursery rhymes in which we are kept in pumpkin shells or crammed into a shoe with a bunch of kids. All of us: Lazy Mary, Contrary Mary, frightened Miss Muffet, empty-headed Bo-Peep—a sorry lot, with little relief on the positive side. Even Mother Goose herself was eccentric.

In school books, the Dick and Jane syndrome reinforced our emerging attitudes. The arithmetic books posed appropriate conundrums: "Ann has three pies . . . Dan has three rockets . . ." We read the nuances between the lines: Ann keeps her eye on the oven; Dan sets his sights on the moon.

Put it all together, it spells conform. Be beautiful, feminine, alluring, passive, supportive. Subvert your energies, dear. Conceal your brains, young lady. Spunky girls finish last on the way to the prom. Tomboys must convert. Boys don't make passes at female smart-asses. We all got the message—finally. If we're fragile, vulnerable and helpless, we'll feel that pea tucked beneath 43 mattresses. The prize is a kingsized bed. And a lifetime of making it up every morning.

The boy reading the same material is victimized by the reverse effects. If she's all dainty and diaphanous, he has to be strong and assertive. If she faints with love for a fullback then he'd better try out for the team. If Mom and the kiddies are at home all day, then who but Dad must work to keep starvation from the door? The pressure is on.

But suppose he isn't up to jousting with his fellows or scaling palace walls? What if he prefers a flute to a football? Tough luck, and that's why Georgie Porgie runs away. Because there's no place for the tender, uncompetitive boy in juvenile books—or in American life.

Children's literature and texts may favor the manchild by investing him with forcefulness, creativity and active virtues. But the concomitant effect is to stunt him emotionally, to teach him that toughness is a prerequisite for manhood, to cheat him of a full and free acquaintance with all forms of culture and to burden him with the identities of soldier and sole support of dependent human beings.

These roles are not negotiable in childhood. Much later, when *The Hardy Boys* and Sports Annuals have been carted off to some charity warehouse, the self-image created by these books is opened to scrutiny—at the psychiatrist's office or in the divorce court.

To break the pattern our children need our help:

To route them to the few realistic books available within each reading category and age level.

To impose an interpretive voice upon their reading experiences.

To seek stories that offer alternate lifestyles and that show men *and* women with cosmic concerns and diverse identities.

To ferret out biographies and history books that give women their rightful place and accord respect to female opinions and perspectives.

You can buy or borrow recommended books such as those listed below. You can pass every book under a Geiger counter for sexist overtones. But you don't have to burn the old stand-bys and the classics in a fit of feminist pique. The simple exercise of adult intelligence and advanced consciousness will do the trick.

As a parent you should become an interpreter of myths. A feminist revisionist. Analyze, discuss, question characterizations. Portions of any fairy tale or story can be salvaged during a critique session with your child.

For example, Dr. Sanger suggests a transformation of *Cinderella* from a tale of a hyperlanguishing female to a constructive fantasy. Look at it this way: Cinderella wasn't a victim. She was a strong young woman and a tolerant, understanding human being. She recognized the pettiness of her stepsisters. She endured her stepmother's cruelty. Because she was sympathetic rather than bitter, she gained an ally—the fairy godmother, who epitomizes our ideal of free choice. Cinderella's reward for perseverence and strength of character is entrée into the castle: in other words, a better life.

As for the bit about marriage being a woman's be-all and end-all, you'll have to deal with that inevitable dénouement as you see fit. Most of the time, I figure it's a fair ending. After all, we don't know what the prince did with the rest of his life either.

167

Sexism and racism, to my way of thinking, are different intensities on the same wavelength. Being barred from medical school or doing compulsory time in the typing pool are some of the ways society sends its women to the back of the bus.

It can be effective to arouse your child's sensibility by drawing a parallel. Most books have ceased portraying black people in servile positions. Elevator operators are no longer all black and research chemists are no longer all white. Flat racial generalizations (lazy, rhythmic, etc.) are no longer tolerated.

And yet—we must point out to our kids—women are still virtually one-dimensional in literature for the young. Female stereotypes are not only endured, they are applauded. Women are helpers, not doers; procreative, not creative. Mothers in ubiquitous aprons cook, clean and beautify themselves to please men. Little girls are nubile maidens in training for Mom's self-effacing role. Rewards are vicariously enjoyed through males. Opinions are limited. Fathers are shown in multi-dimensional pursuits: driving the lawn mower and driving the steam shovel; in the family room and in the conference room. Women never seem to leave the home, yard and supermarket.

While the mother who does not work outside the home is in the minority for the first time, you can count on one hand the books that positively reflect the dual-occupation family. No wonder the 22 million children of working mothers feel somewhat deprived. All the printed evidence suggests that the only normal mother is a stay-at-home mother and that a woman needs only a well-frosted cake to feel fulfilled.

Once conscious of this propaganda, you can externalize your awareness. Start reading seminars for other parents through the school or community center. Inquire into the contents of your child's reading syllabus.

You'll find, as did a Princeton group called Women on Words and Images, that 72 per cent of the stories about individual children are geared to boys; that the overriding conclusions to be drawn from school readers is that girls are always late, give up easily, don't excel in school (contrary to statistical fact), and need a lot of help solving problems and getting things done.

168

You'll discover, as did women at Pandora in Seattle, that math textbooks are full of examples that demean your daughter by inference. Such as

Mary's way: $2 + 2 + 2 + 2 = 8$

Jack's way: $2 \times 4 = 8$

You'll find more than enough reasons to support activist groups that are closing in on publishers and educators. You may even be outraged enough to join a feminist collective to prepare non-sexist reading lists and to launch honest books of your own making.

You might demand that your bookstore and library stock equalitarian literature. Complain to publishers and editors. And don't spare the Board of Education. Remember that when repressive, slanted books are adopted by an entire school system, their contents are invested with divine authority.

The National Organization for Women's Report on Sex Bias in the Public Schools provides appalling evidence of sexism in the entire system, not just in its books. Girls are barred from 85 per cent of the play areas, from several gym activities, from many field and track sports and from most school teams. They are directed instead to volleyball courts, dancing or cheerleading.

Boys get the special assignments, whether on the audiovisual squad, hall patrol or honor guard. While boys may not be welcome in cooking or sewing classes (what male would be caught dead electing them anyway?), girls are barred from shop, metalworking, mechanics and printing courses. Not all exclusions apply in all schools but it's the rare school that has no sex-segregated special classes whatsoever.

In kindergarten and primary grades boys and girls line up separately. Often boys sit with boys and girls with girls. Spelling teams and other groupings are separated by sex. Though this may appear to be a case of separate-but-equal, in reality the sex groupings take on a calcified adversary identity. The boys' group is called upon to move chairs or lug books—though at that age both sexes are found to be comparable in strength. The girls' group is chosen to pass out cookies. The division becomes palpable. Children become polarized into "Them" and "Us."

How can you raise your kids to be free when they're so systematically shackled within the schools? The answer is, you can't. Emancipation from sex-stereotypes is not possible unless all institutions affecting a child's development are brought into harmonious accord. That's why parents are resorting to legal suits to win their daughters' access to wood-working courses or entry into boys' specialty schools or a deserved place on the varsity tennis team. And that's why children's liberation is the next item on our civil rights shopping list.

It will require widespread consciousness-raising courses for teachers. We'll have to stop guidance counselors from programming female students for limited achievement. (Why should gifted girl biology students become science teachers when bright boy students are directed into medical careers?) We'll need more male teachers at the elementary level and more females in administrative posts. Our children must know that men can be fine caretakers of the young and that women can be respected authority figures.

If the schools are often a battleground for the sexes, the television screen is an out-and-out disaster area. Our children are exposed to quiz shows where housewives vie for washing machines or game shows where they make fools of themselves under the patronizing gaze of a male M.C. Situation comedies telecast during children's prime time include such splendid inanities as *I Dream of Jeannie* (a flagrant master-slave relationship between the sexes) or *I Love Lucy* (the die-hard scatterbrain embodying the infantilized woman and the henpecking wife). It's a wasteland all right, but children consider it friendly territory because such programs are targeted at the intellectual level of a six-year-old to begin with.

Even *Sesame Street,* despite its noble educational intentions, teaches role rigidity along with the letters of the alphabet. Susan is almost always in the kitchen. Puppet families are traditional: Dad works, Mom cooks (an inaccurate portrayal of many black and poor families and of middle-class dual-professional families as well). Boy monsters are brave and gruff. Girl monsters are high-pitched and timid. Oscar turns out to be a male chauvinist as well as a grouch. When his garbage-pail home needs a spring cleaning he calls a woman to do it.

And speaking of garbage, the commercials television feeds into our children's minds add up to pure unadulterated rubbish. Often the indictment of exploitive and insulting TV ads has been filed by committed feminists objecting to the assault on women's self-image. However, while most adults have become inured to the high-pressure sales pitch, the crucial point is that children *don't* tune out. They react with interest, not annoyance. So the problem takes on a greater magnitude than that raised by the feminists' outrage. It isn't only woman *now* who is being demeaned by guilt-producing detergent ads or by "feminine hygiene" commercials that play on self-consciousness and self-hatred. It is woman *future*—our daughters, who are being fed this commercial hogwash.

Sexist commercials are an affront to parents and children, not just to feminist women. The 30- or 60-second commercial has been found so effective a sales tool that it forms the foundation of *Sesame Street*'s format for selling knowledge. Obviously, the technique is potent. According to the Boston group Action for Children's Television, your child will see 350,000 TV commercials by the age of eighteen.

Add it all together and you have a bombardment of cultural conditioning: grown-up men buy rugged cars, drink lots of beer, shave their faces and kiss girls who are pretty enough, thin enough or fragrant enough to warrant it; grown-up women diet for love and approval, serve flavorful coffee or lose their husbands to the morning paper, and use the right soap or lose their husbands to a woman with younger skin.

To defumigate TV programming and set a standard for decent commercial messages is a monumental job. A letter to a network executive has as much chance of making waves as a pebble in the ocean. The F.C.C. should care about sexism but its commissioners have licensing, antitrust and equal time on their collective minds. So the target of our wrath must be the sponsors. They must be taken to task for their pejorative view of women in commercials and their financial support of programs that disparage women's role. Consumer power is bargaining power.

It will be a long time before enough women use their dollars to protect their children from media's warped message. Until then it might be wise to monitor the TV fare for sexism as well as sex and violence. A *Flintstones* program showing how wives play dumb to build their husbands' egos can be more harmful to a small child's developing sense of values than a panel discussion of premarital sex or drug addiction. As with children's books, television frequently requires parental supervision and sermonizing. Give the commercials a taste of their own medicine: ridicule. Show children the absurdity of three or four commercials and they'll be talking back to the television set before you know it.

Clearly, the home influence can go only so far. You may renounce role rigidity and set a beautiful example of individuality and gender freedom, only to be defeated when the kid next door calls your free child a dirty name. What is needed, then, is a total eradication of sexism, not only in your house but in the house next door and in the culture as a whole.

The stakes are high. If we fail, it's more of the same. And the same is not good enough for our children. Labeled sexuality and its attendant polarization must go. Sugar and spice and snails and puppy dogs' tails aren't relevant metaphors. Cheating one sex and overburdening the other won't do anymore.

If we win, human liberation is the prize. Our daughters and sons gain the freedom to develop as persons, not role-players. Relationships between the sexes can be the birthright of every child.

For a suggested list of nonsexist books for children, see "A Reading List for Free Children," in Appendix III of this book.

V. Humanized Men

MEN'S MONTHLY CYCLES

THE SINGLE FATHER

MY MOTHER, THE DENTIST

MEN'S MONTHLY CYCLES

(They Have Them Too, You Know)

DR. ESTELLE RAMEY

Sooner or later at every cocktail party polemic on the subject of women, someone (usually male) plays the trump card. "You have to admit," says the accuser, all sweet reason and paternalism, "that women are biologically different from men." This is the cue for cries of "Vive la différence," or other examples of sexual wit, and the argument for social justice being made by the defendant (usually female) tends to get drowned out in the innuendo and laughter.

As an endocrinologist, I found out long ago that men and women are different. But I also found that what is human and the same about the males and females classified as *Homo sapiens* is much greater than the differences. I think we are all beginning to understand that "different" —when applied to females, or to males of other races— has been exaggerated and oddly interpreted in order to come out synonymous with "inferior."

In fact, the accusations and laughter so common in living room debates are almost gestures of religious faith: forms of worshipping the great Freudian tenet, "Anatomy Is Destiny." As a rational justification of sex discrimination becomes harder and harder to find, much less to sustain, the need for the religion of masculine supremacy becomes greater and more intense. The newest wave of

Dr. Ramey is a professor of physiology and biophysics at Georgetown University Medical School. She belongs to the 2 per cent of full professors at American medical schools who are women.

pseudo-biology and pseudo-anthropology to hit the publishing business, a wave typified by Lionel Tiger and his belief that human females should behave in the same way baboon females do, is a self-protective upsurge of this popular religion.

In practice, the religion rests on the belief that women are defective men. They are structurally lacking, since they lack the rod of divinity. (Of course, Mother Goddesses have been worshipped for precisely the reverse reason—that they have wombs, and men do not— but logic has little to do with the impulse to enshrine and justify a power structure.) Furthermore, females lack the consistent and calm behavior of males, because women suffer from a form of periodic lunacy imposed by their lunar sex hormone rhythms. Men, according to this theory, are the natural leaders, being endowed with a biologic stability that rivals that of the rocks.

To be fair, the recurrent drama of menstrual bleeding must have been unnerving to primitive peoples. In man, the shedding of blood is always associated with injury, disease, or death. Only the female half of humanity was seen to have the magical ability to bleed profusely and still rise phoenix-like each month from the gore.

But now that human knowledge has exceeded the invention of elaborate myths to explain the events most obvious in nature, we should be willing to accept and to study the less obvious evidence of cycles, both monthly and daily, that affect all living things—men as well as women, plants as well as animals.

Because men *do* have monthly cycles. The evidence of them may be less dramatic, but the monthly changes are no less real.

In Denmark, for instance, a careful, sixteen-year study was conducted in which male urine was tested for the fluctuating amounts of male sex hormones it contained. The result: a pronounced 30-day rhythm was revealed through the ebb and flow of hormones.

Other studies have tested mood changes in men. More than 40 years ago, for instance, the late Dr. Rex Hersey believed that male factory workers were incorrectly thought to be stable and unchanging in their daily capabilities. For a year, he observed both management and

175

workers, concentrating on a group of men who seemed particularly well-adjusted and at ease in their jobs. Through a combination of four-times-a-day interviews with the workers, regular physical examinations, and a supplementary set of interviews with their families, he arrived at charts for each individual, showing that emotions varied predictably within the rhythm of 24 hours, and within the larger rhythm of a near-monthly cycle of four to six weeks. Low periods were characterized by apathy, indifference, or a tendency to magnify minor problems out of all proportion. High periods were often marked by a feeling of well-being, energy, a lower body weight, and a decreased need for sleep.

Each man tended to deny that he was more or less irritable, more or less amiable, at different points in his cycle, but standardized psychological tests established clearly that he responded very differently to the same life stresses at different times of his cycle. This denial by men of a cyclicity traditionally accepted by women may be a two-edged sword for both men and women.

Female acceptance of, and even obsession with, the monthly cycle may unnecessarily accentuate its effects. Women actively engaged in ego-satisfying work, for instance, report far less discomfort or emotional disarray during their biological ups and downs than women who are bored or relegated to stultifying jobs.

Even the statistical information derived by science is reported in a culturally-influenced way. Monthly discomforts are rightly regarded as "normal" in women, because 60 per cent of all women report them. But the obvious converse—that 40 per cent of all women report *no cycle* symptoms—is emphasized much less. And 40 per cent is a lot of women. It is forever being pointed out, too, that women have a higher incidence of car accidents and suicides during their "periods." However, it is rarely added that the percentage of women who have accidents or commit suicide is much lower than the percentage of men.

Men, on the other hand, also respond to cycles in a way that is a function of their culturally-acquired self-image. They deny it. This reluctance to deal with their biological bondage has probably played down men's monthly symptoms compared to women's, since the human brain is extraordinarily powerful and suggestible. But it has also postponed the study of male cycles by a largely male scientific community, and therefore postponed the practical utilization of biological rhythms in the treatment of disease or in protection against disease, both mental and physical. (Resistance to disease may be different at different points in the cycle, for instance, yet this possibility is rarely considered in treatment. Japanese researchers have discovered psychoses that occur in teenagers and adult men in near-monthly cycles.) Study of men's cycles might even have the socially and commercially useful result of reducing the accident rate.

The directors of the Omi Railway Company of Japan, for instance, are pragmatic students of human behavior and have therefore decided to accept the fact that men have lunar cycles of mood and efficiency. This company operates a private transport system of more than 700 buses and taxis in dense traffic areas of Kyoto and Osaka. Because their operations were plagued with high losses due to accidents, the Omi efficiency experts began in 1969 to make studies of each man and his lunar cycles and to adjust routes and schedules to coincide with the appropriate time of the month for each worker. They report a one-third drop in Omi's accident rate in the past two years, despite the fact that during the same period traffic increased. The benefit to the company has been substantial.

Menopause in men has been studied somewhat more than the effects of their monthly cycles, but not enough. For women, the menopause is an abrupt end to an obvious cyclicity, and it is made more traumatic by various cultural factors: older women are often regarded as having less social value than older men, and women's main role as mother is likely to run out about the time of menopause, as children become independent and leave home. For men, menopause appears to be less traumatic, being largely a social and psychological response to a generalized fear of aging and death. They are likely to be at the height of their careers at this crucial time, in great contrast to most women. (Among women, those with continuous ego-satisfying work suffer menopausal symptoms much less.) But it is also true that there is a gradual decrease in the secretion of testosterone, the male hor-

177

mone, from youth to old age. In some men, the downslope of sex hormone production is steeper than in others. Very little attention has been given to this part of the male life cycle, perhaps again because men—even men of science—have assumed their freedom from cycles. (One wonders sometimes if they prefer not to know.) But a great deal more research into the male menopause needs to be done if men are to be relieved medically from some of its symptoms, and to suffer less from the personal implications of trying to deny biological facts.

So there are, for all living things, lunar cycles, as well as the longer life cycles of childhood, puberty, adulthood, and senescence. But another kind of cycle, the daily or "circadian" one, has often been either ignored or taken for granted by both men and women.

The data just beginning to come out of hospitals and laboratories are rather startling. They show men and women to be in a constant 24-hour rhythmic flux of hormones, moods, strengths, and weaknesses. We sleep and wake, our body temperature rises and falls with our hormones (sex hormones included), and this causes a rise and fall of efficiency and libido. These circadian rhythms are remarkably fixed in time and are difficult to alter by changes in lifestyle. They are also age-linked. The young child has more erratic timing of biological events, and the older person shows signs of disorganization in daily timing. In healthy maturity, however, the adult human changes with clock-like regularity during each day, just as he or she does during each month.

The hormonal cycles that have been most studied are the periodic changes in the adrenal hormones (cortisone, for example), which are called the stress hormones. These vital substances are secreted in largest amounts about the time of waking in the morning, and in the smallest amounts after midnight. Their physiological effects, however, are not felt until several hours after the highs and lows are seen in blood levels of the hormones.

A similar pattern has been reported for the secretion of male and female sex hormones in the course of each day. Testosterone levels are found to be highest in early morning and lowest after midnight. The maximum functional effects seem to be reached several hours after the actual secretion of the hormones. They induce subtle changes in mood and behavior, but men are seldom aware of them. Many psychological tests have shown, however, that daily mood variability is a real and recurrent background to emotional response.

In medicine, relatively little attention is being paid to the significance of these cyclic changes in hormones. Yet there is evidence to show that the timing of the administration of a drug is critical in determining its effects, whether toxic or curative. When a certain dose of amphetamines was given to rats at the daily peak of their body temperature cycle, for instance, it killed 77.6 per cent of them. The same dose, given to litter mates of these animals at the lowest point in their daily activity cycle, killed only 6 per cent. Yet we continue to prescribe and use buckshot capsules that release drugs at the same rate continuously into the blood stream with no regard to changes of sensitivity. Overdoses are probably errors in timing as frequently as errors in dosage. If a person imposes a powerful stimulus on the brain when it is already at peak excitability for that 24-hour cycle, he or she can cause death with the same dose of the drug taken with impunity, at another point in the excitability rhythm.

Cancer cells also seem to be affected by the circadian rhythms. They may be at their highest point of metabolic activity and cell division when normal cells in the same organ are at a low point. This has many implications for therapy, whether with anti-cancer chemicals or with X-rays. It may eventually be possible to time the treatment so that the cancer cells are at the peak of their sensitivity to the destructive agents while the normal cells are most resistant to them. Smaller doses of these toxic agents would thus be more curative, and the unpleasant side effects could be minimized.

Some clinicians and researchers are beginning to suggest that certain kinds of cancers may result from the consequences of altered internal clocks. Cancer cells have abnormal rhythms and are outside the temporal discipline found in healthy tissue. Some people are more sensitive than others to an alteration in their fundamental cyclicity. Given these two facts, investigators propose that inheritance of susceptibility to cancer may be related to a propensity for mis-timing, and that a person's speed of readjustment to time shifts could be an indicator of vulnerability to illnesses of mis-timing. Such individuals, they point out, should probably avoid irregular work-rest schedules and jobs involving rotating shifts. It's still very much in the theoretical stage, but these concepts may prove vital to the preventive medicine of the future.

Emotional problems may also be exaggerated in individuals who frequently alter their cyclicity. (But remember, individual tolerance of such change varies. Ideally, those least suited to such jobs could be pre-selected out.) Workers who often change from night to day shifts have been found to be the most vulnerable to emotional and physical disorders. Next come those workers who remain in the night shift: they are more likely than day workers to have ulcers or nervous disorders. And most healthy are those who work regularly and during the day.

Even the traveler who flies overnight to Tokyo or Peking has significantly deranged his or her circadian rhythms, and cerebral activity is likely to suffer. In addition, individuals vary greatly in their ability to restore normal cycles, sleep-wake patterns, and performance.

Some of men's most cherished tests of stamina have to do with ability to function well without sleep, but these tests of manhood may be doing us all in. Interns, for instance, are traditionally put through round-the-clock work schedules during much of their internship, as if this were part of the training of a real doctor, like the puberty tests of primitive tribes. In fact, a recent study in the *New England Journal of Medicine* indicated that chronic sleep deprivation impaired the interns' performance sharply, no matter how much of a "man" the male or female intern might be. "Sleep-deprived interns," said the study, "felt increased sadness and decreased vigor, egotism and social affection. In addition, numerous psychopathologic symptoms developed . . ."

Internal clocks aren't reset easily. Even after ten hours' sleep for each intern, the previous sleep-deprivation resulted in "decrements on a vigilance task." The article concludes that beyond a small amount of sleep loss emotional and intellectual function deteriorates.

It seems hard for men to admit they are not the

180

masters of nature. During World War II, Dr. Nathaniel Kleitman of the University of Chicago was asked by the Navy to study the sleep patterns of seamen working the traditional four-hour shifts of naval duty. Dr. Kleitman measured body temperature cycles and correlated these changes with efficiency of performance in the four-hour cycle. It turned out to be a terrible physiological way to run a Navy, with enormous cost in efficiency of response. Dr. Kleitman wrote an eloquent scientific report on his findings. The Navy thanked him courteously and has continued the traditional four-hour work cycle to this day.

Given this and a myriad of other evidences of male resistance, it is perhaps optimistic to expect our male-run hierarchies to take lessons from women, or even from the Japanese, when it comes to the less admissible problem of monthly cycles. Such a departure from the mythology of male biological stability might produce in men the same kind of psychological wrench that Copernicus inflicted on them when his theories revealed that man is not, in fact, the center of the universe.

But men—and women—should take heart. What separates us from baboons and other animals, even if Lionel Tiger would rather not admit it, is our very different kind of cerebral cortex. We are *Homo sapiens*: the thinking ones. We share with other living creatures a captivity to time, but as human beings, we alone have the extraordinary plasticity of behavior that results from the unique powers of our cerebral cortex. In other words, our minds can control our behavior to a degree unknown in any other animal. Perhaps we would all be better off if we recognized both the cycles that control humans and the intellectual powers that can mitigate their effects.

Thomas Jefferson had periodic migraine headaches all his life. Abraham Lincoln had periodic depressions. The potential women leaders of this country have cycles, as all living things have, but women do not have the encouragement to mitigate and work around their cycles. Women's chains have been forged by men, not by anatomy.

We should all be informed of the various forces that influence us. As Dylan Thomas wrote,

"Time held me green and dying
Though I sang in my chains like the sea."

THE SINGLE FATHER

JONATHAN WEIGAND

Like all parents—men and women—I had always believed that the business of child-rearing was one of those things, like cooking, shopping, and cleaning the house, which women did; which, in fact, they were born to do. "Believed" is probably too strong a word. Because the truth is that, until a year ago, I had never really given the question much thought one way or the other. Women raising children was a given, an immutable truth. After all, that was the way everyone else did it.

Then, a year ago, as my wife and I were being divorced, I asked for and received permanent custody of our two children, Joanna, five, and Stephen, three. In the beginning, I thought that being a bachelor father would not be all that much different from being a married father (which perhaps says more about men's conception of marriage than it does about my feelings of parenthood). Move into a bigger apartment, hire a live-in maid, and that would be that. The maid would do everything that my wife had done, and I could go on living the lifestyle to which I, if not my wife, had become so thoroughly accustomed, with the perquisites of bachelorhood in the bargain. The difference was that wives cooked, scrubbed, laundered, chauffeured, nursed, entertained, and played with the children for nothing. The maid charged $90 a week, and got the weekends off.

This writer has chosen a pseudonym "Jonathan Weigand" to preserve privacy.

Like I say, that is what I assumed. Suffice it to say that assumption, and a host of others about marriage, parenthood, and love have been blasted away in the last few months. I would be both a liar and a fool if I claimed, after less than a year's time, that I have solved all the problems of raising two young children alone, or that there aren't times when thinking of what lies ahead doesn't scare the hell out of me. The experience of being an "unwed father" has not been as easy as I had originally assumed—not quite. On the other hand, the rewards from trying have been richer than I could ever possibly have imagined.

My experience, if unusual, is not unique. As women discover that fulfillment in their lives can be more than raising children and ministering to a husband, and as men come to know that there is more to parenthood than bringing home a weekly paycheck (just as some of us are coming to know, painfully at first, that our wives are people, too), men taking an active, even dominant role in the rearing of children will become increasingly common. It is not now, however, and that is important for men and women to remember, if they are considering sharing, or, as in my case altogether transferring, child-rearing responsibilities. In addition to the societal attitudes which dictate that men simply don't do this sort of thing (of which more anon), there are serious economic and legal barriers which must be removed if men are to become parents in more than name only. At present, for instance, the divorced man who seeks to raise his children and becomes enmeshed in a child-custody suit (which, luckily, I was spared) must prove not only that he will make a good father, but that his wife is either morally or mentally unfit to raise the children. Even then, other obstacles remain. In New York State, where the laws are not atypical, a husband can be ordered to continue to pay alimony to his former wife, even if she won't have anything whatever to do with raising the children.

As a consequence, a bachelor father confronts a considerable financial burden, since, in addition to alimony, a good housekeeper will probably cost about $400 a month and day-care tuition can run to that much a month or more. But money is only part of the problem, and a small part at that. The chief difficulty is one of attitude—society's and one's own.

Perhaps the most wrenching realization, at least for me, is that raising children, if not a full-time job, comes very close to it. Day care and a maid, both of which I have used, can certainly help, but only help. A housekeeper can be affectionate with the kids, efficient with the housework; in short, wonderful in every respect, but she cannot—nor, indeed, should she—provide the love of one parent, let alone two. And children caught up in a divorce need constantly to be reassured that they are loved and wanted and cared for, that the sudden departure of one of their parents, for reasons they cannot begin to comprehend, does not mean that they have been abandoned. This reassurance is crucial. For children assume, in the absence of any contradictory evidence, that they are to blame for Mommy and Daddy's not living together any more; that Mommy didn't leave Daddy but *them*. In short, in the aftermath of a divorce, children, more than at any time in their lives, need someone to lean on, to grab hold of, someone who loves them, and on whom they can totally rely. In short, they need a parent.

And they need one as close to full time as possible, which, for a man, means business cannot go on as usual, either literally or figuratively. As a journalist, I had been accustomed to jetting in and out of town on a few hour's notice. As a single father, I found that each one of the trips was a torment for the kids. Even so ordinary a thing as leaving for work in the morning could be a source of tiny tears and clinging hugs. It was not surprising that the children were hanging on to me. I was all that they had left.

Fortunately, because I make my living as a writer, I have been able to adjust my professional lifestyle to accommodate theirs, rather than the other way around, which is the usual arrangement between a father and his children, or, for that matter, between a husband and wife. I now free-lance, working a great deal of the time at home, setting my schedule by their needs.

The transition from full-time career person to father/career person has gone surprisingly well; "surprisingly," because, like most men, I was wholly involved in my work—actually almost consumed by it. My career provided me not only with income, but status, ego-gratification, competition, and what I imagined was the deepest kind of satisfaction a person could experience: the sensuality of a job done well. What I have discovered, to my considerable astonishment, and to the total bewilderment of my employers, is that I don't miss careerism at all. I have not given up on the work ethic, and writing continues to be a source of enormous pride. What has changed is that what once was a compulsion has become a pleasure that I can either take or leave. The children, in effect, "forced" me to put my personal and professional lives in proper perspective. Given the opportunity—as well as the insight—I think that most men would make the same choices that I have. But that is only supposition. Because, right now, they never have the chance. By casting women as the exclusive raisers of children, "society" (an unhappy word meaning all of us) has taken the decision out of their hands.

So total is the acceptance of this arrangement, that a very real problem has been explaining my seeming deviation from the norm. When friends, male and female, discover that my children and I are living together, the invariable reaction is one of shock, followed by sentiments of sympathy ("Oh, you poor boy") and offers of baby-sitters and the telephone numbers of unattached young women.

The object of all this concern, however well-intentioned, is to keep me as far from my children as possible. In the long term, my friends simply want me to get married again, and the sooner the better. There are moments when I feel like the woman who reaches 30 and somehow has avoided being married, engaged, or divorced. No one can understand how either one of us did it. The assumption is that there must be something terribly wrong with us, like chronic halitosis.

Ironically (or maybe not so ironically, come to think of it), women are usually more horrified than men. A number of women, open to virtually every other idea, simply cannot bring themselves to understand how, as they put it, a "woman could do such a thing." They are

185

scandalized that a wife could "abandon" her children to, of all things, a man.

What really unsettles people is my telling them that raising children was not forced on me, that, on the contrary, it came out of a joint decision by my wife and me, and that she loves the children and continues, though at a distance, to play a significant role in their lives. Their jaws are still sagging when I add, triumphantly now, that I like this arrangement just fine, and that thanks for the telephone numbers, but that I have no current intention or pressing need of getting married.

"But think of the children," comes the immediate rejoinder. "They need a woman." But do they really? Until that question is answered definitively, I am willing to accept the premise that the absence of a mother does not mean the disappearance of the so-called maternal instinct. Because, with my own family, it is there; the only difference is that it comes from a man, rather than a woman. The children, while they certainly miss and love their mother, do not seem to have been emotionally disfigured by her departure. They might well be if they thought that her not being with them meant—as most people are quick to assume—that she did not love them. But I have taken some pains, as has my former wife, to insure that they don't make this equation. Mainly, we have talked to the children, explaining in direct, simple terms why they are living with Daddy and why their mommy won't be seeing them as often. She still calls them frequently, an event that is greeted with great joy, and they, in turn, spend part of each day's playtime making her presents and letters. In all our play and conversations, she is regarded as still being very much a part of the family and their experience—which, indeed, she is.

There are times when I wish she were far closer at hand, if only to give strength to my opinions. I have, for instance, become quite concerned about the children, especially Joanna, being set in traditional sex roles. Already, at the age of four, she likes frilly dresses, "baking" cookies, in the sandbox, and dreaming of being a princess when she grows up. If anything, I try to steer her on the opposite course, pointing out the virtues of pants and gently hinting that perhaps there is a better market for doctors,

186

lawyers, and writers than there is for princesses, even cute little blonde princesses. I also make a point of sharing the cooking and cleaning with the housekeeper, lest the children assume that such things are exclusively for women, be they mommies or not. (It is hard convincing Jo of that, however. Not long ago, when I was up to my elbows in dishwater, she came into the kitchen and demanded that I stop cleaning up. "That's work for girls, Daddy," she insisted.) Television, which I have long suspected as the source of Jo's princess ambitions, now comes under careful scrutiny. Programs like the "Flintstones" and the "Jetsons," the worst of the chauvinst lot of cartoons, have been summarily banished, and the children have been conditioned to change the channel whenever a "Barbie" or "Ken" commercial comes on.

But it is a terrible balance. I don't want Joanna (or Stephen) growing up like Mannix, either. Is there anything inherently wrong with frilly dresses? Why shouldn't a little girl bake cookies in the sandbox, so long as she swings from the jungle gym like a monkey? I have read all the books, listened to all the experts, and agonized in my own mind over these and dozens of other questions. Finally, I have proceeded, haltingly, clumsily, but always full of the exhilaration that I am at least doing something.

What I am doing has no formal rules and is not according to any theory, at least none that I have ever read. Around our house, we live with a few guidelines, stringent enough so that the children (as well as their father) are aware of the limits of the permissible, yet loose enough so that they can be bent when the occasion demands it. If there is one hard-and-fast principle, it is that we share everything we have together, from our feelings to our Coke. I am never afraid of saying that I am sorry to the children, or confessing when I have made some goof, like burning the dinner beyond repair. In turn, they are honest with me, even to the point of owning up when they were merely not "kind" to one another. Since we have no one to do all the housework for us, we each have chores, and there is no distinction between what Joanna does and what Stevie does. Nearly everything we do, in fact, is together. There have even been days when I couldn't work at home, and when we didn't want to leave one another, that I simply took them with me, they playing in one office while I worked in another. But togetherness has its limits. Some things a three- and four-year-old cannot provide. And there are moments when, if I hear one more fairy tale or see one more episode of "Sesame Street," I know—and the children sense—I will go crazy. They give me privacy then, with neither hurt nor resentment. They know that when Daddy asks to be alone, he really means it. And just as they respect my wishes, so, too, do I respect theirs.

Ours, of course, is a special situation, and no one knows that better than the children. They talk about it, and the reasons their mommy went away and how they wish we could all be a family again; but that, if we can't, that's okay, too. I never discourage this kind of conversation, and, as honestly as I can, I try to answer, though in a general sort of way, their questions about why they have one parent and the other kids have two. Interestingly, one thing they have never asked is why I do the things other mommies do, like going to the park or taking them to school. They, at least, if not my friends, seem to have accepted me as a surrogate mother.

Naturally, it goes without saying that my kids are the best in the world. They are always watching out for each other (and for me) and are sweet and generous to an absolute fault. I would like to take credit for all these wonderful traits, or at least smile bashfully and say it was my wife's doing. But the actual explanation, I think, lies with the kids themselves. They know that their family life is different from that of other kids. And they realize that their father is under heavier than usual pressures because of it. (God knows, I couldn't hide them, even if I wanted to.) So, if this family is going to make it, each member has to pull a little more than what would ordinarily be his or her own weight. By being good—better perhaps than children should have to be—they are doing what they perceive as their part.

As three people caught up together, we are, I think closer, more loving, and open than a "normal" family would otherwise be. And, at the same time, I think we are older than our years, more savvy and independent.

Sure, there are problems, and sometimes it is the

most trivial ones that seem the most insurmountable. Like, in a restaurant, what do you do when your little girl says she has to go "pee-pee"? Take her to the men's john, or the women's? The first time that happened, I thought I was going to cry in frustration. I debated it long enough until Jo finally wet her pants. Now we use the men's johns at gas stations, where, thank God, we are quite alone.

Stevie presents some special difficulties. For the first year and a half of his life, I spent most of my time on overseas assignment. As a consequence, he grew close to his mother, and, when we first began living alone, he used that relationship as a lever for getting what he wanted. When something would not go his way, Stevie would announce, "I am going to live with Mommy," knowing that he was hitting me at my most vulnerable spot. Then, one day, when I was feeling particularly low, Stevie again made his threat, and, in some exasperation, I replied, "Fine, go ahead," and began packing a suitcase for him. Crying, he ran to me and hugged me. A cruel solution, perhaps, but he has not used that ruse again; *nor* have I.

Some things I will never get fully used to. I doubt, for instance, that I will ever be entirely comfortable sitting in the park with all the other mommies and wondering where the hell their husbands are. One day I counted 27 mothers within the confines of our small park, seven nannies, and one other man. He was a drunk. I have also given up taking the children to afternoon birthday parties. The last one I attended was with four other mommies, two of them pregnant, one of them trying, and a fourth just delivered. For an hour and a half, I shifted uncomfortably while everyone discussed their friends' cesarean sections. By the time the last teapot was drained, I was feeling guilty for not having had labor pains.

The problem is not women. There is a reason why they always seem to be pregnant, or seem to spend so much of their time talking about the latest recipes, what happened on "Love of Life" yesterday, or what their husbands are doing at the Equitable. They are put into that routine and find it very difficult to escape from it.

189

But I am lucky. In a sense, I have the best of both worlds, personal and professional, and when either one becomes too overpowering, I can retreat into the other for refreshment and stimulation. Having a career is more than an economic necessity. It makes me a better parent, too. Because if I didn't have the intellectual excitement and personal satisfaction that comes from working, I would be a pretty dull person. More to the point, perhaps, I would be a damned unhappy one, and inevitably that unhappiness would show up in my dealings with the children. As it is now, I do not feel bogged down by them. On the contrary, they enliven my spirit. And, I think they know that they do. They know that they aren't a burden. They know that when Daddy plays with them, it is never because he has to, but because he wants to.

So, I am not a typical mommy. Indeed, I am not a mother at all, typical or otherwise, and I can never hope to do and be all the things that mothers are. Fatherhood is difficult enough. My children, I think, understand that, and, for the moment at least, accept it. What happens when they grow into adolescence and beyond is another question. How will I explain menstruation, contraception, pregnancy, and all the other things that mothers traditionally explain to their daughters? Better, I hope, than either one of my own parents explained sex to me.

That is easy to say, and when it comes right down to it, not all that difficult to do. If parenthood can be reduced to a series of problems to be overcome—from making enough money to pay the rent to cooking dinner to bandaging bruises to explaining the mysteries of sex—and if "success" as a parent is measured by the ability to solve those problems, one can very quickly become arrogant about his abilities as a parent. I have sometimes felt that way myself. Inevitably, it is the children who bring me up short, who remind me that I am not such a know-it-all after all. They do so in a variety of ways. Sometimes, it's as direct as a simple statement: "Daddy, you can't talk to little children that way." Usually, though, it is more elusive: the hug that lasts too long, the scraped knee that even a dozen kisses can't heal, and, most painful of all, the tearful mention of Mommy.

Parenthood is more than problem-solving. I am not sure, at this stage, of what it all is, but I think, at least, that I can see a dim outline of what it ought to be. At base level, parenthood should be a love affair, with all the warmth, affection, openness, and respect for persons that one brings to a love affair. What one puts in, invests of self, should flow back to one, not because one is due it, but because love and parenthood are affairs among equals who care about each other. I know, certainly, that because of my relationship with my children, I am a different person than I was a year ago—different and richer. My friends claim that I have mellowed, that I appear less driven and cocksure, that I am more reflective and questioning. I guess that assessment is right, more or less. Certainly, I hope it is.

Even if it isn't right in all the flattering details, some things have changed wholly for me. Whatever happens from here, whether I do marry again or whether we three continue on alone, I will never again feel quite the same about a number of things. Each day with my children, I am discovering things I didn't know were there. I know now that this parenthood business—as I used to refer to it when I was married, with a mixture of ignorance, mystery, and contempt—is something very special and precious among persons, and much too important to be left either to fathers or mothers alone.

MY MOTHER, THE DENTIST

NICHOLAS VON HOFFMAN

If you like your mother and respect your mother as well as love her, she's a tough topic to write about. You don't have that great flow of Freudian lore and resentment to help you. The consequence is that your mother is likely to come out looking like one of those most-unforgettable-person pieces in the *Reader's Digest*.

But *my* mother is. And that's not just the only child, mindful of what it takes to rear a boy by yourself, who says that. My oldest son agrees. After every visit, he sits down, gives his locks a smiling shake, and says in the soft tones of astonishment. "Damn, Grandmother's got it together. She's something else. She knew it all years ago, didn't she?"

"All" in this instance means a vast number of things, like how to cook squid, preventive medicine, the Rockefellers and the destruction of New York, how to appreciate a really good piece of fruit, and how to live in joy and justice without ever relinquishing your own independent judgment. And this last is so hard when you are a woman dentist and it's twenty or thirty years ago and you're convinced that the manuufactured food people eat is sickening and killing them. A man thinks these things, and they call him unorthodox. A woman does, and she's a batty dame in tennis shoes.

Nicholas von Hoffman worked as a labor organizer with Saul Alinsky. He is now a columnist for C.B.S. Radio and for "The Washington Post."

It took me a long time to realize my mother was an unusual person. After all, your mother is your mother, and a lot of people die without coming to see their parents as distinct people. Until I was in high school, it didn't even hit me as exceptional that she was a dentist. I was always vaguely surprised to hear my friends say they went to men dentists, and to this day I get a little uncomfortable when a male D.D.S. put his big hairy fingers in my mouth.

If Mother had advanced ideas, she managed to live up to them without being either weird or didactic. Not that she wouldn't talk to me about these things. She did, but in the way someone does who knows how to rear a child. That is, she was always talking to me because we were friends. Sometimes, she'd fling down *The World-Telegram* after she'd read of some new war, some new massacre of innocents. "Why don't they give the women a chance to run things?" she'd ask. "Don't tell me," she'd say, as if you safely could when Mother was going at full throttle. "They'll never stop these wars as long as the men run things."

But it wasn't always anger. Sometimes it was sadness. "Women are suckers," she'd tell me after we'd bumped into some tale of a barbarously treated female. "They allow themselves to be used." Mother's feminism could be violent as hell. After all, she arrived at her opinions because she'd seen men acting so shitty, to use one of her unambiguous expressions. But it wasn't just that. She'd thought it through.

She explained how *her* mother was regarded as a minor scandal by her fellow villagers in Pennsylvania because she took *The New York Times* and hated housework so much the beds never got made till ten o'clock at night. I wasn't very old when it was clear to me that my grandmother was frequently an unhappy person, mostly because men wouldn't let her do the things she wanted to do.

Mother grew up promising herself the same thing wouldn't happen to her. It wasn't easy, more than 50 years ago, to be a young woman without money and get through dental school. She and her new D.D.S. degree finally did land a job in a dentist's office because, she says, her boss regarded her as a novelty.

There were a lot of amazing women in Mother's genera-

193

tion, but the most astonishing were the ones who fought off female bondage and didn't have money or didn't come from upper-middle-class families. The self-made women. That's what Mother is.

She didn't go into dentistry to make money, but to serve. When she wasn't working, she was reading, thinking, being curious, and changing her mind. Decades before it was fashionable, Mother was worrying about medical delivery systems for poor people. Because she decided there was no way to provide dental care in the needed volume, she got interested in preventive care through diet. She pretty much had to go it alone, but it's just not in her to be permanently discouraged. She might be down and angry after one meeting, but then she'd be off again looking for kindred minds.

Looking back, I'm amazed at her patience and her amiability. Though she'd had to work and concentrate with such force to make her career, she didn't pass the success anxiety on to me. At exam time, when I'd drag myself off to school hating it and anticipating new academic failures, she'd say, "Remember the motto: 70 is as good as 100." She believed in work, hard work, good work, but for yourself, not to get high marks or make a splashy career.

She hadn't fought free of the traditional woman's role in order to become a female replica of a man, destructively competitive with other women. Mother's always had a lot of close women friends—a fellow dentist, a geology professor, a writer, a social worker—women in a wide variety of occupations. On the other hand, she didn't want me living only around women. Regardless of men's fallen state, her son ultimately had to grow up and be one. Some women who have to bring up boy children alone get very panicky at this thought and end up rearing super males who act like helpless pigs at home and brutes outside.

That's hardly the sort of person Mother was hoping to visit on the world. She wanted this male offspring of hers to develop in ways consistent with his nature. She had no ideal way a man should act, although she certainly thought he ought to be able to cook, sew and clean house. Everybody ought to be able to do these things, she used to say, and not wander around in a helpless condition. I never thought my male essence was violated by having to keep house. On the other hand, Mother had inherited Grandmother's distaste for this kind of work, and she passed it on to me. "The best electrical appliance in the world," she'd say when we'd talk about housework, "is a maid."

That remark may get a lot of hackles up, but if Mother hadn't had a maid, she couldn't have practiced dentistry. I'm glad she did for other reasons. Watching my mother and maids and cleaning women, I learned a lot about how to treat people.

Even then in New York, the white people with money were bitching that their maids stole and broke things and were dirty, unreliable and absent. Mother's maids never stole or were dirty or unreliable or absent. The reason wasn't just that she was unfailingly polite, it was that she respected their area of work. She assumed that they knew how to do it, just as she did hers. "There's nothing demeaning about being a servant," she'd say. Every Christmas, Mother gets a card from a maid who worked for her more than twenty-five years ago. Her life is full of such testimonials from all kinds of poor people she's tried to help. They are especially moving to me because I know Mother is poor, too.

Sometimes Mother attempted to introduce me to male activities. That's how I went to my first baseball game. She says she didn't do it to get me interested in the game, but to stimulate me to get me off my backside. I was a fat, stationary kid. Whatever her intentions, the result was that I transferred my sitting to the Polo Grounds. After that, I could sometimes cajole Mother into coming with me, although it would be an understatement to say she wasn't taken with the game.

Still, whenever she came, she had a good time. She has a good time wherever she goes because she talks to everybody. I remember one night game at Ebbets Field when, breaking out of my trance along around the sixth inning, I noticed Mother peering into the mouth of the friendly taxi driver next to her, and giving advice.

Mother is one of the few New Yorkers I've ever known who use cultural resources. The Cloisters, the Staten Island Ferry, grand opera, a certain saloon in Hoboken where they used to sell delicious steamed clams and melted butter, the museums and theaters. She knew all the good free places and the good inexpensive places and, to the limit of her thin pocketbook, the expensive ones. I think she took me to every important theatrical production during the time of my growing up.

Once, she did surprise me. After supper, she said we were going to get on the subway, go up to Madison Square Garden and see Joe Louis fight. For a woman who decried football because of what the players did to each other's teeth, it was an incomprehensible act. But we sat up in the highest balcony and had a great time watching Joe Louis knock some nameless somebody out.

I think if Mother hadn't been that way, she would have driven me crazy. I couldn't have stood it if she'd been mercilessly consistent with her principles. She hated fighting, but she liked and admired Joe Louis. I don't think she could say exactly why, although I do remember her putting down *The World-Telegram* one night and saying, "I like that name—the Brown Bomber." Ordinarily, Mother abhors any kind of bomber, as a lifelong pacifist properly should, but a year or so ago when some Weatherpeople set off a bomb in the General Motors building, Mother was unashamedly disappointed that they hadn't razed the place.

Principles aren't written-down statements of moral conduct with her, but working values that collide at high velocities. They don't get reconciled according to a table of descending priorities, but are fought out and temporarily reconciled on a case-by-case basis.

You never knew beforehand how those collision cases were going to turn out. Take the question of men. As is often the case with children growing up with one parent, I went through a period when I wanted to marry Mother off. I'd got it into my head she'd be happier, even though she'd long since made it clear that she considered marriage an even more odious institution than the Chase Manhattan Bank—and there is nothing lower than that with Mother except Mayor Lindsay and *The New York Times*.

The candidate I'd fixed on was an old vaudeville tap dancer: a wonderfully kind, good, non-Male Chauvinist

Pig who was always able to get box seats at Yankee Stadium. He'd come for dinner and bring flowers, and we would eat and Mother would yawn. She told me that he was very sweet, but he bored her to tears.

Mother's preference in men ran toward guys with all the classic male vices—big, loud men who expected to be waited on. But they were interesting. My favorite was an enormously picturesque Greek artist with an infinite and exciting monologue on politics, painting, cuisine, labor unions, good French prose style, history and gossip, but even I had figured out that nobody could cohabit with him. Just sitting in a chair reading a newspaper, he could demolish a room. What he'd do to a kitchen in the process of making a cup of coffee was indescribable. Whenever he came, Mother and I would spend the time alternately mopping up after him and being fascinated.

A man of extraordinary charity, he would tromp through a blizzard to make you leek soup when you were sick, but he was still a hopeless M.C.P., and on a grand scale. "Annabelle," he would say to Mother in his heavy accent. "Get this. Do that!" She'd take it for a while and then she'd turn on him and chew him up.

I loved it, but I could see Mother's point when she told me that the men you could live with you wouldn't want, and the men you would want you couldn't live with. It was better to be alone and independent—and maybe that's true if you have Mother's spirit.

There are probably a lot of good mothers who are liberated, or who treat their cleaning women well, or who make their lives a service for others. There are other mothers who reach her age and write Dick Gregory's name in for the Presidency, as she did. But not many. And even fewer who get taken to parties by women forty and fifty years younger to sit and pass the J. around, declining to puff it because, "It took me years to break the cigarette habit and I don't want to get started smoking again."

All of this makes her fun and reveals her ability to feel what other people are feeling. Other mothers are like that, too, just as there are other mothers imaginative and hopeful enough to try out all kinds of groups in everything from politics to nutrition. But what really made her such a good parent was the serenity that came from her self-realization as a woman. Certainly there were times when Mother was angry and tired, and when her back was killing her from standing too long at the dentist's chair. But through all of that daily friction, she knew who she was, she was satisfied with the person she'd made herself into, and therefore she was absolutely unintimidated by how anybody else thought she should live.

That was an enormous help to me. It meant she was strong enough to allow me freedom. She wasn't recouping her life or her mistakes through me. She would let me know what she thought, but I didn't have to think it with her. It takes a lot of strength to do that. At eight, I was spending my allowance on toy soldiers and my time on comics. At fourteen, I was inviting one of New York's best-known homosexual writers home to dinner.

And always, Mother let me decide, just as she'd struggled to decide. That's something I don't believe your unemancipated woman can do. She can spoil her children, love them through the hard times, pretend not to see, but that's letting them get away with something. It's not showing them how to be free.

Ah, these liberated women. They make great dentists. And wonderful mothers.

VI. Women, Lost and Found

*MARILYN—THE WOMAN
WHO DIED TOO SOON*

*RECONSIDERING
SYLVIA PLATH*

*THE MYTH OF
THE BLACK MATRIARCH*

*THE RADICALIZATION OF
SIMONE DE BEAUVOIR*

MARILYN

*The Woman Who
Died Too Soon*

GLORIA STEINEM

MORE THAN TEN YEARS AFTER THE DEATH OF MARILYN MONROE, SHE HAS BEGUN TO LIVE AGAIN. WOMEN ARE RE-ASSESSING HER LIFE AND WORK WITH NEW EYES. POTEN-TIALLY, SHE WAS ONE OF THE MOST POWERFUL WOMEN OF THIS CENTURY, YET SHE COULD NOT USE THAT POWER EVEN TO HELP HERSELF. WE HAVE BEGUN TO TAKE HER SERIOUSLY AT LAST. TO LOOK AT HER LIFE, AND ASK WHY?

Saturday afternoon movies. No matter how poorly made or incredible the plot, they were a refuge from my neigh-borhood and all my teen-age miseries. Serials that never ended, Doris Day, cheap travelogues, sci-fi features with zippers in the monster suits: I loved them all, believed them all, and never dreamed of leaving until the screen went sickeningly blank.

But I walked out on Marilyn Monroe. I remember her on the screen, huge as a colossus doll, mincing and whis-pering and simply hoping her way into total availability, total vulnerability. Watching her, I felt angry, even hu-miliated, but I didn't understand why.

After all, Jane Russell was in the movie, too (a very bad taste version of "Gentlemen Prefer Blondes"), so it

Gloria Steinem has been a free-lance writer for more than ten years. Since 1969, she has also traveled the country lec-turing on the Women's Movement. She is an editor of "Ms." This article on Marilyn Monroe is based on the research insight, and longtime interest of Harriet Lyons of the "Ms." staff.

wasn't just the vulnerability that all big-breasted women seem to share. (Women prefer actresses who are smaller, neater—the Audrey Hepburns of the world—but it isn't because we're jealous of the *zoftig* ones as men suppose. It's just that we would rather identify with a woman we don't have to worry about, someone who doesn't seem in constant danger.) Compared to Marilyn, Jane Russell seemed in control of her body, and even of the absurd movie situations.

Perhaps it was the uncertainty in the eyes of this big, blonde child-woman; the terrible need for approval that made her different from a Jane Russell. How dare she expose the neediness that women feel, and try so hard to conceal? How dare she, a movie star, be just as unconfident as I was?

So I disliked her, and avoided her movies, as we avoid that which reflects our fears about ourselves. If there were jokes made on her name and image when I was around, I joined in, contributing to the put-down, and laughing to show that I was nothing like her. Nothing at all.

Later, I, too, got out of my neighborhood, just as she had got out of a much worse life of lovelessness and foster homes. I didn't do it, as she did, through nude calendar photographs and starlet bits. (Even if there had been such opportunities for mildly pretty girls in Toledo, Ohio, I would never have had the courage to make myself so vulnerable.) Yes, I was American enough to have show-business dreams: the boys in my neighborhood hoped to get out of a lifetime in the factories through sports; the girls imagined show-business careers, if they dreamed of anything other than marrying a few steps up in the world. But a brief high school career as a dancer on the Toledo show-business circuit, or what passed for show business there, seemed hopeless even to me. In the end, it was luck and an encouraging mother and a facility with words that got me out—a facility that helped me fake my way through college entrance exams for which I was totally unprepared.

But there's not much more confidence in girls who scrape past college boards than there is in those who, like Marilyn Monroe, have to parade past beauty contest judges instead. By the time I saw her again, I was a student sneaking in to watch the celebrated members of The Actors

Studio do scenes from what seemed to me very impressive and highbrow plays; Arthur Miller and Eugene O'Neill were to be served up that day. She was a student, too— a pupil of Lee Strasberg, leader of The Actors Studio and foremost American guru of the Stanislavski method— though her status as movie star and sex symbol seemed to keep her from being taken seriously, even there. She was allowed to observe, but not to do scenes with her colleagues.

So the two of us sat there, mutually awed, I think, in the presence of High Culture and such theater people as Ben Gazzara and Rip Torn; mutually trying to fade into the woodwork.

I remember thinking that Strasberg and his actors

THE REAL MARILYN

The quotations that appear at the bottoms of these pages are taken from the articles, notes, and recollections of interviewers and friends who talked with Marilyn Monroe. One of the friends was Patricia Newcomb, who contributed most of all to this personal record. As Marilyn Monroe's publicity agent, Ms. Newcomb arranged and was present at major interviews. As her friend, she talked with Marilyn Monroe daily, and was one of the last persons to see her alive.

WORK

Why do I want to be an actress? Well, even when I was a child I loved playing pretend games, and I led all the other children into making up play games, and taking the different parts. And I'd listen to "The Lone Ranger" and get terribly excited. Not at the horses and the chases and the guns but—you know—the drama. *The wondering of how it would be for each person in that situation.*

Later on, I learned that all the time I thought I was just playing, I was acting. And I thought, Gee, acting is play! Of course, it isn't—there are techniques to be learned, and it's hard work. But it still seems sort of like play to me, and something you want terribly to do.

seemed to take pleasure in ignoring this great and powerful movie star who had come to learn. Their greetings to
her were a little too studiously casual; their whispers to
each other about her being there a little too self-conscious
and condescending. Though she stayed in the back of the
room, her blonde head swathed in a black scarf, and her
body hidden in a shapeless black sweater and slacks, she
gradually became a presence, if only because the group
was trying so hard not to look; to remain oblivious and
cool.

As we filed slowly out of the shabby room, Marilyn
listened eagerly to the professional postmortem that Ben
Gazzara and others were carrying on ahead of us, her
fingers nervously tracing a face that was luminous and

---

*I guess people think that why I'm late is some kind of
arrogance and I think it is the opposite of arrogance. . . .
I do want to be prepared when I get there to give a good
performance.*

———

*They tell you to cry one tear, and if you feel two and
therefore cry two, it's no good. If you change "the" to
"a" in your lines, they correct you. An actress is not a machine, but they treat you like one. A money machine.*

———

*You can meet working people who want to know what it
is like. . . . I don't like to disillusion them and tell them it's
sometimes nearly impossible. They kind of look toward
you for something that's away from their everyday life.*

———

*Some actor once said about me that kissing me was like
kissing Hitler. Well, I think that's his problem. If I have
to do intimate love scenes with somebody who really has
these kinds of feelings toward me, then my fantasy can
come into play . . . out with him, in with my fantasy. He
was never there.*

totally free of makeup, as if she were trying to hide her-self to apologize for being there. I was suddenly glad she hadn't participated, and therefore hadn't been subject to the criticism of this rather vulturous group. (Perhaps it was an unschooled, unprofessional reaction, but I hadn't enjoyed watching Strasberg encourage an intimate love scene, and then pick apart the actor and actress with humiliating authority.) Summoning my nerve, I did ask the shy, blonde woman in front of me if she could imagine playing a scene for this group.

"Oh, no," Marilyn said, her voice childish, but much less whispery than its version on the screen, "I admire all these people so much. I'm just not good enough." Then, after a few beats of silence: "Lee Strasberg is a genius, you know. I plan to do what he says."

THE REAL MARILYN (cont'd.)

Even if all I had to do in a scene was just to come in and say, "Hi," I've always felt the people ought to get their money's worth, that this is an obligation of mine, to give them the best you can get from me.

ON BEING A SEX SYMBOL

When I was eleven, the whole world which was always closed to me . . . suddenly opened up. Even the girls paid a little attention to me just because they thought, Hmmmmm, she's to be dealt with! I've never deliberately done anything about the way I walk. People say I walk all wiggly and wobbly. I don't know what they mean. I just walk. In high school the other girls asked me, "Why do you walk down the hall that way?" I guess the boys must have been watching me and it made the other girls jealous, but I said, "I learned to walk when I was ten months old, and I've been walking that way ever since."

I react to men, but I don't do it because I'm trying to prove I'm a woman.

Her marriage to Arthur Miller seemed quite understandable to me and to other women; even those who were threatened by Miller's casting off of a middle-aged wife to take a younger, far more glamorous one. If you can't be taken seriously in your work, if you have an intellectual insecurity complex, then marry a man who provides that serious and intellectual identity: it's a traditional female option, far more acceptable, and easier, than trying to achieve that identity on one's own.

Of course, Marilyn's image didn't really gain seriousness and intellectuality. Women don't gain serious status much more easily by sexual association than they do by hard work. (At least, not unless the serious man dies, and we become keepers of the flame. As Margaret Mead has pointed out, widows are almost the only women this

---

If that part about my being a sex symbol is true, it ought to help at the box office, but I don't want to be too commercial about it. After all, it's a responsibility, too—being a symbol.

All my stepchildren carried the burden of my fame. Sometimes they would read terrible things about me and I'd worry whether it would hurt them. I'd rather they ask me these things straight out and I'll answer all their questions.

I don't mind being burdened with being glamorous and sexual. But what goes with it can be a burden . . . people . . . expect an awful lot for very little. A sex symbol becomes a thing. . . . . I just hate to be a thing.

MARRIAGE

I was never used to being happy, so that wasn't something I ever took for granted. I did sort of think marriage did that.

country honors with authority.) Even Marilyn's brave refusal to be intimidated by Hollywood threats that she would never work in films again if she married Miller, who was then a "subversive" being called to testify before the the House Un-American Activities Committee, was considered so much less brave than Miller's refusal to testify that it was barely reported at all.

Probably, she didn't take her own bravery seriously, either. She might be giving up her livelihood, the work that meant so much to her, but she was about to give that up for marriage anyway. As Mrs. Arthur Miller, she retired to a Connecticut farm, and tried hard to limit her life to his solitary work habits, his friends, and his two

---

THE REAL MARILYN (cont'd.)

For a man and a wife to live intimately together is not an easy thing at best. If it's not just exactly right in every way it's practically impossible. . . .

At the beginning of our marriage [to Arthur Miller], there was a pupil-teacher relationship. I learned a great deal from it, but there was more to the marriage than that.

A formal education is never a basic cause of a marital problem; it is the emotional background which matters.

A wife is there if she's "there," even when she isn't there . . . that is, it isn't the quantity of time that matters, it's the quality of the relationship.

PRIVACY

I restore myself when I'm alone. A career is born in public—talent in privacy.

children. Only when they badly needed money did she come out of retirement, mainly to act in "The Misfits," a film written by Miller.

The public interpretation was often different: she was an egocentric actress forcing one of America's most important playwrights to tailor a screenplay to her inferior talents; that was the gossip-column story here and in Europe. But her own pattern argues the case for her. In two previous marriages—to an aircraft factory worker at the age of sixteen, and to Joe DiMaggio years later—she had cut herself off from the world and put all her energies into being a housewife. When it didn't work out, she blamed it on herself, not on the role, and added the

---

You're always running into people's unconscious. Let's take some actors—or directors. Usually, they don't say it to me, they say it to the newspapers because that's a bigger play. You know, if they're only insulting me to my face that doesn't make a big enough play because all I have to do is say, "See you around, like never."

People feel fame gives them some kind of privilege to walk up to you and say anything to you, of any kind of nature—and it won't hurt your feelings—like it's happening to your clothing.

Sometimes, it gets pretty rough. Right after I had a gall bladder operation, the crowds in the street pushed at me so hard that it opened up the incision again.

FUTURE PLANS

I'm going to play Sadie Thompson in "Rain" for television. I'm really excited about doing the part—she's so interesting. She was a girl who knew how to be gay, even when she was sad. And that's important—you know?

failure to her insecurities. "I have too many fantasies to be a housewife," she sadly told a woman friend. And finally, to an interviewer: "I guess I *am* a fantasy."

"The Misfits" contained some facets of the real Marilyn —honesty, an innocence and belief that survived all experience to the contrary, kindness toward and understanding of other women, a fascination with plants and animals. It also showed her acting ability to me for the first time, and I began to see her earlier movies: those few in which, unlike "Gentlemen Prefer Blondes," she wasn't called upon to act the female impersonator.

She was there in the world, a life force we had come to accept and count on, whether we respected her or not,

---

THE REAL MARILYN (cont'd.)

I don't think of myself as a comedienne only, and I don't want to do just light roles, always. Some people say I should, maybe because they've never seen me do more serious things. But I can. I did Anna Christie at The Actors Studio. And anyway, the serious and the sad and comedy are all so tied together in life.

I don't want to make money, I just want to be wonderful. I'm not going into any kind of racket. But I certainly am going to have something to do with the motion picture industry from now on.

I will not discuss psychoanalysis except to say that I believe in the Freudian interpretation. I hope at some future time to make a glowing report on the wonders that psychiarists can do for you.

208

whether we were embarrassed by her or wanted to protect her. And then she was gone. I remember being told, in the middle of a chaotic student political meeting in Europe, that she was dead. I remember that precise moment on August 5th, 1962—the people around me, what the room looked like—and I've discovered that many other people remember that moment of hearing the news, too; a phenomenon usually reserved by us for the death of Presidents. She was an actress, a person on whom no one's fate depended, and yet her energy and terrible openness to life had made some connection with strangers.

In New York, within days after her body was discovered, eight young and beautiful women took their

---

Another new thing is shopping. I was never much interested in clothes, except for public appearances . . . but the other day, I went into a Fifth Avenue store I'd never been into in my life—and I bought a pale yellow sweater. I never wear yellow, but now I will. And I never used to wear blue, but I do now. And I've found out it's fun to go shopping. It's such a feminine thing to do.

Love is . . . a relationship. A woman needs to . . . well, to support a man, emotionally I mean. And a man needs to be strong. This is partly what it means to be masculine or feminine. I think it's terribly important to feel feminine, to act feminine. . . . Men need women to be feminine.

Being thirty-six years old is just great, as long as kids and men still whistle. There has to be some change with time. I wonder why they don't put more stress on casting older parts—not just spring lovers? I want to become a marvelous character actress, like Marie Dressler.

lives in individual incidents clearly patterned after Marilyn Monroe's death, some of them leaving notes to make that connection clear.

Two years later, Arthur Miller's autobiographical play, *After the Fall,* brought Marilyn back to life in the character of Maggie. But somehow that Maggie didn't seem the same. She had Marilyn's pathetic insecurity, the same need to use her sexual self as almost her only way of getting recognition, of feeling alive. But, perhaps naturally, the play was about Miller's suffering, not Marilyn's. He honestly included some of his own destructive acts. (He had kept a writer's diary of his movie-star wife, for instance, and Marilyn's discovery of it was an emotional blow; the beginning of the end for that marriage. It made her wonder if her husband wasn't just exploiting her in a more intellectual way than most men.) But the message of the play was more Miller's view of his attempts to shore up a creature of almost endless insecurities; someone

---

THE REAL MARILYN (cont'd.)

I need lots of new things, and when I get them, I'm going to begin having some small dinner parties— some candlelight dinner parties. I want a crystal chandelier with real candles in it over the mirrored table. . . . I want big comfortable club chairs. Not delicate, spindly little things, but big. You know why? For a man to sit in!

A woman can't be alone. She needs a man.

First, I'm trying to prove to myself that I'm a person. Then maybe I'll convince myself that I'm an actress. But I don't have to do anything yet. I'm going to take time to stand still and look around, to breathe a little, not to hurry. I don't have to do anything. I don't have to decide now. There's time.

How about life begins at forty?

ON BEING TAKEN SERIOUSLY

I'm beginning to look at things—really look. To find the real inside center of me—and then to look out at the world in a new way. It makes you more tolerant to look. Tolerance is one of the most important things in the world.

doomed beyond his helping by a mysterious lack of confidence in herself.

To women, that lack was less mysterious, even with the consciousness of more than ten years ago. Writer Diana Trilling, who had never met Marilyn, wrote an essay that struck many of Marilyn's friends as a more accurate portrayal than that of Maggie. She wrote of the public's "mockery of [Marilyn's] wish to be educated"; the sexual awareness that came from outside herself, from men's reactions, "leaving a great emptiness where a true sexuality would have supplied her with a sense of herself as a person with connection and content"; and she also questioned whether Marilyn had really wanted to die, or only to be asleep, not to be alive, through the suffering and loneliness of that particular Saturday night.

Diana Trilling also recorded that feeling of connection to Marilyn's loneliness felt by many strangers ("especially women to whose protectiveness her extreme vulnerability

----

I don't mind making jokes, but I don't like being looked at as one. I want to be an artist—an actress with integrity. My work is the only ground I've ever had to stand on. I seem to have a whole superstructure with no foundation —but I'm working on the foundation.

At the conclusion of her last interview, Patricia Newcomb reports that Marilyn asked: *Couldn't we end this interview with what I really want to say? That what the world really needs is a real feeling of kinship—everybody: stars, laborers, Negroes, Jews, Arabs. We are all brothers. If we could end this article saying just that, we'd get down to what we should all be talking about.*

Please don't make me a joke. End the interview with what I believe.

These quotes were compiled from: *Life Magazine*, August, 1962; *Redbook*, August, 1962; *Saturday Evening Post*, May, 1956; *Norma Jean* by Fred Lawrence Guiles (McGraw-Hill, 1969).
 Previously unpublished quotes were supplied by Margaret Parton and Patricia Newcomb.

spoke so directly"), so much so that they fantasized their ability to save her, had only they been there. "But we were the friends," Trilling writes sadly, "of whom she knew nothing."

Now that women are changing their vision of themselves, they have begun to reevaluate the life of Marilyn Monroe. Might the new confidence in women's autonomy, without depending totally on the approval and validation of men, have helped a thirty-six-year-old woman of talent, the woman Marilyn Monroe was when she died, to stand on her own and resist the ridicule? To stop depending on sexual attractiveness for proof that she was alive and important, and therefore to face aging with confidence? To question the Freudian analysts whom she turned to in her distress?

Most of all, we wonder if the support of other women could have helped. Her early experience of men was not good: she was the illegitimate daughter of a man who would not even contribute for her baby clothes; her mother's earliest memory of her father, Marilyn's grandfather, was his smashing a pet kitten against the fireplace in a fit of anger; Marilyn herself said she was sexually attacked while still a child; and she was married off at sixteen because her foster family could not take care of her. Yet she was forced always to depend on the goodwill and recognition of men, even to be interpreted by them in writing, because she feared that sexual competition made women dislike her.

We are too late. We cannot know. But women are learning from the life of one Norma Jean Baker. We are taking her seriously at last.

RECONSIDERING
SYLVIA PLATH

HARRIET ROSENSTEIN

Because an enormous amount has been written about her recently, much of it in the tone of embattled advocacy, it is difficult just now to talk about Sylvia Plath. There has been so much side-taking surrounding her work and the conduct of her life that further commentary may serve only to heighten the volume rather than the clarity of the debate. Then, too, there is the problem of language. To deal with the Plath phenomenon, words like "rage," "anguish," and "contempt" have been so frequently invoked that the vocabulary of extreme feeling has been numbed, if not exhausted, through a kind of critical overkill. Without it, one sometimes wonders, how is Plath to be approached? She is rarely quiet, hardly mild; she virtually gives us her life from line to line, and those lines seem to demand an absolutism of response equal to her own.

For the passions impelling many writers, whether they admire her work or loathe it, whether they knew her well or slightly or not at all, are those we ordinarily associate with great public issues or overwhelming private crises. It is as if she were some collective hallucination—a Lourdes miracle or an apocalyptic horsewoman—momentarily illuminating the landscape for some, darkening it for others, and leaving behind her an audience furiously divided be-

Harriet Rosenstein is writing a book on Sylvia Plath to be published by Alfred A. Knopf. She is also a writer of fiction.

tween apostles and infidels. Among the apostles there are sects, between the infidels, schisms; taken together, they threaten to drown out their subject.

Sylvia Plath, less than a decade after her death, is the center of a Holy War. With the American publication of *Winter Trees* (Harper & Row) one can only imagine the controversy's getting louder and wonder how Plath would have responded to it all.

There is no disputing her genius or her artistic courage; those questions have been settled by many of the poems she wrote in the last year or so of her life, some initially collected in *Ariel,* and others now published in *Winter Trees*. She is a singular poet, irrespective of sex. But it *is* worth disputing the world view her verse and fiction insist on. And that is a difficult task these days, if only because violent outrage and equally violent despair seem inevitable responses to our era. All the horrors committed in the name of national honor or the sanctity of the family or individual integrity have caught up with us, and it is easy to locate in Sylvia Plath denunciations more eloquent, hopelessness more overpowering, than we could ever utter.

This sense of being spoken for surely illuminates the sectarian fervor with which Plath has been taken up by feminists here and abroad—as does the fact that she is the first female poet to create a body of verse about women, scores of them. More than a century after Victorians like Browning were writing dramatic monologues about bishops and dukes (while, it's worth noting, his wife Elizabeth was toting up the ways she loved him), Plath has given us a vivid mythology of women. No small achievement. Nor, certainly, is the manner in which she has performed it. For no other woman, at least in the history of English verse, has had the audacity to mate the least "feminine" aspects of the female sensibility—the capacity for sheer brute anger, for example—with the least "poetic" aspects of the female experience—stinking diapers or menstrual blood. There is a liberation here. Yet there is also the liability of error. It arises in exaggerating not the extent of her artistry but that of her vision. To those feminists who unfurl Plath's name like a battle banner, who read her writings and her biography as a single manifesto, who interpret her suicide as a function of her sexual oppression, Sylvia Plath has become an icon and supposedly a model to us all. Theirs is an error as self-indulgent as it is self-defeating. It is only fair to Plath to get things straight.

What that means is making discriminations between those passages in which we feel that Plath genuinely hits on the universals of the female estate and those in which she speaks for nobody but herself. It means drawing the line between those brilliantly caught details, however bitter or hurtful, that we affirm out of experience or imagination, and those we cannot accept without acquiescing in destructiveness, in Plath's oscillation between fury with the self and with the universe. It means distinguishing among forms of victimization, some culturally inherited and thus eradicable, some unique, self-induced, and savored for their own sake. It means assessing Plath's portraits of women: their range of action and choice, their relation to men, to children, and to their fellow women. These are large issues; this discussion can only approach them. Hopefully, women will go on to read the works themselves.

There are now available four books of verse: *The Colossus* (1960), *Ariel* (1966), *Crossing the Water* (1971), and *Winter Trees,* different from its predecessors in that it contains a brief verse play, the only one she wrote, called *Three Women.* There are scattered short stories, none terribly good, in American and English periodicals that, one assumes, eventually will be collected. And there is *The Bell Jar,* the novel by which most Americans know her as they will probably never know her verse.

What about *The Bell Jar?* Because its themes, as well as its women, are those she returns to with infinitely greater authority in her poetry, it is an excellent place to begin. The book was published in England under a pseudonym shortly before Sylvia Plath's death in 1963. Although she made no large claims for it and although it was received cooly enough then, it has since become a mandatory text, widely praised and still more widely read. She had to write it, did so, in fact, twice—in an American manuscript she completed and burned a bare two years after the event it describes, and then, with the presumptive detachment that time, geography, and reflection had

215

allowed her, wrote it again in England. One feels, however, that the initial version must not have been terribly different from the last, that the bell jar never fully lifted. The novel is a fairly literal account of the breakdown, suicide attempts, and hospitalization that Sylvia Plath experienced following her junior year at Smith. Its themes are hardly laughing matters, yet she wanted it to amuse, even told a friend that when she read the proofs she "roared and roared, it was so funny."

To face head-on the psychosis by which she had been overtaken as a girl must have threatened the precarious stabilities she had achieved as a woman. Thus the book was weighted with satire verging on parody. (Which is not to say that suffering and wit are incompatible; Plath's verse proves quite the opposite. Or that its frigid humor is constant; the book is jammed with images whose vividness and bite suggest the late poetry at its best.) But it is the particular tone the novel often takes—a shallow jauntiness about even the most excruciating states—that makes it sound like pieces she wrote for the Smith humor magazine and, perhaps, that makes it available to many readers who would ordinarily flee the literature of madness. For a major element accounting for the novel's artistic hollowness accounts as well for its popular success. Plath wanted her heroine, Esther Greenwood, to seem less aberrant than symptomatic. She hoped to imply that for any girl with half a brain, coming of age in the fifties was a brutalizing experience. By making her private horrors funny, Plath also makes them general, exemplary. The book's humor, chilling though it is, has the curious effect of undercutting, even rationalizing, its fundamental irrationality.

Thus we find a heroine less sophisticated, less intelligent, less original that her creator was at 19: a canny, repressed, super-achiever, trailing her A's and honors like a chain of wilted forget-me-nots from the green suburbs and schools of Massachusetts to a New York guest editorship. Esther is greedy for experience and things: stuffing in all the free banquet food she can get (she develops ptomaine), holding on to the gifts—personalized makeup kits and steel-springed strapless bras—that *Ladies' Day* gives away (she wears neither), and casting about for someone to relieve her of her virginity, preferably a foreigner (she finds a Peruvian misogynist who hurls her, hymen intact, into the mud). The city is manipulative, libidinous, and predatory as she can never be. Its demands are even tougher than those she spent a bitter lifetime fulfilling and its rewards equally questionable. Surrounded by zombies, dolts, sensualists, and taskmasters, paralyzed by a multiplicity of choices and a multiplicity of fears, she feels her certainties wither, her sanity slip.

She knows what she doesn't want. Despite the urgings of her widowed mother who teaches shorthand and typing, Esther rejects the secretarial skills: *My mother kept telling me nobody wanted a plain English major. But an English major who knew shorthand was something else again. Everybody would want her. She would be in demand among all the up-and-coming young men and she would transcribe letter after thrilling letter. The trouble was, I hated the idea of serving men. . . . I wanted to dictate my own thrilling letters.* Domesticity, as interpreted by her former boyfriend, is equally stultifying:
I also remembered Buddy Willard saying in a sinister, knowing way that after I had children I would feel differently, I wouldn't want to write poems any more. So I began to think maybe it was true that when you were married and had children it was like being brainwashed, and afterwards you went about as numb as a slave in some private, totalitarian state.
Or,
I never wanted to get married. The last thing I wanted was infinite security and to be the place an arrow shoots off from. I wanted change and excitement and to shoot off in all directions myself, like the colored arrows from a Fourth of July rocket. To all of which we say Hurrah! Here is a 19-year-old who doesn't want to be Jane Powell or Debbie Reynolds, who wants control of her own destiny, if only she can decide what it will be. We identify with her late adolescent miseries in a city—indeed a culture— of spray net, steel-springed bras, and each life-denying constraint they imply. And with her refusal to be sold on the gold standard of virginity peddled by her era and epitomized by a *Reader's Digest* article passed on to Esther by her mother. "The main point of the article was

that a man's world is different from a woman's world. . . .
This woman lawyer said the best men wanted to be pure
for their wives, and even if they weren't pure, they wanted
to be the ones to teach their wives about sex. Of course
they would try to persuade a girl to have sex and say they
would marry her later, but as soon as she gave in, they
would lose all respect for her. . . . Now the one thing this
article didn't seem to me to consider was how a girl felt."
Esther's final observation is underscored when Buddy, a
medical student, escorts her to a delivery room at her request; throughout the birth, the mother makes an "un-
human whooing noise" while her doctor encourages her to
push down like "a good girl." When Esther learns that
the woman was so drugged that she will never remember
her labor,

*I thought it sounded just like the sort of drug a man would
invent. Here was a woman in terrible pain, obviously
feeling every bit of it or she wouldn't groan like that, and
she would go straight home and start another baby, because the drug would make her forget how bad the pain
had been, when all the time, in some secret part of her,
that long, blind, doorless and windowless corridor of
pain was waiting to open up and shut her in again.**

The novel is full of images like that last one: closed
corridors, closed elevators, closed bus doors, the enclosure
of the bell jar itself. (It is no accident that Esther describes
in almost identical terms her college, the Deer Island prison, and the mental hospital in which she is treated. She
mentions "enrolling" in the asylum and, with awful ap-
propriateness, receives a scholarship even there.) Esther
wants out—to be the colored rocket arrows—and yet
when the time comes, it is not up but under that she
travels—into a crawl space in her mother's cellar, where
she heaves herself and a bottle of barbiturates into a dank,
dark hole. She does so because the value of 19 years of

* The passage is also remarkable stylistically. It splits down the
middle, as the novel so often does, between schoolgirl idiom—
"go straight home and start another baby"—and protracted, intensely felt metaphor. The person who speaks the first half of
the sentence would never have been capable of the second.

218

fanatical achievement has disintegrated along with the identity that was founded on it, because she cannot write her novel or even a letter, because a psychiatrist who runs an electroshock factory has jolted her into hideous oblivion after two meetings at $25 a shot, because she cannot sleep or eat or make contact with any human being.

Yet Esther's isolation is nothing new. The style of her madness is true to the terms of her sanity; she has survived thus far through a detachment overlaying her fundamental terror of intimacy. While still the Golden Girl, accepting gifts and special attentions from prominent women, she feared them because "they all wanted to adopt me in some way, and, for the price of their care and influence have me resemble them." So too with equals. Esther rejects one acquaintance and decides to put her faith in another: "I would have nothing to do with her. Deep down, I would be loyal to Betsy. . . . It was Betsy I resembled at heart." To like is to *be like,* to resemble. In the extreme, it is to *become* the other and to lose identity altogether. And that is a possibility both alluring and terrifying to someone overtaken by self-loathing. Thus Esther looks everywhere for female models and finds none, less the result of an impoverished culture than of her own impoverished ego. She does not dare connect with another person for fear that she will disappear outright, will become only the mirror of another's wishes. One shudders at the affective barrenness that such a state necessitates. More terrible still, that same detachment characterizes Esther's relation even to herself once her mind has gone. She describes her situation with almost clinical objectivity; symptoms are presented as if someone else were undergoing them: "I squinted at the page. The letters grew barbs and rams' horns. I watched them jiggle up and down in a silly way." Or with that old appalling man-hating humor: "It was just like a man to do it with a gun. A fat chance I had of laying my hands on a gun. And even if I did, I wouldn't have a clue as to what part of me to shoot at." We feel her pain so sharply because she cannot bear to approach it.

But to stop here, to insist, as certain feminist readers have, that Esther is a victim pure and simple, is to lapse into Esther's own paranoia. To claim that her culture has driven her crazy by foreclosing her freedoms—authenticity, spontaneity, dissent, sexuality, what-have-you—is to treat *The Bell Jar* as a tract and to indulge oneself rather as Sylvia Plath did in composing it. Esther's madness, people say, is the only appropriate response to a value-system intent on crushing the spirit and dulling the senses; it becomes, in this light, a transcendent sanity. And for all the novel tells us, that might as well be true. Its world of elitist colleges and slick women's magazines and genital fumbling and familial pieties, where everybody seems lobotomized already, is hardly the place to want to get "well" enough to return to. But one has to ask of the sane, recovered Esther who narrates her tale what she seems never to ask herself: whether the failings were all out there or whether the crucial failing is one of vision—still vehemently clung to—within herself. Not to ask the question is to participate in the free-floating anger that is the novel's medium, an anger mysteriously generated, promiscuously directed, that neither her culture nor her experience nor even her madness adequately explains.

While Esther is still pursuing the American Dream, is, indeed, its paragon, her great pleasures are hot baths and anchovy paste. But beyond that, what? Does she like anything? Not men, not children, few, if any, women. Not poetry or art or learning, though she talks about them, thinks of dedicating her life to them. Not humane politics—the Rosenbergs and Eisenhower exist in the novel as structural gimmicks. The pleasure of her sanity, like that of her madness (remember her kicking the black ward-attendant who serves two kinds of beans for dinner?), is malice. Esther cherishes her inexplicable rage at arrangements—one cannot call them relationships—she herself has acquiesced in, even initiated. A graphic example. Seemingly cured, still oppressed by her virginity, Esther settles on "the proper man," a professor qualified by intelligence, experience, and utter anonymity, and thus decides "to seduce him." (If this is not the "chauvinistic" reduction of a person to a set of genitalia, what is?) Grotesquely, she hemorrhages till her shoes overflow. She is rushed to an emergency room for treatment and later, to punish the man for a choice she made, an action she

220

precipitated, Esther demands nothing less than blood money, tracking him down with the hospital bill until he capitulates because "he's a mathematics professor—he won't want to leave any loose ends." The style of Esther's speech—that callow, grim wit of proper men and loose ends—betrays as much as it camouflages the anger by which it is energized.

Nor is her scorn limited simply to a male-dominated system offering bogus or deferred gratification to its female populace: the student/secretary/virginity/slave-marriage/drugged-childbirth/good-girl syndrome that her seduction is intended to eradicate.* Women too are seen as manipulative, trivial, hypocritical, contemptible. Before she breaks down, during her hospitalization, and as she speaks to us from the plateau of recovery crowned by motherhood (her baby plays with a vintage *Ladies' Day* giveaway as the book begins), Esther is actively seeking confrontations of her fundamental contempt for things human. With the single exception of Dr. Nolan, the woman who carries Esther through and past her madness, the novel's population, male and female alike, is the object of derision.

A week before her release from the institution, presumably restored, Esther recites the list of those women who have tried to assist her: a faculty poet who has championed her, a novelist who has subsidized her education and hospitalization, a *Ladies' Day* editor who has encouraged her, a previous employer who has tried to offer solace at the asylum. She reduces the lot to "weird old women."

... *the famous woman poet at my college lived with another woman—a stumpy old Classical scholar with a cropped Dutch cut. And when I had told the poet I might well get married and have a pack of children some day, she stared at me in horror. "But what about your career?" she had cried.*

....*My head ached. Why did I attract these weird old women? There was the famous poet, and Philomena*

* As she is fitted for a diaphragm, Esther thinks: "I am climbing to freedom, freedom from fear, freedom from marrying the wrong person . . . just because of sex. . . . I was my own woman."

221

Guinea, and Jay Cee, and the Christian Scientist lady and lord knows who. . . .

These are the women, Esther still maintains, who want to possess her soul. But just how defenseless or misunderstood is she, has she ever been? Two pages after this malicious catalog, herself convinced that poetry and motherhood cannot mix, Esther tells us: "If I had to wait on a baby all day, I would go mad." Yet she derides the poet for having uttered the same sentiments; derides her sexually, too, in that implicit slur of the poet's friendship with a cropped-cut Classics scholar. Listen to Esther describing the first letter she wrote to her college patron:

I wrote what the leaves looked like in autumn when I bicycled out into the hills, and how wonderful it was to live on a campus instead of commuting by bus to a city college and having to live at home, and how all knowledge was opening up before me and perhaps one day I would be able to write great books the way she did.

I had read one of Mrs. Guinea's books in the town library and it was crammed from beginning to end with long, suspenseful questions: "Would Evelyn discern that Gladys knew Roger in her past? wondered Hector feverishly." . . . These books earned Philomena Guinea . . . millions and millions of dollars.

Here is no amateur at flattery, no literary innocent. The calculated naïveté of Esther's note compounded with her private derision of those "great books" makes it seem pretty unlikely that P. Guinea or Jay Cee or anybody else will swallow Esther up, and "for the price of their care and influence, have [her] resemble them." Her fear of engulfment was a reason for her collapse, but Esther— the sane Esther—persists in getting things backwards. She has been far more endangered, all along, by her contemptuous detachment from others than by their designs on her destiny.

There are other women in the novel, also mocked. Dodo Conway, a neighbor, who has committed a breach of taste in producing six children, which error she compounds by feeding them marshmallow fluff. Betsy, a fellow guest editor and Kansas corn queen, despised because the mindless wholesomeness to which Esther sometimes aspires is hers by nature. Doreen, another *Ladies' Day* apprentice, all suntan and silver hair and sexual appetite, whose instant liaison with a disc jockey so repels Esther that she returns to her hotel to steam it all away.

. . . I guess I feel about a hot bath the way those religious people feel about holy water. . . . All that liquor and those sticky kisses I saw and the dirt that settled on my skin on the way back [were] turning into something pure.

The longer I lay there in the clear hot water the purer I felt, and when I stepped out at last and wrapped myself in one of the big, soft, white, hotel bath-towels I felt pure and sweet as a new baby.

Sticky kisses. Purgatorial baths. Whiteness. Babies. That sexuality contaminates is merely an extension of Esther's notion of human relatedness. It's not just kisses that stick. It's people. Her horror of male domination, the "freedom" she thinks she's won with her diaphragm—laudable in the abstract—remain, tragically, only that. Abstractions, little bell jars, shielding Esther from intimacies odious while she is sane, lethal once she is mad. Men or women, authority figures or equals, it is all the same. Doreen, whose lustiness and contempt for convention Esther admires until Doreen acts on them, is renounced. She becomes an obscenity: sticky kisses. And that, in turn, becomes a code for the universe. Esther must cleanse herself of the world's dirt and become—what?—a baby.

The image of the baby is at the heart of Esther's pathology. She certainly does not look to their creation to redeem her: "Children made me sick"; they smile "little piggy smiles"; they drive their mothers mad. She does not simply crave the return to an earlier, remembered innocence. Nor does she wish simply to start all over again, as an experienced adult inhabiting an infant's uncorrupted body. Esther first discovers the "baby" she wants at the base of Mount Pisgah, in the novel a ski slope, and in the Old Testament the peak overlooking the Dead Sea. Although she has no idea how to maneuver, Esther sets out to ski:

The thought that I might kill myself formed in my mind as coolly as a tree or a flower. . . . I pushed myself into a flight I knew I couldn't stop by skill or any belated access of will. . . . I felt my lungs inflate. . . . I thought, "That's what it is to be happy."

*People and trees receded on either hand like the dark
sides of a tunnel as I hurtled on to the still, bright point
at the end of it, the pebble at the bottom of the well, the
white sweet baby cradled in its mother's belly. . . .*

Esther has said that she wanted excitement, "to shoot off
in all directions myself, like the colored arrows from a
Fourth of July rocket." Here she does so, but in a single
blanched direction. And finally she is happy. Her lungs
inflate; she is most alive as she speeds toward fatality. Like
a woman in labor who cannot contradict her body's des-
tination, Esther abandons her will and hurtles toward the
irrevocable. She is both mother and child, making the
same reverse passage that later, in wretchedness rather
than exhilaration, she makes to the cellar. Through a
dark tunnel, back to her own womb, to meet the sweet
and saintly baby who is her offspring, her twin, her puri-
fication, her death.

The baby Esther envisions is one with the process of
her pathology. Here pain and the release from pain are
equally sought—pain because it purges, release because it
rewards the sufferer. The pain is that of labor; the release,
of delivery. Together, in a fantasied act of magic they
generate a transcendent self. It is this magic wish that
ultimately propels Esther into that damp, earthen hole
in her mother's cellar, to be hauled out alive only by extraordinary chance. It is the magic by which she hopes to
conceive immaculately and bear dangerously not another,
not a real baby, but a redeemed version of herself. Esther,
the tainted mother, dies in giving birth to Esther, the un-
tainted infant. And because the world inevitably corrupts,
that "baby" must be released into the sole pure sphere
there is: death. Esther, in her madness, wishes to im-
pregnate herself with herself, to enter her own womb and
to deliver the offspring, pure and sweet, into the whiteness
of nonentity. To be at once the Father, the Madonna, and
the Holy Ghost.

This is terrifying stuff. One would like to approach it
more as a puzzle of images, a hallucinated crossword
game, than as the condition of somebody's psyche. Plath
rather invites the game, offering her most seductively lyri-
cal outpourings about the blood Esther spills, the death
she craves, bringing the beauty and excitement of it all

home to us in such a fashion that true life does seem to come only through self-mutilation, self-immolation. The suburbs are, emphatically, pale by comparison. Then, too, no one but Esther is allowed full presence in the book. Plath's characters are drawn just enough to verify their flatness, to validate therefore the flatness of the fifties and Esther's mad retreat. Better the flight down Mount Pisgah than the trek to meaningless security in a landscape so arbitrarily delimited. Esther's recovery and release from hospital are as unconvincing as they are unprepared for; no less magical than the suicidal fantasy that brought her there. Equally inexplicable is her desire to return to the wasteland of reality. And that, probably, because Plath herself could not muster the imaginative resources necessary to enrich a world that she had gone to such lengths to sterilize.

Sylvia Plath's genre is not the novel, which, traditionally, at least, has depended on the pretense of objectivity to lend it the status of truth: a little world seen full and clear. Plath's sensibilities are stifled by so much space; she simply hasn't the patience or the interest to decorate it. People's motives and their things matter to her art only as they relate to her own arbitrary, protean subjectivity. She is a lyric poet: what is considered cheating in realistic fiction is *de rigueur* in lyric poetry. Her best verse never toys with the Sanforized objectivity or broad canvases that are the novelist's pride. Instead, hers is a genius for condensation, for the astonishing image that emerges under the pressure of intensely felt experience. No explanations. No causality. No bric-a-brac. (And here she far exceeds lyric expectations.) A novelist's teacup is ordinarily only that; in Plath's hands it is a symbol thrust at us with visionary intensity. When then she presents us with a world of women, they and their things are there larger than life, locked in the perception of an instant. And Plath has the enormous courage of her subjectivity: she always lets us know it is she doing the seeing and feeling. She takes the standard deprecation of "female subjectivity" and turns it into triumph.

Plath's women. Although some of them in the novel or her verse have no counterparts in her experience, Plath knows them all, literally, inside out. From the spinsters of

The Colossus to the glassy narcissists of the later poems, Sylvia Plath is externalizing versions of herself. (An observation *not* to be confused with split personalities, the return of the repressed or any other psychoanalytic pigeonhole.) She gives us either divergent self-images, "old whore petticoats," she calls them in "Fever 103°," or real others, whether pitied or loathed or admired, who reflect those images. "Enigmatical/Shifting my clarities . . . I gleam like a mirror" ("Purdah"). Each female figure is a facet of Plath, a momentary clarity, but none totally defines her, nor, for that matter, do all of them taken together. Thus, her women emerge with the authority of long familiarity but their limitations are necessarily her own.

This point needs to be made for a couple of reasons. The first is that many critics somehow assume that Plath in this or that poem finally "becomes herself." Usually, gloatingly, they locate that "real" self in a series of works in which the speakers are furiously destructive. "This," they cry, like an army of triumphant Sherlock Holmeses, "is the true Sylvia Plath!" They should look at "The Detective," in *Winter Trees;* there Holmes corrects his Watson: "This is a case without a body./The body does not come into it at all." Plath's is a body of work rich and manifold; we cannot doubt that she was any less so in her life. Esther Greenwood is not identical to Sylvia Plath; nor is Lady Lazarus; nor the passion-drained speaker of "Mystic," who asks, "Is there no great love, only tenderness?"

The point also needs to be made directly to many women readers, both to dispel vicarious identification with *their* "real Plath" and to indicate precisely the limits of her subjective renderings of womanhood. For the continuum on which she places her women, though highly populated, is hardly broad. Think of the range of female roles in *The Bell Jar*: mother-wife, secretary, teacher, student, seductress, writer, physician. Remember, too, that of that group only one woman, Dr. Nolan, wins Esther's respect because she has managed to act meaningfully in a male field without capitulating to standards not her own. Each of the women associated with literature—Jay Cee as an editor, Philomena Guinea as a novelist, and the college poet (as a lesbian?)—wins Esther's scorn. The novel's characters undergo metamorphoses and multiplication in the verse, but their options are rather limited than expanded. From the first volume on, we encounter virgins, spinsters, widows, gossips, prostitutes, sexual rivals, secretaries, students, eternal mothers, maiden aunts, predatory older women. Only a handful of poems are clearly concerned with a woman whose task is the writing of poetry. And in the place of Dr. Nolan, the redemptive Wise Woman, we find redemptive Death Women: visionaries perceiving only doom; witches reveling in their own pyres; the moon-mother imperviously dictating mortal cycles; Lady Lazarus, rejoicing in her cyclic bouts with death as much as in her murderousness of men. Beyond a fleeting attempt at transcendence through the love of one's children, death—violent or dispassionate—is the only redemptive vision Plath achieves. Women's lot, in the verse, exceeds Esther's worst fears in the novel. There are no models here.

Nor is there much affection. Sometimes women are hated with reason—in "The Other," for example—because they are sexual rivals. Most often, though, the degree of animus seems utterly excessive—diatribes against an old lady alcoholic whose "room is lousy with flowers," in "Leaving Early," or against a prying neighbor in "Eavesdropper"—offering no contextual rationale for their sheer, surging invective. None, that is, except one—and that, crucial. Plath's speakers feel implicated in the odiousness they love to lacerate; what they most hate in themselves they vilify in others and then refer inward again. Hence the "Eavesdropper," a "little whore tongue," a "boggling Belge troll," a "Flea body!" with "eyes like mice/Flicking over my property," is ironically, yet accurately recognized in the last line as the speaker's "Toad-stone! Sister bitch! Sweet neighbor!"

Sisterhood for Plath has a single constituent: victimization. There is strength neither in one's own womanhood nor in community with others. Women's vulnerability —to their own bodily processes, to their men, to their children, to their culturally assigned roles—turns them into either rag dolls worthy of scorn, bitches worthy of fair fight, manipulators worthy of caution, rivals worthy

227

of hate, or, all too rarely, equals, worthy of compassion. One of the few exceptions to the rule of "Sister bitch" is heard in "The Babysitters," where the speaker addresses a friend from years past about the miserable exploitation they shared. "Little put-upon sisters," they were. But a proud assertion of womanhood among women is not to be found. Only negations like this one: "I stand in a column/Of winged, unmiraculous women,/Honey drudgers. I am no drudge/Though for years I have eaten dust/ And dried plates with my dense hair." One assumes that the feminist dedication to Plath's verse is rooted in lines like these, where the drudgery, thanklessness, and diminution of domesticity are bitterly condemned. Or bitterly satirized, as they are in "The Applicant."

> Now your head, excuse me, is empty.
> I have the ticket for that.
> Come here, sweetie, out of the closet.
> Well, what do you think of that?
> Naked as paper to start
>
> But in twenty-five years she'll be silver,
> In fifty, gold,
> A living doll, everywhere you look.
> It can sew, it can cook,
> It can talk, talk, talk.
>
> It works, there is nothing wrong with it.
> You have a hole, it's a poultice.
> You have an eye, it's an image.
> My boy, it's your last resort.
> Will you marry it, marry it, marry it.

That glittering scorn, of course, cuts both ways. "My boy" may be contemptible, a collection of emptinesses waiting to be filled, but the true hatred here is for the female, for the woman so naked of self-esteem that she has allowed herself to become an "it," a not-so-living doll. At the furthest reaches of the feminist response to Sylvia Plath, there is pleasure in the terrible cry that ends "Lady Lazarus": "Out of the ash/I rise with my red hair/ And I eat men like air." And there is false comfort in Plath's assertion that intuition (female) is superior to intellection (male), a theme she states baldly and, it has to be said, badly, in *Three Women*.

A secretary, one of the play's three speakers, remembers from her bed in a maternity ward the men in her office.

There was something about them like cardboard, and now
    I had caught it.
That flat, flat, flatness from which ideas, destructions,
Bulldozers, guillotines, white chambers of shrieks proceed,
Endlessly proceed—and the cold angels, the abstractions. . . .

I see the Father conversing with the Son.
Such flatness cannot but be holy.
"Let us make a heaven," they say.
"Let us flatten and launder the grossness from these souls."

That second passage is salvaged through wit, and a woman's sort of wit it is—who else could so deflate divinity via detergents? But consider the assumption here. It is vastly important to *Three Women*, to a portion of Plath's mature world view and perhaps to some feminist ideologists. Men are flat; what does that say? That they are out of touch with whatever is rounded or cyclical—the earth, the womb, the menstrual cycle, the developing fetus, the delivered child. And in their envious one-dimensionality, men conceive systems of thought or of faith that render women's truths gross, repugnant, no truths at all. Women experience their bodies and their blood. Men do not, cannot, thus they concoct philosophies that sanction the spilling of blood, the defiling of gross flesh: guillotines and torture rooms. Because men cannot create, they must destroy; they are bulldozers flattening everything in sight. This argument squarely divides the turf. Who would not flee the brain for the uterus if this is where abstraction leads? But the thesis is utterly specious because it assumes an either/or position that will advance women no more than men. And it glorifies the very mindlessness and reliance on pure feeling of which men have long smugly accused women. In and of itself, abstract thinking

229

is no more destructive than it is "masculine." That thought and feeling are, in our time, increasingly divorced is a human tragedy. That they must be united is a human necessity. For feminists to jump on the intuition bandwagon is merely to follow the bulldozers. And it is to ignore Plath's own affinities for rational system-making, on the one hand, and violent impulse, on the other.

The secretary, already the victim of many miscarriages, delivers a stillborn child, as if she had in fact "caught" the sterility of the male world she detests. The remaining speakers give birth. One, an unmarried student, associated thus with the world of deathly abstraction, leaves behind her daughter for adoption. The other woman is unidentified; we assume that she is married, though she makes no reference either to husband or lover. (A significant omission.) It is she who speaks the lines most striking and most beautiful in Plath's verse drama, and who, from the first, has been the emblem of the earth, of blood-knowledge. Before the birth she is "slow as the world," immersed in a "great event" that requires neither thought nor attention. Returned to her country home with her son, she utters a plea and benediction immensely tender, intensely felt.

How long can I be a wall around my green property?
How long can my hands
Be a bandage to his hurt, and my words
Bright birds in the sky, consoling, consoling?
It is a terrible thing
To be so open: it is as if my heart
Put on a face and walked into the world. . . .

I shall meditate upon normality.
I shall meditate upon my little son. . . .

I do not will him to be exceptional.
It is the exception that interests the devil.
It is the exception that climbs the sorrowful hill
Or sits in the desert and hurts his mother's heart.

These are lines of rare beauty and poignancy in *Three*

Women, the longest and surely the weakest work in *Winter Trees.* It is, in the main, a garbled compendium of images, reflections, and states of mind that Plath was to put to stunning effect in later, briefer lyrics. But its importance to this discussion is as an index of sorts. All three women speak for Plath. Perhaps that is one reason we have such trouble distinguishing one from another until we have read far into the play. The secretary—threatened by living children, interpreting her barrenness as a guilty fault, despising male authority, leaving the hospital "tasting the bitterness between my teeth./The incalculable malice of the everyday"—is as true a facet of her creator as the Cambridge undergraduate—horrified, too, of sex and of men and of her daughter as well. The infant's "cries are hooks that catch and grate like cats. . . . Scratching at my sleep like arrows . . . and entering my side." She prefers her Cambridge "black gown . . . a little funeral: It shows that I am serious." And certainly the mother, praying to keep away the winds of pain or uniqueness from her little son, is Plath again. The "heroine" of *Three Women,* if such a term is applicable, is the loving, all-too-wise mother. She knows that she can protect only so long, that suffering for her own or anybody else's child is inevitable, that the best to be hoped for is a safe, sweet dullness in her boy.

The metamorphosis in point of view from *The Bell Jar* to the late poems is astounding. Now it is the real infant, not some mad fantasy, in whom all hope, purity, and beauty inhere. But still the redemptive possibility is external to an ongoing self; before in the death-baby, now in the living child. Motherhood becomes woman's highest calling. The secretary has lost not only her child. She has lost her identity altogether: "I see myself as a shadow, neither man nor woman." The student defensively dismisses her daughter as "an old wound," a "dream [that] did not mean a thing," then wonders "What is it I miss?/ Shall I ever find it, whatever it is?" Only the third speaker can rejoice: "I am simple again, I believe in miracles." Throughout *Winter Trees* childbearing becomes a proof of authentic love, a gesture beyond narcissistic self-gratification, even a declaration of moral worth. The "Childless Woman" is indicted because "Spiderlike, I spin mirrors,/

Loyal to my own image,/Uttering nothing but blood." The womb must be filled. Otherwise one becomes one's own divinity. Motherhood is the closest Sylvia Plath comes to any talk of female transcendence in this volume. How poignantly conventional that expectation is. How shortsighted. And, within the book itself, how shortlived.

The book is filled with babies; sometimes, as in "Child," we hear the voice of *Three Women's* mother, her fears less for the infant himself than for the legacy of despair into which he has been born. The quality of love here seems absolute as the clarity of her child's eye.

> *Your clear eye is the one absolutely beautiful thing.*
> *I want to fill it with colors and ducks,*
> *The zoo of the new*
>
> *Whose names you meditate—*
> *April snowdrop, Indian pipe,*
> *Little*
>
> *Stalk without wrinkle,*
> *Pool in which images*
> *Should be grand and classical*
>
> *Not this troublous*
> *Wringing of hands, this dark*
> *Ceiling without a star.*

The first lines are an exquisitely simple statement. Then, like many of the verses in *Winter Trees*, "Child" breaks at midpoint; in this case, between wish and reality. For the mother is both behind and beyond the child's eye, making tragic interpretations. The universe has closed in and shut down; there is no vista further than the psychic room by which she is enclosed, the dark ceiling without a star. This poem is so delicate—a tiny perfection—that one hesitates to touch it. Like the mother's song in the play, though, it leaves a question.

In both works the infant is so much the mother's that her bleak expectations are made to seem inevitable for her son; the child becomes an implicit vessel and perpetuator of his mother's pessimism. Intense maternal devotion

232

notwithstanding, this is a love that cannot imagine the separateness of child from mother, that cannot envision a fate for the child different from that the mother suffers.

Only such an incapacity to separate herself from her son could account for the lines spoken to another infant in the monologue "By Candlelight." "This is the fluid in which we meet each other,/ This haloey radiance that seems to breathe." How is one to understand the wish behind those images? More directly, how is one *not* to understand the wishful meaning of the shared fluid, the room *qua* womb haloing the two in candlelight?

At other times in *Winter Trees* we hear the conflicting voices of *Three Women's* mother and student within a single poem. The speaker of "Brasilia," for example, first refers to a series of mammoth metal sculptures erected there, utterly inhuman in scale, substance, and flatness. They become ominously prophetic, the source of a negative prayer like that in the play.

> *Will they occur,*
> *These people with torsos of steel*
> *Winged elbows and eyeholes*
>
> *Awaiting masses of cloud to give them expression,*
> *These super-people!—*

She asks no such destiny for her child.

> *O You who eat*
>
> *People like light rays, leave*
> *This one*
> *Mirror safe, unredeemed*
>
> *By the dove's annihilation,*
> *The glory*
> *The power, the glory.*

The very power of those stanzas is instantly recognizable as Plath's. The brevity of line, the incantatory conclusion, the perfection of that image, "O You who eat/People like light rays," at once terrifyingly abstract and concrete (like the sculptures themselves), soldered together by its sounds, hammered out by its rhythms—Plath at her best. Yet listen, too, to the other voice in the poem, resenting her own victimage rather than warding off her son's.

> *And my baby a nail*
> *Driven in, driven in.*
> *He shrieks in his grease*
> *Bones nosing for distances.*

> *And I, nearly extinct,*
> *His three teeth cutting*

> *Themselves on my thumb—*

Like the futural super-people, the child devours and destroys; his mother a female Christ, crucified by the "nail driven in." There is arrogance in the analogy, excess in the degree of suffering the speaker experiences, and loathing for the child. "Brasilia" envisions the universe as an ongoing crucifixion, its first victim, Mary, martyred to her Son before He was martyred to the world.

Plath's martyrdoms. We remember the monumental forms they take in many of the *Ariel* poems. *Winter Trees* is cut more to human scale. The emotions are often vast but ordinarily free of transcendental tags. There is less intent here to enlarge upon situations already laden with almost insupportable feeling. Fewer mythic or historic parallels are invoked, fewer threats made. Murder and suicide are in the air, but more tentatively. Actions are not taken. *Ariel's* great scenes form the fifth act of a revenge tragedy; *Winter Trees* is a complete domestic drama. *Three Women* aside, and with slight rearrangement, its contents would form a coherent scenario of marital upheaval, infidelity, desertion. Everything is here: the loathed, callous, womanizing husband, his mistress, prying neighbors who thrive on calamity, children loved for their beauties but hated for the burdens they impose, and the wife herself, the center of the action, alternately paralyzed by despair, braced by irony, and vivified by the enormity of her rage. Everything flows here except hope.

The scenario properly begins with "Event," a poem of extraordinary strength; its definiteness of line and image, its succession of stark declarations—each hard, bare, pained—give it the substance of the tooled block from which woodcuts are made, the precision of angle and shading of the woodcut itself. The scene is black and white; its only tint, the baby's red face. The couple are back to back, the moonlight on their bed forming a "chalk cliff/In whose rift we lie." The husband sleeps; the wife absorbs the night, waiting for signs. An owl cries. The baby cries. "Intolerable vowels enter my heart." The wife "walks in a ring,/A groove of old faults, deep and bitter." At once her marriage band and her unconfirmed fears, the ring of bitterness could be circled endlessly without breakthrough. Everything is frozen and apart; stars, icy apple bloom, the moon, the marriage. "Love cannot come here." Nor can the woman travel any further. "My limbs, also, have left me./Who has dismembered us?/The dark is melting. We touch like cripples." Paraphrase cannot do the poem justice. (And that is true for a good many of the works here. One wants to quote them whole, one after another.) There is, in truth, no event in the poem outside the touch of its last line. What is recorded is a psychic event—the question finally asked not of what, but of who, has created the rift. "Event's" premise, sustained through poems of some emotional range throughout *Winter Trees,* is that marriage quite literally makes of two people one flesh. The detachment of either means the mutilation of the other: a genuine dismemberment. The agony, the outrage, the unforgivingness of so many of these and *Ariel*'s verses surely emerges from an almost animal astonishment that the limbs or heart, once symbiotically shared, have been wrenched away, leaving both body and spirit bloody fractions.

For the wife in "Mystic," no relief has come. Still "the air is a mill of hooks—/Questions without answer." Her passion extinguished, her faith in its resurrection annulled, she asks: "Once one has been seized up/ . . . and used,/Used utterly, in the sun's conflagrations,/What is the remedy?" It is not meditation; thought simply multiplies the griefs and confusions: "Is there no way out of the mind?" Then certain knowledge comes—of duplicity, of bastardy. And the woman's brain, once "a great surgeon [is] now a tattooist,"

Tattooing over and over the same blue grievances,
The snakes, the babies, the tits
On mermaids and two-legged dreamgirls.
The surgeon is quiet, he does not speak.
He has seen too much death, his hands are full of it.

Here, in "The Courage of Shutting Up," Plath's speaker
becomes a kind of quick-change artist, shifting from the
idiomatic invective of which she is queen (tits and two-
legged dreamgirls) to the stern plain-style of the last
two lines. And from here to virtuoso wit, simultaneously
self-deprecating, self-lacerating, and self-loving.

Then there is that antique billhook, the tongue,
Indefatigable, purple. Must it be cut out?
It has nine tails, it is dangerous.
And the noise it flays from the air, once it gets going.

It is a marvelous object—
The things it has pierced in its time.

And in this time as well. Yet that piercing tongue is
turned as much against the speaker as it is against her
object. We find protracted here, as we did ultimately in
"Eavesdropper," a confusion between the injurious other
and the injured speaker. And this is a fairly frequent phenomenon in Plath's verse. Victim and victimizer keep
changing roles; responsibility cannot be assessed. Anger
boomerangs; rage is turned inward. "The discs of the
brain revolve, like the muzzles of cannon," we are told;
yet what happens? The discs, recordings of "bastardies,
usages, desertions and doubleness," keep turning beneath
the mind's needle. Intellect becomes an ally in self-
extinction—meticulously, excruciatingly, tattooing grievances—tattooing itself and the tongue and eventually the
identity out of existence. There is false pride and true
self-destructiveness in such a posture. The speaker's eyes
once contained "death rays," but those are now "folded
like flags/Of a country no longer heard of,/An obstinate
independency/Insolvent among the mountains." Obsti-
nacy indeed. Martyrdom self-invoked. Murderous wishes
omnipotently held, omnipotently withdrawn. The speaker

of "Event" experienced herself the victim of a partial death. Now her "groove of old faults" has become a revolving disc whose message is outright murder. The poem ends with a declaration of cease-fire, white flags folded, yet the reader is left with the fall-out. Flashing hatred, flashing wit, violent impulse, sheer silliness, egregious pride, bewilderingly mixed. Clearly the speaker takes pleasure in the display of self-lacerating "courage" as much as in the display of wit. One wishes to respond with another of Plath's own lines: "O heart, such disorganization!"

There are more fireworks, worse discoveries, deeper sufferings. The (reconstructed) scenario ends with a poem whose excellence arises from its weird blend of ironic detachment, horror, and pathos, of images that just manage to cohere despite their disparate sources: the cups and carpets of the family-house, the nerve-curlers and convulsors of the mad-house, the dissolution of the death-house. In "The Detective," Plath steps back. Her speakers are male: Holmes and Dr. Watson, come to investigate the utter disappearance of a family. (One remembers the antithetical male figures in "Death & Co.," there trying to seduce and threaten the woman into mortality. The gentlemen of "The Detective" are a follow-up team.) Watson is still stupid, looking for the large and obvious. Holmes, a man of subtlety, as always solves the insoluble through miraculous inductions. He has, at times, Plath's voice—her directness and her lyricism—and, appropriately enough, it is through a sort of "female" intuition that he solves the case. Yet, it is a man who makes the final analysis, who has the ultimate say on reality. Watson, greedy for the horrible, asks: "Which of the poisons is it? Did it electrify?" But Holmes, recognizing that "this is the valley of death, though the cows thrive," and that there was a killer, maintains still that "No one is dead./ There is no body in the house at all."

The pun in that last line is what makes possible the poem's ironies and its capacity to pain. It is the death of, rather than the death in, a family that is the subject. For this sort of killing, weapons are unnecessary. Spirit-murder takes place in kitchens, amid the smells of furniture polish and neat rows of cups.

237

This is the smell of years burning here in the kitchen,
These are the deceits, tacked up like family
photographs. . . .

The desolation of the scene is amplified by a radio playing in an empty room; it "talks to itself like an elderly relative." What does Holmes make of this instant desolation?

It is a case of vaporization.
The mouth first, its absence reported
In the second year. It had been insatiable
And in punishment was hung out like brown fruit
To wrinkle and dry.

The breasts were next.
The milk came yellow, then blue and sweet as water.
These were harder, two white stones.
There was no absence of lips, there were two children,
But their bones showed and the moon smiled.

This, then, has been a punishment. The killing has been gradual but merited. That ironically domesticated image of dried fruit holds the line between self-mockery and self-pity; but it is experienced as a judgment, nonetheless. The wife has asked what she needed, but she needed too much. Plath's late poetry is full of mouths, open, demanding, never satisfied. Those of children, of flowers, of animals, of other women, of men, and of her speakers. One's sense always is that the universe is insatiable because the speaker herself is insatiable. No amount of food, real or symbolic, can fill the emptiness within. And every demand from outside threatens to deplete her still further, provocations thus to terror or rage. Her fate—her dissolution—has in this and many other poems the ring of inevitability. For one so needy and so needed—"there was no absence of lips, there were two children"—punitive abandonment must sooner or later come. And that means death. All nurture gone. Thus, too, death for the children, suggested in a line that is quintessential Plath—"But their bones showed and the moon smiled." Spare, encoded, stripped to monosyllables and "intolerable vowels"—all the malice of comic processes are fixed here. And then they expand in the final stanza.

> *Then the dry wood, the gates,*
> *The brown motherly furrows, the whole estate.*
> *There is only the moon, embalmed in phosphorus.*
> *We walk on air, Watson.*
> *There is only a crow in a tree. Make notes.*

What notes are we to make? Initially, to overcome the morbid curiosity about Plath's suicide, the question she anticipates with some derision in the opening of "The Detective": "What was she doing when it blew in?" The circumstances of her life and death have real significance only to the genesis of her poetry, surely not to her falsely assigned role as feminist heroine. Next, to consider dispassionately both what she has to say and how she says it. As poet she is sometimes able to make miracles out of impossible materials—the family-house, the mad-house, the death-house. We cannot overpraise her great *Ariel* poems: the series on bees, "A Birthday Present," "The Moon and the Yew Tree," "Edge," "Morning Song," others, too. Nor can women undervalue those lines where Plath scourges the common female estate in tones and language no other woman has had the courage to hurl onto the page. But to rest here, to designate her the doomed oracle of liberation, the woman who saw it all and died thereby, is to ignore everything isolating, immobilizing, and life-denying in her work. There the ego and the universe are identical, both finally devoid of intrinsic options. The female self is weak in all things except rage at her immobility. Yet she is unable either to make contact with or to function in the larger world. Thus, she takes what life she can from a tiny group of people who, in turn, take life from her. Although creativity might offer a way out, we are told that "The blood jet is poetry/There is no stopping it." The ongoing self cannot change; the world will not change; the moon merely smiles. The only transformation possible amidst all this stasis is that which the blood affords.

The final notes. First, a profound sense of loss that a woman of genius, capable of such uncanny beauties and such inspired furies that her work has measurably extended the range of English poetry, abandoned her art at 30. *Winter Trees* attests that loss. Its title poem, "Event," "Mystic," "Child," and "The Other," a poem of great complexity and brilliance, are superb works. Second, an overwhelming compassion for the anguish the woman must have experienced at the end of her life. Of those who write vengefully about Plath's lifelong love affair with death, one can only ask whether their hypothesis renders her suicide any the less terrible, her sufferings any the less real, or their resources of pity any the less impoverished. Her loss is, simply, a tragedy. Listening to "Apprehensions," one of the finest works in this new volume, we sense the dimensions of her private tragedy and of the common tragedy we all experience in her loss.

There is this white wall, above which the sky creates
    itself—
Infinite, green, utterly untouchable.
Angels swim in it, and the stars, in indifference also.
They are my medium.
The sun dissolves on this wall, bleeding its lights.

A grey wall now, clawed and bloody.
Is there no way out of the mind?
Steps at my back spiral into a well.
There are no trees or birds in this world,
There is only a sourness.

This red wall winces continually:
A red fish, opening and closing.
Two grey, papery bags—
This is what I am made of, this and a terror
Of being wheeled off under crosses and a rain of pietas.

On a black wall, unidentifiable birds
Swivel their heads and cry.
There is no talk of immortality among these!
Cold blanks approach us:
They move in a hurry.

THE MYTH OF
THE BLACK MATRIARCH

ANGELA DAVIS

BEFORE ARREST TURNED ANGELA DAVIS INTO AN INTER-
NATIONAL SYMBOL, SHE WAS A SCHOLAR; A BRILLIANT AND
CONTROVERSIAL TEACHER OF PHILOSOPHY AT THE UNIVER-
SITY OF CALIFORNIA. DURING THE LONG MONTHS IN HER
PRISON CELL, SHE TRIED TO CONTINUE THAT SCHOLARSHIP.
SHE WROTE ESSAYS ON REVOLUTIONARY PHILOSOPHIES,
HISTORY, AND A POLITICAL DIARY—ALL WITHOUT OPPOR-
TUNITY FOR THE LENGTHY RESEARCH THAT HER TRAINING
HAD TAUGHT HER TO VALUE. FOR THAT REASON, SHE
PREFERRED TO CALL THIS ESSAY SIMPLY "REFLECTIONS."

BUT TO WOMEN WHO READ IT IN A SCHOLARLY JOURNAL,
THESE "REFLECTIONS" BECAME A SOURCE OF INSIGHT AND
SELF-RESPECT. AT LAST, A VIEW OF BLACK WOMEN THAT
WASN'T SEEN THROUGH RACIST OR PATRIARCHAL EYES. AT
LAST, A BLACK WOMAN SCHOLAR WRITING ABOUT HER OWN
HISTORY.

A FEW PRECIOUS COPIES OF THIS ESSAY WERE PASSED
FROM HAND TO HAND, ESPECIALLY AMONG BLACK WOMEN.
"MS." IS GRATEFUL TO "THE BLACK SCHOLAR" FOR ALLOW-
ING US TO ANSWER THE MANY REQUESTS TO PUBLISH A
MAJOR PORTION OF IT HERE.

---

*Angela Davis grew up in Birmingham, Alabama, graduated
from Brandeis, and studied abroad. She taught philosophy at
UCLA and edited, with Bettina Aptheker, "If They Come
in the Morning: Voices of Resistance." Two of her lectures
have been reprinted in "Lectures on Liberation," published by
The New York Committee to Free Angela Davis.*

The paucity of literature on the black woman is outrageous. But we must also contend with the fact that too many of these rare studies reinforce fictitious clichés. They give credence to grossly distorted categories through which the black woman continues to be perceived. In the words of sociologists Nathan and Julia Hare, "she has been labeled 'aggressive' or 'matriarchal' by white scholars and 'castrating female' by [some] blacks." Many have recently sought to remedy this situation. But for the time being, at least, we are still confronted with these reified images of ourselves, and we must still assume the responsibility of shattering them.

The matriarch has been repeatedly invoked as one of the fatal by-products of slavery. When the Moynihan Report consecrated this myth with Washington's stamp of approval, its propagandistic mission should have been apparent. Yet even outside establishment ideology and also among black people, unfortunate references to the matriarchate can still be encountered. Occasionally, there is even acknowledgment of the "tangle of pathology" it supposedly engendered. According to Patrick Moynihan and others, this black matriarchate defines the roots of our oppression as a people.

Lingering beneath the notion of the black matriarch is an unspoken indictment of our female forebears as having actively assented to slavery. The "emasculating female" cliché has its roots in the fallacious inference that the black woman related to the slaveholding class as collaborator.

Nothing could be further from the truth. In the most fundamental sense, the slave system did not—and could not—engender and recognize a matriarchal family structure. Inherent in the very concept of the matriarchy is "power." It would have been exceedingly risky for the slaveholding class to openly acknowledge symbols of authority—female symbols no less than male.

The American brand of slavery strove toward a rigidified disorganization in family life, just as it had to proscribe all potential social structures within which black

This article excerpted from "Reflections on the Black Woman's Role in the Community of Slaves," in *The Black Scholar*, December, 1971. This issue was devoted to articles about the black woman, and copies and subscriptions ($10 a year) are available from *The Black Scholar*, P.O. Box 908, Sausalito, Calif.

people might forge a collective and conscious existence. Mothers and fathers were brutally separated; children, when they became of age, were branded and frequently severed from their mothers. That the mother was "the only legitimate parent of her child" did not therefore mean that she was even permitted to guide that child to maturity.

The designation of the black woman as a matriarch is a cruel misnomer. It is a misnomer because it implies stable kinship structures within which the mother exercises decisive authority. It is cruel because it ignores the profound traumas the black woman must have experienced when she had to surrender her childbearing to alien and predatory economic interests.

Even the broadest construction of the matriarch concept would not render it applicable to the black slave woman. But it should not be inferred that she therefore played no significant role in the community of slaves. By virtue of the brutal force of circumstances, the black woman was assigned the mission of promoting the consciousness and practice of resistance. A great deal has been said about the black man and resistance, but very little about the unique relationship black women bore to the resistance struggles during slavery.

In the living quarters, the major responsibilities "naturally" fell to her. It was the woman who was charged with keeping the "home" in order. This role was dictated by the male supremacist ideology of white society in America, but it was also woven into the patriarchal traditions of Africa. As her biological destiny, the woman bore the fruits of intercourse; as her social destiny, she cooked, sewed, washed, cleaned house, raised the children. Traditionally the labor of females, domestic work is supposed to confirm their inferiority.

But with the black slave woman, there is a strange twist of affairs: in the infinite anguish of ministering to the needs of the men and children around her (who were not necessarily members of her family), she was performing the only labor of the slave community which could not be directly claimed by the oppressor. There was no compensation for work in the fields; it served no useful purpose for the slaves. Domestic labor was the only meaningful labor for the slave community.

Precisely through performing the drudgery which has long been a central expression of the socially conditioned inferiority of women, the black woman in chains could help to lay the foundation for some degree of autonomy, both for herself and her men. Even as she was suffering under her unique oppression as female, she was thrust by the force of circumstances into the center of the slave community. She was, therefore, essential to the *survival* of the community. Her survival-oriented activities were themselves a form of resistance.

It is true that she was a victim of the myth that only the woman, with her diminished capacity for mental and physical labor, should do degrading household work. Yet, the alleged benefits of the ideology of femininity did not accrue to her. She was not sheltered or protected. She could not remain oblivious to the desperate struggle for existence unfolding outside the "home." She was also there in the fields, alongside the man, toiling under the lash from sunup to sundown.

This was one of the supreme ironies of slavery. In order to approach its strategic goal—to extract the greatest possible surplus from the labor of the slaves—the black woman had to be released from the chains of the myth of femininity. In the words of W.E.B. Du Bois, ". . . our women in black had freedom contemptuously thrust upon them." In order to function as slave, the black woman had to be annulled as woman, that is, as woman in her historical stance of wardship under the entire male hierarchy. The sheer force of things rendered her equal to her man. Male supremacist structures could not become deeply embedded in the internal workings of the slave system.

Though the ruling class was male and rabidly chauvinistic, the slave system could not confer upon the black man the appearance of a privileged position vis-à-vis the black woman. The man slave could not be the unquestioned superior within the "family" or community, for there was no such thing as the "family" allowed among the slaves. The black woman was therefore wholly integrated into the productive force.

Even in the posture of motherhood—otherwise the occasion for hypocritical adoration—the black woman was treated with no greater compassion and with no less severity than her man. She shared in the deformed equality of equal oppression.

But out of this was forged quite undeliberately, yet inexorably, a state of affairs which could unharness an immense potential in the black woman. Expending indispensable labor for the enrichment of her oppressor, she could attain a practical awareness of the oppressor's utter dependence on her—for the master needs the slave far more than the slave needs the master. At the same time she could realize that, while her productive activity was wholly subordinated to the will of the master, it was nevertheless proof of her ability to transform things. Stripped of the palliative feminine veneer which might have encouraged a passive performance of domestic tasks, she was now uniquely capable of weaving into the warp and woof of domestic life a profound consciousness of resistance.

With the contributions of strong black women, the slave community as a whole could achieve heights unscalable within the families of the white oppressed or even within the patriarchal kinship groups of Africa. Latently or actively, it was always a community of resistance. It frequently erupted in insurgency, but was daily animated by the minor acts of sabotage which harassed the slave master.

To say that the oppression of black slave women necessarily incorporated open forms of counterinsurgency is not as extravagant as it might initially appear. It is an indication of the magnitude of her role as caretaker of a household of resistance—of the degree to which she could concretely encourage those around her to keep their eyes on freedom.

With the sole exceptions of Harriet Tubman and Sojourner Truth, black women of the slave era remain more or less enshrouded in unrevealed history. Even General Tubman's role has been consistently minimized. She was a far greater warrior against slavery than is suggested by the prevalent misconception that her only outstanding contribution was to make nineteen trips into the South, bringing over 300 slaves to their freedom.

In 1970, Earl Conrad wrote in *The Black Scholar*: "[She] was head of the Intelligence Service in the Department of the South throughout the Civil War; she is the only American woman to lead troops black and white on the field of battle, as she did in the Department of the South. . . . She was a compelling and stirring orator in the councils of the abolitionists and the antislavers, a favorite of the antislavery conferences."

The participation of the black woman in the overt and explosive upheavals which constantly rocked the slave system must be much better studied and documented than it has been in the past.

Much has been said about the sexual abuses to which the black woman was forced to submit. They are generally explained as an outgrowth of the male supremacy of Southern culture. The purity of white womanhood could not be violated by the aggressive sexual activity desired by the white male, so his instinctual urges found expression in his relationships with his property—the black slave woman, who had to become his unwilling concubine. No doubt there is an element of truth in these statements, but it is equally important to unearth the meaning of these sexual abuses from the point of view of the woman who was assaulted.

In keeping with the theme of these reflections, I submit that the slave master's sexual domination of the black woman contained an unveiled element of counterinsurgency. To understand the basis for this assertion, the slave woman's oppression must be restated and recaptured. The prime factor was the total and violent expropriation of her labor.

Secondly, as a female, she was the housekeeper in the living quarters. In this sense, she was already doubly oppressed. However, having been wrested from passive, "feminine" existence by the sheer force of things— literally by forced labor—confining domestic tasks were incommensurable with what she had become. That is to say, by virtue of her participation in production, she would not act the part of the passive female, but could

246

experience the same need as her men to challenge her subjugation.

The slave master would attempt to thwart this process. He knew that, as a female, this slave woman could be particularly vulnerable in her sexual existence. Although he would not pet her and deck her out in frills, the white master could endeavor to reestablish her femaleness by reducing her to the level of her biological being. With his sexual assaults to establish her as a female *animal*, he could try to destroy her proclivities toward resistance.

Copulation, reduced by the white man to an animal-like act, was symbolic of the effort to conquer the resistance the black woman could unleash. The master subjected her to the most elemental form of terrorism distinctly suited to the female: rape. Given the already terroristic texture of plantation life, the slave woman would be most unguarded as a potential victim of rape. Furthermore, she might be most conveniently manipulable if the master contrived a ransom system, forcing her to pay with her body for food, diminished severity in treatment, and the safety of her children.

The integration of rape into the legitimate social life of the slaves harks back to the "right of the first night," the *jus primae noctis*. The feudal lord manifested and reinforced his domination over the serfs by asserting his authority to have sexual intercourse with all the females. The right itself referred specifically to all freshly married women. But while the right to the first night eventually evolved into an economic institution, the feudal "virgin tax," the American slaveholder's sexual domination never lost its openly terroristic character.

Politically, the rape of the black woman was more than an attack upon her. Indirectly, its target was also the slave community as a whole. In launching the sexual war on the woman, the master not only asserted his sovereignty over a critically important figure of the slave community, but he also aimed a blow against the black man. The latter's instinct (now stripped of its male supremacist implications) would be frustrated and violated.

As W.E.B. Du Bois wrote in his book, *Darkwater: Voices from Within the Veil*:

"I shall forgive the South much in its final judgment

247

day: I shall forgive its slavery, for slavery is a world-old habit; I shall forgive its fighting for a well-lost cause, and for remembering that struggle with tender tears; I shall forgive its so-called pride of race, the passion of its hot blood, and even its dear, old, laughable strutting and posing; but one thing I shall never forgive, neither in this world nor the world to come: its wanton and continued and persistent insulting of the black womanhood which it sought and seeks to prostitute to its lust."

The retaliatory import of the rape for the black man was entrapment in an untenable situation. Clearly, the master hoped that once the black man was struck by his manifest inability to rescue his woman from sexual assaults of the master, he would begin to experience deep-seated doubts about his ability to resist at all.

An intricate and savage web of oppression intruded at every moment into the black woman's life during slavery. Yet a single theme appears at every juncture: the woman transcending, refusing, fighting back, asserting herself over and against terrifying obstacles. It was not her comrade brother against whom her incredible strength was directed. She fought alongside her man, accepting or providing guidance according to her talents and the nature of their tasks. She was in no sense an authoritarian figure; neither her domestic role nor her acts of resistance could relegate the man to the shadows. On the contrary, she herself had only been forced to leave behind the shadowy realm of female passivity in order to assume her rightful place beside the insurgent male.

This portrait cannot, of course, represent every individual slave woman. It is a portrait of the potentials and possibilities inherent in the situation to which slave women were anchored. Invariably, there were those who did not realize this potential. There were those who were indifferent and a few who were outright traitors. But certainly they were not the vast majority. The image of black women enchaining their men and actually cultivating relationships with the oppressor is a cruel fabrication which must be called by its right name. It is an ideological weapon designed to impair our capacity for resistance today by foisting upon us the ideal of male supremacy.

248

Under the impact of racism, the black woman has been continually forced to inject herself into the desperate struggle for existence. She, like her man, has been compelled to work for wages, providing for her family as she previously provided for the slaveholding class. The infinitely onerous nature of this equality should never be overlooked. For the black woman has always been harnessed to household chores. Yet, she could never be defined by her uniquely "female" responsibilities.

As a result, black women have made significant contributions to struggles against the racism and the dehumanizing exploitation of a wrongly organized society. In fact, the intense levels of resistance historically maintained by black people—and thus the historical function of the Black Liberation Struggle as harbinger of change throughout the society—are due in part to the greater *objective* equality between the black man and woman.

Official and unofficial attempts to blunt the effects of the egalitarian tendencies between the black man and woman should come as no surprise. The matriarch concept, embracing the "female castrator" cliché is a weapon of open ideological warfare. Black men and women alike remain its potential victims—men unconsciously lunging at the woman, equating her with the myth; women sinking back into the shadows, lest an aggressive posture resurrect the myth.

The myth must be consciously repudiated. The black woman in her true historical contours must be resurrected. We, the black women of today, must accept the full weight of a legacy wrought in blood by our mothers in chains. As heirs to a tradition of perseverance and heroic resistance, we must hasten to take our place wherever our people are forging toward freedom.

THE RADICALIZATION OF SIMONE DE BEAUVOIR

ALICE SCHWARZER

Translated by Helen Eustis

TWENTY-FOUR YEARS AGO, SIMONE DE BEAUVOIR PUB-
LISHED "THE SECOND SEX," A CLASSIC STUDY OF WOMEN'S
CONDITION. THE BOOK CHANGED MINDS AND POSSIBLY
HISTORY, BUT THE AUTHOR HERSELF REMAINED A DISTANT
FIGURE; A WOMAN GREATLY ADMIRED, BUT LITTLE KNOWN
EVEN TO THE VERY WOMEN'S GROUPS HER WORK HAD
HELPED TO START. SHE WAS THE LONE WOMAN IN THE
MALE INTELLECTUAL CIRCLES OF FRANCE.

HERE, FOR THE FIRST TIME, SIMONE DE BEAUVOIR RE-
VEALS A RECENT AND VERY PERSONAL REVOLUTION. WITH
ALICE SCHWARZER, AN ACTIVIST IN THE FRENCHWOMAN'S
LIBERATION MOVEMENT, SHE DISCUSSES HER CONVERSION
TO FEMINISM, HER CHANGED POLITICAL PHILOSOPHY, AND
HER PLANS TO JOIN WOMEN AT LAST.

Schwarzer: When you wrote *The Second Sex* in 1949 you
believed that socialism was the only true remedy for the
inequality of the sexes. Then in November 1971, 22
years later, you became actively involved in the feminist
movement by taking part in the international women's
march in Paris. Why?
Beauvoir: Because I realized that in the past 20 years,
the position of women in France had not really changed
and that socialism, as it has evolved—for example, in
Russia—hasn't changed women's position, either. Frenchwomen had won a few minor legal victories in terms of
marriage and divorce; contraceptive devices had been dis-

tributed, but very inadequately, since only 7 percent of Frenchwomen use the Pill. There may be a few more women working than before, but not many, and they are secretaries rather than heads of businesses, and nurses more often than doctors. They are almost completely barred from the most interesting careers, and their advancement is blocked even in those professions they can enter. All these factors made me reconsider. Also, before the Women's Liberation Movement formed in 1970, the women's groups in France were reformist and legalistic. I had no desire to join them. The new feminism, however, is radical. It reiterates the 1968 slogan—change life today; don't gamble on the future; act now.

When the women of MLF [The Frenchwomen's Liberation Movement] got in touch with me, they asked me to help formulate an abortion manifesto, making public the fact that I and others had had abortions. I thought that this was a valid way of drawing attention to the problem. So it was quite natural that I should decide to march with the militants of the MLF, and to support their slogans: free abortion on demand, free contraception, voluntary motherhood.

Schwarzer: You spoke of the situation in Russia. What are women's lives like there?

Beauvoir: Almost all Soviet women work, and those who don't—the wives of a few highly placed functionaries and other important men—are looked down upon by the rest. Soviet women are very proud of working. They have quite extensive social and political responsibilities and a sense of these responsibilities. However, the number of women with any real power in the Central Committee or in the Assemblies is very small in relation to the number of men. For the most part, women practice the least agreeable and least respected professions. In Russia, almost all the doctors are women. This is because the medical profession is extremely hard, tiring, and poorly remunerated by the state. Women are herded into medicine or teaching—more important careers, like the sciences, engineering, etc., are much less accessible to them. On one hand, women are not professionally equal to men. On the other, responsibility for housework and care of children falls entirely upon them, exactly as in other countries. Perhaps even more so than in France, where a woman in a comparable position would have a house-keeper. One must conclude that even in the Soviet Union there is no real equality between men and women.

Schwarzer: Why is that so?

Beauvoir: Well, first of all, the socialist countries are not really socialistic. The socialism Marx dreamed of, that would truly change mankind, has not been realized any-where. The means of production have changed hands, but as time goes on we see that this is not really enough to change society, change humanity. So in spite of a different economic system, the traditional roles of man and woman remain the same. This relates to the fact that men have deeply internalized the idea of their own superiority. They are not ready to give up what I call their superiority com-plex. To validate themselves, they need to see woman as inferior. And she is so used to thinking of herself as in-ferior that only a few women dare to fight for equality.

Schwarzer: There are many misunderstandings about the concept of feminism. What is your definition?

Beauvoir: At the end of *The Second Sex,* I said I wasn't a feminist because I thought that the solution to women's problems must depend on the socialist evolution of society. By feminist, I meant fighting for specifically feminine de-mands independent of the class struggle. Today my defi-nition is the same, but I have come to realize that we must fight for an improvement in woman's actual situation before achieving the socialism we hope for. Besides this, I realized that even in the socialist countries, women's equality has not been won. So it is necessary for women to fight for their rights. That is why I have now joined the MLF.

Another reason is that even in the French leftist move-ments, there is serious inequality between men and women. Women always do the humblest, most boring, and least visible jobs. The men speak, write articles, do the most interesting things, and have the greatest responsibilities. In the bosom of these movements, in principle formed to liberate everybody—including youth and women—women remain inferior.

It goes even further. Many male leftists are aggressively hostile to Women's Liberation. They despise us and let us know it. The first time a feminist meeting was held in Vincennes, a number of male leftists broke into the hall shouting, "Power to the phallus!" I think they are beginning to revise that position, just because women are demonstrating that they can conduct a militant action independent of men.

Schwarzer: What are your reactions to the new feminists, the young radical women in the movement?

Beauvoir: In America, where the movement is most advanced, there is a whole range of tendencies—from Betty Friedan, who is fairly conservative, to what is called S.C.U.M. (Society for Cutting Up Men), a movement to emasculate men. In France, too, at the heart of the movement there are a number of different tendencies. My own is to want to link Women's Liberation with the class struggle. I feel that women's struggle, while it is unique, is connected to the wider one in which they must join with men. As a result, I reject any wholesale repudiation of men.

Schwarzer: What do you think of the principle of women-only in meetings? Most parts of the Women's Movement have adopted it for the time being.

Beauvoir: I think that, for the moment, it's a good thing for several reasons. First, if men were admitted to these groups, they wouldn't be able to restrain their masculine compulsion to dominate, to impose. At the same time, many women, consciously or unconsciously, still have certain feelings of inferiority, a certain timidity; many women would not dare to express themselves freely in front of men. Specifically, it is vital that they should not feel judged by the individual men who share their individual lives, because they also need to liberate themselves from them. For the moment, neither men's nor women's mentalities permit really honest discussion in mixed groups.

Schwarzer: But isn't the temporary exclusion of men also a political question? Since they represent the system—and since it is also the individual man who oppresses a woman—don't the feminists consider them "the first enemy" in this primary stage?

Beauvoir: Yes, but it's very complicated, because, as Marx said of capitalists, they are victims, too. But it is too abstract to say, as I've thought sometimes, that only the system is to blame. Men are to blame, too. The man of today did not establish this patriarchal regime, but he profits by it, even when he criticizes it. And he has made it very much a part of his own thinking.

One must blame the system, but at the same time be wary of men, and not let them take over our activities, our potentialities. The system and men both must be attacked. Even when a man is a feminist, one must keep one's distance and watch out for paternalism. Women don't want to be *granted* equality, they want to *win* it. Which is not the same thing at all.

Schwarzer: In your own life, do you have this hatred and mistrust for men?

Beauvoir: No. I have always gotten along very well with the men in my life. Many of the women I know in the MLF have no hatred for men either, just an attitude of caution, a determination not to allow themselves to be devoured.

Schwarzer: Do you think it's a good thing, politically, that some women go farther?

Beauvoir: Actually, it isn't a bad thing at all that there are women who repudiate men. They will influence those who are inclined to compromise.

Schwarzer: What do you think about the argument that sexual relations with men are oppressive?

Beauvoir: Is it really true that all sexual relations between men and women are oppressive? Instead of refusing all such relations, couldn't one work toward having a kind which would not be oppressive? I find it absurd to assume that all coitus is rape. By saying that, one agrees to the masculine myth that a man's sex is a sword, a weapon. The real problem is to find new sexual relationships which will not be oppressive.

Schwarzer: You said in a commentary on *The Second Sex* that the problem of femininity had not touched you personally, and that you felt you were in a "highly impartial position." Did you mean that a woman can, as an individual, escape her feminine condition? On the professional level and in her relations with others?

Beauvoir: Escape her condition as a woman? No! But actually I've been very lucky. I've escaped most of woman's bondages: maternity, the life of a housewife. Also, in my day there were fewer women who pursued advanced studies. To have a postgraduate degree in philosophy was to be in a privileged position as a woman. I received immediate recognition from men—they were ready to accept friendship with a woman who had succeeded on their own level, because it was so exceptional. Now that many women are advanced students, men are afraid of losing their own status. More generally, if you admit, as I do, that a woman is not obliged to be a wife and mother to have a complete and happy life, there are a certain number of women who can achieve full lives without submitting to women's limitations.

Schwarzer: You once said, "The greatest success of my life is Sartre." Yet you express a great need for independence and a fear of being dominated. Although egalitarian relations between men and women are so difficult to establish, do you think that you achieved them?

Beauvoir: Yes. Or rather, the problem never came up, because Sartre is in no way an oppressor. If I had loved someone other than Sartre, I still would not have allowed myself to be oppressed. Some women escape masculine domination by means of their professional autonomy. Some arrive at a balanced relation with one man. Others have meaningless affairs.

Schwarzer: You have spoken of women being an inferior class . . .

Beauvoir: Not a class. In *The Second Sex,* I said that women are an inferior *caste.* In principle, one can leave one class to move into another, but caste is the group into which one is born and which one cannot leave. If you are a woman, you can never become a man. And the way in which women are treated on the economic, social, and political levels makes an inferior caste of them.

Schwarzer: What do you think of the political analyses that equate patriarchal oppression of women as unpaid domestic labor with the capitalist use of workers?

Beauvoir: I don't think those analyses are accurate. Housework produces no profit—it's a different situation from that of the worker who is robbed of the profit from his work. I would like to know exactly what relationship exists between the two. Women's entire future strategy will depend on it.

This particular point has not been examined thoroughly enough in any of the books I've read; only Shulamith Firestone, who is less well known than Millett or Greer, has suggested something new. In her book *The Dialectic of Sex,* she associates Women's Liberation with children's liberation. This is right because women will not be liberated until they are liberated from children, and children are at the same time to some degree liberated from adults.

Schwarzer: How do you see the relationship between the class war and the war between the sexes?

Beauvoir: Abolishing capitalism will not mean abolishing the patriarchal tradition as long as the family is preserved. I believe that not only must we change the ownership of the means of production, but that we must also change the family structure. And even in China this has not been done. It is true that they got rid of the feudal family, which made great changes in woman's condition. But to the extent that they still accept the conjugal family, which is basically a legacy of the patriarchal family, I don't believe that Chinese women have been liberated at all. I am in complete agreement with the attempts which have been made by women and some men to replace the family by either communes or whatever forms remain to be invented.

Schwarzer: Would you say that, while the class struggle doesn't necessarily change woman's condition, radical feminism and the reexamination of the social structure would resolve the class struggle?

Beauvoir: No, not necessarily. If one begins by abolishing family structures, it is very probable that capitalism would be deeply shaken. But that will not be enough to reorganize the means of production, the conditions of work, and the relationships of human beings to each other. There has not yet been enough analysis of this point because the women who were active in feminism were middle-class women who weren't thinking in economic terms. In economics, on the other hand, we've been too content with Marxist formulas to ask the important question. When socialism is achieved, will there then be equality between men and women?

When *The Second Sex* was published, I was very much surprised to find it badly received by the left. I remember an objection from the Trotskyites. They said that the problem of woman is not a true problem. There is no point in raising it. When the revolution comes, women will find their place quite naturally.

Also the Communists, with whom I was in very bad political repute at that time, ridiculed me harshly. They wrote articles about how the workingwoman of Billancourt had no time for or interest in the woman problem. After the revolution, women would be the equals of men. But what was to happen to women in the meantime didn't interest them.

Schwarzer: In concrete terms, what possibilities for liberation do you see for the individual woman?

Beauvoir: The first thing is work. Then refuse marriage if possible. After all, I could have married Sartre. But I believe that we were wise not to have done so. When you are married, people see you as married, and you begin to see yourselves as married. This is quite different from the relationship you have with society when you are not married. Marriage is dangerous for a woman. Having said this, I acknowledge that a woman may have reasons for marrying—if she wants to have children, for example. It's still very difficult to bring children into the world when the parents aren't married; they encounter hardships.

To be really independent, what counts is to have a profession, to work. It means that when you are married, if you wish to divorce, you can leave; you can support your children; you can make a life for yourself. But work is not the solution for everything. It has both liberating and dehumanizing aspects. As a result, women often have to choose between two forms of dehumanization: being a housewife or working in a factory. Work is not a general panacea; nevertheless, it is the first condition for independence. When women strike in factories, as they did in Troyes and Nantes, they become conscious of their power, their autonomy, and as a result they are less submissive at home. It's all connected.

Schwarzer: Can women limit liberation to the individual level?

Beauvoir: Individual emancipation is not enough. Women must go on to collective action. I have not done so myself until now because there had been no organized movement in which I could believe. But writing *The Second*

257

Sex, after all, was an act beyond my own personal liberation. I wrote that book out of concern for the whole feminine condition, not just to understand what the situation of women was, but also as an act to help other women understand themselves. During the past 20 years, I have answered a great number of letters from women who told me that my book helped them very much to understand their situation, to resist, to make decisions for themselves.

In France and elsewhere, most women are very conservative. They want to be "feminine." However, new conditions in housework are liberating women a little and leaving them time to think: they must be led further, into revolt. In a capitalist country, women will never get jobs while there is unemployment among men. That is why I think that women's equality cannot be won unless there is a total overthrow of the system.

I think the Women's Movement, like the student movement, which was limited at first but later ignited strikes all over the country, could cause an explosion. If women manage to get a foothold in the world of work, they will really shake up the system. For the moment, the weakness of the French and the American movement, too, is that they include very few working-class women.

Schwarzer: Are you in favor of violence in the women's struggle?

Beauvoir: In the present situation, yes, up to a point, because men use violence toward women, both in language and in action. They attack women, they rape them, they insult them. Women should defend themselves with violence. Some are learning karate and other ways of fighting. I am in favor of that. They will feel much more at ease in their own skins and in the world when they don't feel helpless in the face of aggression.

Schwarzer: You often speak of American women. Have you had much contact with them?

Beauvoir: Yes. First of all through their books. We have to admit that the American movement is more advanced. I've received many letters from Americans, and invitations to go to America. But my reply to them is: I am working with Frenchwomen. I must first work at home.

Schwarzer: Now that you consider yourself a militant feminist, what immediate action do you plan?

Beauvoir: First, we are holding special meetings to expose the crimes committed against woman. The first two meetings dealt with problems of maternity, contraception, and abortion. A committee of inquiry interrogated witnesses—biologists, sociologists, psychiatrists, doctors, midwives—and, most important, women who had suffered directly from the conditions that this society has imposed on womankind.

We hope to convince the public that women must be assured the right to procreate freely, that is, the public must help provide the expenses of maternity—child-care centers, especially—and the right to refuse undesired pregnancies through contraceptive devices and abortion. We demand that these be free, and that only the individual woman decide whether or not to make use of them. But contraception and abortion are only a point of departure for women's larger liberation.

Later on we will be organizing meetings at which we will expose the exploitation of female labor: the housewife's, the white collar worker's, and the women of the working class.

Schwarzer: In *The Second Sex* you quoted Rimbaud's vision of a future world in which woman would be liberated. What do you think that new world will be like?

Beauvoir: Women's Liberation will surely bring about new kinds of relationships between human beings, and men as well as women will be changed. Women, and men too, must become human beings first and foremost. The differences which exist between them are no more important than the differences which exist between individual women, or individual men.

I don't believe that when women have won equality they will develop specifically feminine values. The fact is that culture, civilization, and universal values have been made by men because they were the ones who represented universality. When the proletariat rejected the bourgeoisie as a dominant class, they did not reject the entire bourgeois heritage, and in the same way, women, when they have won equality with men, will have to make use of some of the tools created by men. It is true that in creating universal values—I would call mathematical science a universal value, for example—men have very often given them a specifically masculine, male, virile character and have confused the two in a very subtle, sly way. It becomes a matter of separating the two, of getting rid of the contamination.

Schwarzer: After the publication of *The Second Sex,* you were often reproached for not having developed any battle plan for women, for having gone no farther than analysis.

Beauvoir: That is true. I recognize this as a shortcoming in the book. I stopped on a note of vague confidence in the future, in the revolution, and in socialism.

Schwarzer: And today?

Beauvoir: Today I've changed my mind. I have become truly a feminist.

VII. Appendices

APPENDIX I:
HOW Ms. MAGAZINE
GOT STARTED

First, there were some women writers and editors who began to ask questions. Why were the media, including women's magazines, so rarely or so superficially interested in the big changes happening to women? Why was our own work so unconnected to our lives? Why were we always playing the game by somebody else's (the publisher's, the advertiser's) rules?

Then there were questions from activists: women who were trying to raise money for an information service and self-help projects, particularly for poor or isolated women, and having very little luck. Mightn't a newsletter or magazine serve to link up women, provide a forum for new ideas, and generate income as well?

The two groups met several times early in 1971. Whether we were editors or potential readers, we all agreed that we wanted a new kind of publication, one that was both owned by and honest about women. Gradually, the idea of a full-fledged national magazine developed; a publication created and controlled by women that could be as serious, outrageous, satisfying, practical, sad, funky, intimate, global, compassionate, and full of change as women's lives really are.

We began to hold meetings—many meetings—and we made big plans. Then we spent many months making appointments, looking for backing from groups that invest in new ventures—and just as many months getting turned down. Flat. We usually heard one or several reasons like these from potential investors:

. . . all around us, magazines are failing; why spend money to buck the tide?

. . . even though local or "special interest" magazines are making money (curiously, anything directed at the female 53 percent of the population is regarded as "special interest"), they are bad investments compared to, say, apartment buildings, computer hardware, and the like;

. . . the more we insisted on retaining at least 51 percent of the stock, the more everyone told us that investors don't give money without getting control; who ever heard of a national magazine controlled by its staff?

. . . setting aside some of the profits (supposing there were any) to go back to the Women's Movement is so unbusinesslike as to be downright crazy—even publications made necessary by other reform or revolutionary movements haven't managed that;

. . . and finally, the investors said, there are probably only ten or twenty thousand women in the country interested in changing economic and social discrimination against women anyway; certainly not enough to support a nationwide magazine.

We got discouraged, but there was some support: friendly magazine people who thought we should try to find "public-spirited" money; women in advertising who were themselves trying to create ads that were a service to women instead of an embarrassment; and feminist speakers who had been traveling around the country and sensed that a mass audience was there. Most of all, there were the several women writers, editors, and many all-purpose feminist volunteers who were willing to contribute their talents in return for little except hope.

Then two concrete things happened. First, Katherine Graham, one of the few women publishers in the country, was willing to pretend that a few shares of stock in a nonexistent magazine were worth buying; a fiction that allowed us money for some of our out-of-pocket expenses. Second, Clay Felker, editor and publisher of New York, a weekly metropolitan magazine, suggested an unusual idea: New York would help us to produce a sample issue to prove that we could create a new kind of magazine, and that women would buy it. We would have the chance to win—or fail—in a nationwide test.

263

In more detail, *New York* offered to bear the full risk of the $125,000 necessary to pay printers, binders, engravers, paper mills, distributors, writers, artists, and all the other elements vital to turning out 300,000 copies of a Preview Issue. (Plus supplying the great asset of *New York's* production staff, without which the expenses would have been much higher.) In return, some of the *Ms.* articles and features would appear first as an insert in the year-end issue of *New York,* half of the newsstand profits (if any) of our own Preview Issue would go to *New York,* and so would all of the advertising proceeds. Though *Ms.* editors would be working without pay, we were assured of editorial control. The ads were to be *New York's* usual ones; otherwise, all the pages were ours.

It was an odd way to introduce a magazine, but a generous and unusual offer—the first time, as far as we knew, that one magazine had given birth to another without the "quid pro quo" of editorial control, or some permanent financial interest.

The Preview Issue

In a small office, with four people working full time and the rest of us helping when we could get away from our jobs, the Preview Issue was put together, start to finish, in two months.

The one-room office was crowded and sometimes heavy with concern that we would somehow deplete the strength of the Women's Movement by creating a test issue that did poorly, but it also had an atmosphere of camaraderie; of people doing what they cared about. Could there possibly be 100,000 women in the country who wanted this unconventional magazine? We had been listening to doomsayers for so long that we ourselves sometimes doubted it, but there was little time to worry and no way to turn back.

When the insert from our Preview Issue appeared as part of *New York* in December, 1971, the issue set a newsstand sales record; more than *New York* had ever sold before.

Of course, said the doomsayers, women in a metropolitan area might be interested. But would we appeal to the women of Ohio or Arizona or Iowa?

The complete and autonomous Preview Issue of *Ms.* —dated "Spring 1972," because it was designed to remain on the newsstand for at least two months—was distributed nationally in January, 1972. It was a new entity on the newsstands and we wanted to make sure women knew about it. But when authors and editors visited various towns and cities to speak about the magazine, we were met with phone calls: "Where it is?" "We can't find a copy." "What newsstands are selling it?"

Worriedly, we called the distributor—and the truth finally dawned on us. The 300,000 copies supposed to last on the newsstands for at least eight weeks had virtually disappeared in eight days. *Ms.* had sold out.

Letters began to pour into our crowded office: more than 20,000 long, literate, rough, disparate, funny, tragic and very personal letters from women all over the country, including Ohio, Arizona and Iowa. They identified with the magazine, as with a friend, and had accepted it as their own.

Though inundated with mail, we still didn't realize how unusual its quantity and quality was until we asked the editor of another women's magazine—with a circulation of seven million, compared to our 300,000—how much editorial response each issue got. "About 2,000 letters," she said, "and a lot of them not very worthwhile. Four thousand letters of any kind is quite extraordinary."

Obviously, the need for an honest magazine by and about women was greater and deeper than we had thought. As much out of instinct as skill, we had connected with a great and deep cultural change. We were experiencing it ourselves—and we were not alone.

After the Preview Issue, we spent another three months looking for investors who believed in the need for such a magazine, and would therefore give us the backing we now knew we must have to get it going on a regular basis. We had one important condition: that the investor be willing to back us without taking financial and editorial control in return.

In spite of the endless appointments and months of looking, we can't take credit for finding Warner Communications. They found us. We are grateful to them for exploring many kinds of new media. And we are especially impressed that they took the unusual position of becoming the major investor, but minority stockholder; thus providing all the money without demanding the decision vote in return. It was a step forward for women and for journalism.

Even with Warner's help, however, we had to reach the break-even point with a third of the money, and in a third of the time, that most national magazines have required. (The average seems to be $3 million and three years before a publication begins to show profit.) And our hope is to be able to give a healthy percentage of our profits back to the Women's Movement; to programs and projects that can help change women's lives.

Six months after the Preview Issue, we had moved out of our one-room office to larger rooms in the same building; hired the people who had been working for so long, and new staff besides, and produced an issue dated July, 1972—the first of our regular monthly productions. In it, we reported to our readers exactly what our financial and editorial status was, the mistakes we had made, and our plans for the next issues. It was a step toward open journalism, and one we have continued through periodic Personal Reports.

As for our content, you see a sampling of it in this collection. But we have many more plans for the future, and we are continuing to learn.

We are also continuing to be inundated with mail. More than 100 unsolicited manuscripts come in every day. Unlike most magazines, we read these contributions carefully, but are still more than a month behind in reading and replying. Then there are the thousands of reader letters that come in each week. Sometimes it seems we must make a choice: either get out a magazine, or answer our mail. But we do treasure this personal response, and make an effort to publish as many letters as we can.

In some cases, we use our Personal Reports to answer the most frequent questions. For instance:

Is the office really free of the traditional chain-of-

command? Yes, we can say that we are managing to be reasonably efficient without the imposition of a hierarchy; a pattern that imitates patriarchy anyway, and is no longer workable, at home or in the office. We list ourselves alphabetically on the masthead, divided only according to area of expertise. Decisions affecting a particular area are made by that group's members together; decisions affecting more than one area are made by members of the groups involved. This isn't as difficult as it sounds: either there is a consensus quickly, or a few people who care passionately succeed in convincing the rest. The important thing is that the magazine gets the benefit of many people's knowledge and ideas—not just of one or a few.

As for the chores of office life, we each do as much of our own phone-answering, letter-writing, and coffee-making as commonsense and deadlines will allow. Though there are staff members who do far more typing of manuscripts than others, they also take part in editorial decisions, represent the magazine at conferences or on television shows, and write articles themselves. It means an end to airtight job categories, no opportunity to learn new skills, and secrecy about who's getting what salary. Most of us have suffered through years of the conventional, authoritarian kind of work day. Our freer alternative isn't perfect but it is an enormous, life-giving relief.

Who Are the Readers of Ms.?

We have found, from newsstand and subscription patterns, that the distribution of our readership pretty much follows that of the population, with the same relationship among urban, suburban, and rural: interest isn't confined to the East and West coasts, as people unfamiliar with the Women's Movement suppose. The only area with proportionately fewer readers is the South. Within each locale, the sales are greater wherever women gather: campuses, office buildings, supermarkets, and the like.

We are often asked about our readership among men, and also among black and other minority women. It's difficult to know real percentages and race can't be told from subscriber lists; men tend not to subscribe for themselves (they read their wives' or friends' copies, or buy single issues on the newsstand). But there are indicators. About 10 percent of our mail comes from men, for instance, and about 20 percent from women who identify themselves as black or other Third World women.

To find out more about ages, incomes, and life situations of our readers, we conducted a survey of our subscribers. Eighty-nine percent are between the ages of 18 and 49, and 71% are presently married. Only 15% belong to groups associated with the Women's Movement: we hope that means we are reaching out to new women, in addition to those who have access to feminist organizations and support.

Beyond the statistics, one thing stands out clearly: the intensity of interest our readers have in *Ms*. Not only do they write unprecedented numbers of letters in response to each article, poem, or story, but they take advertising pages almost as seriously as editorial pages. The ad letters we received in response to the Preview Issue concentrated on ads that didn't fit the editorial content; ads that seemed to say women spent all their money on make-up, clothes and the like. But since we've been able to go out after our own ads—ads that show women realistically and feature the full range of products women buy, not just feminine ones—we have had a predominately positive response. In either case, we pass all letters along to the companies concerned, and they do listen. Advertising practices are changing, and they will have to change much more—not because of this magazine's rather minor needs, but because advertising words and images are such a pervasive influence on our expectations and those of our children.

And there must be many readers with consciousness and a generous spirit. We have received hundreds of contributions, ranging from 50 cents to $100, to help pay for subscriptions for women who can't yet afford them. We matched some contributions with requests from women who have written to tell us that they need free subscriptions. Others are used to send subscriptions to women's prisons (about 30 so far), plus some individual female and male prisoners who have responded to the magazine, and rehabilitation centers for young people. Still others make subscriptions available to members of organizations such as the National Committee on Household Employment and the National Welfare Rights Organization.

Books and Other Projects

This *Ms. Reader* is our second full-fledged book. Our first book, *Wonder Woman,* began as a story and cover in our July issue and grew into a big book of classic Wonder Woman stories that had been long out of print.

We also have a record, called "Free To Be . . . You and Me." It was put together by Marlo Thomas, who wanted to contribute to the Women's Movement, and to the childhood of a much-loved niece by volunteering her talents to a children's record. Marlo gradually gathered original songs and poems by such talented people as Carol Hall, Mary Rodgers, Bruce Hart, and Sheldon Harnick. Then she enlisted other performers: Carol Channing, Diana Ross, Mel Brooks, Robert Morse, Alan Alda, and Shirley Jones, among others. The result is a joyous and delightful record.

We always intended to establish a foundation that would allow a portion of eventual income created by this magazine to go back to the Women's Movement. (Since *Ms.* succeeded in breaking even in one year, we hope to be able to contribute soon.) The record album gave us the means to set up a foundation because Marlo and the other creative people involved wanted to contribute part of the money they would normally receive. So we have established the Ms. Foundation for Women, Inc. A variety of feminists will steer its course.

The Future

We continue to examine our actions and attitudes, assessing our gains, and analyzing our mistakes to see how we can best contribute to changing women's lives for the better and to exploring feminist goals. Perhaps the truth is, for us and for women everywhere, that none of us yet knows how to achieve all our feminist goals, and therefore ultimately humanist ones. Consciousness is not an absolute state, but a continual process of becoming. But we hope that *Ms.*—and the books and projects that grow from it—will continue to be a forum for exploration and a source of contribution to the ideals of the Women's Movement in the months and years to come.

After all, it's a very deep, basic, and long-term kind of change we are after. Eliminating the patriarchal and racist base of existing social systems requires a revolution, not a reform. But it's not a revolution we die for—it's one we live and work for. Every day.

APPENDIX II:
Ms. AS A FORM OF ADDRESS

For more than twenty years *Ms.* has appeared in secretarial handbooks as the suggested form of address when a woman's marital status is unknown; a sort of neutral combination of *Miss* and *Mrs.*

Now, *Ms.* is being adopted as a standard form of address by women who want to be recognized as individuals, rather than being identified by their relationship with a man. After all, if *Mr.* is enough to indicate "male," then *Ms.* should be enough to indicate "female."

A proposal often referred to as the "Ms. bill" has been introduced in Congress by New York's Congresswoman Bella Abzug. It would forbid any agency of the Federal Government from using prefixes that indicate marital status. Congressman Jonathan Bingham, also of New York, has introduced a bill that would forbid requiring females registering to vote in any Federal election to disclose their marital status unless men were also required to disclose theirs.

The U.S. Government Printing office has taken a step forward. Its style book now lists *Ms.* as an acceptable term for use in government publications.

In practice, *Ms.* is used with a woman's given name: *Ms. Jane Jones,* say, or *Ms. Jane Wilson Jones.* It doesn't make sense to say *Ms. John Jones*: a woman identified only as her husband's wife is obviously a Mrs.

Of course, titles are going out of style altogether. Thus, even when addressing a married couple, it is easier to write *Jane* and *John Jones,* without any prefixes at all. But on

271

occasions such as voting, when sex must be given but males are not required to reveal their marital status, the use of *Ms.* provides equal treatment for women.

Ms. is pronounced "miz." When asking someone to write it down, however, women find it easier to say the initials: "M.S." Otherwise, the result in writing turns out to be *Miz,* just as *Mister* might have been written down in full before *Mr.* was popularly accepted. To designate the magazine, either *Ms.* or *Miz* is fine.

The use of *Ms.* isn't meant to protect either the married or the unmarried woman from social pressure—only to signify a female human being. It's symbolic, and important. There's a lot in a name.

APPENDIX III:
SOME SUGGESTED READING

Books

Ingrid Bengis, *Combat in the Erogenous Zone* (Knopf, 1972). A highly personal, honest account of one woman's journey toward liberation.

*Caroline Bird, *Born Female: The High Cost of Keeping Women Down* (McKay, 1971). A basic text of current feminist thought, especially valuable for breaking down myths used against women in the work force.
* Available in paperback.

*Boston Women's Health Book Collective, *Our Bodies, Ourselves* (Simon & Schuster, 1973). A basic self-help health course for and about women.

Phyllis Chesler, *Women and Madness* (Doubleday, 1972). Explores the relationship between sex-role stereotyping and mental illness; challenges the existing definitions of normalcy and madness imposed on women, especially those from poor and Third World backgrounds.

*Elizabeth Gould Davis, *The First Sex* (Putnam, 1971). Traces women's contribution to civilization from the first millenium forward, raising basic arguments against a patriarchal interpretation of history.

*Karen DeCrow, *The Young Woman's Guide to Liberation: Alternatives to the Half-Life While the Choice is Still Yours* (Pegasus, 1971). A very readable guide to feminism, with emphasis on the everyday experiences of high school age women.

* Available in paperback.

273

*Shulamith Firestone, *The Dialectic of Sex: The Case for Feminist Revolution* (Morrow, 1970). A feminist adapts Marxist analytical techniques to the needs of women and children; an original theoretical work.

*Eleanor Flexner, *A Century of Struggle: The Women's Rights Movement in the United States* (Atheneum, 1968). A history of the first wave of American feminism.

*Ellen Frankfort, *Vaginal Politics* (Quadrangle, 1972). A patient's guide to survival in the patriarchal world of doctors and hospitals.

*Betty Friedan, *The Feminine Mystique* (Norton, 1963). A report on the middle and upper-income white housewives of the '50s who began to question the waste of their education and talent; Freudian interpretations of women.

*Vivian Gornick and Barbara K. Moran, eds., *Woman in Sexist Society:* Studies in Power and Powerlessness (Basic Books, 1971). A far-ranging anthology of information and personal experience.

*Germaine Greer, *The Female Eunuch* (McGraw-Hill, 1971). How women as wives, employees mothers and lovers are emotionally and intellectually crippled by patriarchy.

Judith Hole and Ellen Levine, *Rebirth of Feminism* (Quadrangle, 1972). A history of the contemporary feminist movement.

Gerda Lerner, *Black Women in White America* (Pantheon, 1972), Black women recount their victories and defeats in the historical fight against racism and sexism.

*Kate Millet, *Sexual Politics* (Doubleday, 1970). How the patriarchal bias operates in culture, with case studies of prominent male writers and philosophers.

*Robin Morgan, ed., *Sisterhood Is Powerful: An Anthology of Writing from the Women's Liberation Movement* (Random, 1970). A good introduction to the issues of the Women's Movement. Includes "Double Jeopardy: To Be Black and Female" by Francis Beal.

*Diane Schulder and Florynce Kennedy, *Abortion Rap* (McGraw-Hill, 1971). Women testify honestly about their abortion experiences and their confrontations with anti-female forces along the way.

* Available in paperback.

*Barbara Seaman, *Free and Female* (Coward, 1972). Discusses female sexuality, and covers the whole spectrum of the contemporary woman's sex life.

Other Published Materials

N. M. Guli, "Liberation—For Half a Race?" *Crisis*, April-May, 1971, vol. 78 no. 3. A summary of the economic and social position of black women.

Aileen Hernandez, "Sister and Brother: Getting Ahead Together," *Contact*, Fall, 1972. The interest of Blacks in Women's Liberation.

Pamela Newman and Maxine Williams, "Black Woman's Liberation," Pathfinder Press, 14 West Street, New York, N.Y. 10014.

If you cannot find the books and other publications listed above in your local bookstore, they can be ordered from *Feminist Book Mart*, 162-11 Ninth Street, Whitestone, New York, N.Y. 11357. For a listing of additional reprints and pamphlets, write to KNOW, P.O. Box 86031, Pittsburgh Pa. 15221.

A Reading List for Free Children

Because "Ms. Magazine" publishes "A Story for Free Children" in each issue—that is, a story that is free of sex and race stereotypes—many parents, teachers, and children have written to ask us for more such reading. Letty Cottin Pogrebin, a "Ms." editor who is especially interested in role-free education for children, has prepared this bibliography as a helpful beginning. She has included in it recommendations by Nancy Barron (University of Missouri Graduate Center for Research in Social Behavior); Feminists on Children's Media and their bibliography "Little Miss Muffet Fights Back;"* Rhonna Goodman (Vocational High School Specialist, New York Public Library); Lillian Morrison (Coordinator of Young Adult Services, New York Public Library); Aileen O'Brien Murphy (Children's Literature Specialist, N.Y. Public Library).

*To order a copy of "Little Miss Muffet Fights Back" send 50¢ in coin plus a stamped, addressed 4 x 9½" envelope to Feminists on Children's Media, P.O. Box 4315, Grand Central Station, N.Y., N.Y. 10017.

Tuning in early: Pre-school picture books
and beginner readers

All Kinds of Mothers. Cecily Brownstone (McKay). Black and white mothers, working and stay-home mothers all have an important quality in common—their love for their children.

Ann Can Fly. Frederick Phleger (Random). Dad gives Ann a piloting lesson on their way to camp.

Clever Polly and the Stupid Wolf. Catherine Storr (Puffin). Girl outwits wolf—suggesting that intelligence pays for females too.

Jellybeans for Breakfast. Miriam Young (Parents). Two girls share fantasies about their future adventures, including a trip to the moon.

Jenny's Secret Place. Sara Evans Boyte (Lollipop Power).† What makes a five-year-old girl bequeath her private daydreaming hideaway to her little brother?

Jumbo the Boy and Arnold the Elephant. Dan Greenburg (Bobbs-Merrill). Baby boy and baby elephant are mixed-up in the hospital nursery. A whimsical story showing both fathers and mothers tending the mismatched offspring.

Madeline's Rescue. Ludwig Bemelmans (Viking). Strong-willed Madeline, her friends and housemother set their proper French boarding school adither for love of a dog.

Martin's Father. Margrit Eichler (Lollipop Power). Household chores, games and outdoor adventures are shared by a boy and his father.

Mommies at Work. Eve Merriam (Scholastic). Busy moms in various occupations, trades and professions. A must!

Noisy Nancy Norris and *Noisy Nancy Norris and Nick.* Lou Ann Gaeddert (Doubleday). Two books about irrepressible Nancy who is as inventive as she is boisterous.

Quiet on Account of Dinosaur. Jane Thayer (Morrow). Girl dinosaur maven grows up to become a world-famous scientist.

†For a brochure listing the publications of Lollipop Power, the Feminist collective, send a stamped, addressed envelope to: P.O. Box 1171, Chapel Hill, N.C. 27514.

Rosa-Too-Little. Sue Felt (Doubleday). Learning to write is a huge challenge for a Puerto Rican girl who desperately wants a library card.

The Dragon and the Doctor. Barbara Danish (Feminist Press)‡. A fantasy with a twist; the doctor is a little girl.

The Little Duster. Bill Charmatz (Macmillan). A grown man cleans up his messy apartment with the inadvertent aid of a dog who resembles a feather duster.

The Man Who Didn't Wash His Dishes. Phyllis Krasilovsky (Scholastic). Cooking for himself is no problem, but cleaning up afterwards is.

The Temper Tantrum Book. Edna Mitchell Preston (Viking). Lionel Lion and Cathaleen Kangaroo prove that anger, frustration and humor know no sex.

Humanized fiction: Girls who think and act; Boys who feel and care

I. For young readers or read-aloud

L. Frank Baum, *The Wizard of Oz*. (Reilly & Lee Co.). Dorothy leads the search for brains, heart, courage and honesty. A fantasy for feminists and humanists of all ages.

Betsy Byars, *Go and Hush the Baby* (Viking). Babysitting can be fun for a big brother (ages 5–8).

Astrid Lindgren, *Pippi Longstocking* (Viking). The escapades of an unreconstructed tomboy. (6–11).

Betty Miles and Joan Blos, *Just Think!* (Knopf). Mothers who work, fathers who enjoy the kids, athletic girls, a child care center . . . just think—reality! (4–8).

Kay Thompson, *Eloise*. The hilarious, not-at-all lady-like adventures of the 6-year-old who lives, for Lord's sake, in the Plaza Hotel. (5 and up)

II. For the middle grades

Vera & Bill Cleaver, *Lady Ellen Grae* (Lippincott). An ingratiating tomboy resists all attempts at socialization. (9–12)

‡For information about the publications of The Feminist Press send a stamped addressed envelope to Box 334, Old Westbury, New York 11568.

Alberta Wilson Constant, *The Motoring Millers* (Crowell). A young girl from a madcap family wins an auto race. (9–12)

Louise Fitzhugh, *Harriet the Spy* (Harper). An aspiring author spies on her neighbors and learns about herself. (8–12)

Maria Gripe, *The Night Daddy* (Delacorte). An eccentric young man babysits for a girl whose mother works nights. (8–12)

Sonia Levitin, *Rita, The Weekend Rat* (Atheneum). Cynthia overcomes her belief that girls are not as interesting as boys. (9–12)

Evelyn C. Nevin, *The Extraordinary Adventures of Chee Chee McNerney* (Four Winds). Mystery and excitement abound as a girl and her hunting party search for gold in Alaska. (9–11)

Scott O'Dell, *Island of Blue Dolphins* (Houghton). A strong Indian girl survives 18 years alone on an island. (9–12)

Ivan Southall, *Walk a Mile and Get Nowhere* (Bradbury). A 13-year-old tests his manhood and finds that machismo is meaningless. (10+)

III. For Young Adults—age 12 and up

Honor Arundel, *The Longest Weekend* (Nelson). A pregnant girl refuses to marry until the father of her child is mature enough to be her husband.

Hila Colman, *Daughter of Discontent* (Morrow). A 17-year-old girl must reexamine her attitude toward her domineering father and men in general.

John Donovan, *I'll Get There. It Better Be Worth the Trip* (Harper). Despite a negative view of women, the novel includes sensitive treatment of a boy's loneliness and of a suggestion of homosexuality.

Betsy Madden, *The All-American Coeds* (Criterion). How the crackerjack girls' basketball team of a black high school triumphs over the rule against coed competition.

Judith Merril, *Daughters of Earth* (Doubleday). The first of three science fiction stories shows women astronauts on equal footing with men.

Charles Portis, *True Grit* (Simon & Schuster). A spunky frontier girl is pledged to avenge her father's murder.

Elizabeth George Speare, *The Witch of Blackbird Pond* (Houghton). A high-spirited girl is accused of witchcraft.

Dorothy Uhnak, *The Witness* (Simon & Schuster). A plainclothes-woman solves a murder committed during a street demonstration. The author is an ex-policewoman.

Maia Wojciechowska, *Don't Play Dead Before You Have To* (Harper). A sympathetic teen-aged boy becomes father and mother to a neglected 5-year-old.

Let us now praise famous women: Biography and Autobiography

Jacqueline Auriol, *I Live To Fly* (Dutton). The only female test pilot in the world describes her comeback. (12 +)

Ella Kaiser Carruth, *She Wanted To Read: The Story of Mary McCleod Bethune* (Abingdon). The black woman who organized the National Council of Negro Women. (8–12)

Leah Lurie Heyn, *Challenge To Become a Doctor: The Story of Elizabeth Blackwell* (Feminist Press). Well-illustrated biography of the first woman doctor. (8–12)

Charles Graves, *Nellie Bly* (Garrard). The first woman reporter and her fight against sex discrimination. (7–9)

Philip Sterling, *Sea and Earth: The Life of Rachel Carson* (Crowell). Author of *a Silent Spring*. (12+)

Milton Meltzer, *Tongue of Flame: The Life of Lydia Maria Child* (Crowell). The unsung political writer and author of the first anti-slavery book published in America. (12 +)

Susan Brownmiller, *Shirley Chisholm* (Doubleday). The first black woman to be elected to the U.S. Congress. (9–13)

Shirley Chisholm, *Unbought and Unbossed* (Houghton). Her life in her words—by the woman who found her sex an even greater burden than her race. (14 +)

Conchita Cintron, *Memoirs of a Bullfighter* (Holt). The world's only successful woman torero describes her exclusion from the bullrings of Spain. (12–16)

Bernadette Devlin, *The Price of My Soul* (Knopf). The young Irish revolutionary tells her experiences in parliament. (12 +)

Agnes DeMille, *To a Young Dancer* (Little Brown). Heartaches and big breaks in the world of dance. (12 +)

Peggy Mann, *Amelia Earhart: First Lady of Flight* (Coward-McCann). The aviator who disappeared over the Pacific. (8–11)

Marianna Norris, *Dona Felisa: A Biography of The Mayor of San Juan* (Dodd Mead). First Puerto Rican woman to exercise the right to vote in her country. Mayor of San Juan 1945–68. (8–10)

Alix Shulman, *To the Barricades: The Anarchist Life of Emma Goldman* (Crowell). The 19th century revolutionary whose causes—women's rights, peace, birth control—are still with us. (12–15)

Irving Werstein, *Labor's Defiant Lady: The Story of Mother Jones* (Crowell). The militant trade union organizer who fought for the 8-hour day and against child labor. (12–15)

Polly Anne & Stewart Graff, *Helen Keller: Toward the Light* (Garrard). The remarkable handicapped woman and her loyal teacher Anne Sullivan. (6–9)

Terry Morris, *Shalom, Golda* (Hawthorn). Israel's Prime Minister Golda Meir from her beginnings in a small Russian town to her development as a world leader. (10–15)

Toby Shafter, *Edna St. Vincent Millay* (Messner). The tomboy who grew up to become a Pulitzer Prize-winning poet. (12 +)

Dorothy Sterling, *Lucretia Mott* (Doubleday). The Quaker preacher who crusaded for Abolition and Women's Suffrage for over 50 years. (12 +)

Stella K. Hershan, *A Woman of Quality: Eleanor Roosevelt* (Crown). Stories of the effect the First Lady had on the lives of many. (12 +)

Lawrence Lader & Milton Meltzer, *Margaret Sanger: Pioneer of Birth Control* (Crowell). The patron saint of planned parenthood. (12–15)

Carmen Moore, *Somebody's Angel Child: The Story of Bessie Smith* (Crowell). The rise and fall of the great blues singer. (12–15)

Alice Fleming, *The Senator From Maine: Margaret Chase Smith* (Crowell). The only woman in the U.S. Senate. (8–13)

Judith Strick Dribben, *A Girl Called Judith Strick* (Cowles). The Jewish girl who spied against the Nazis, endured a concentration camp and lived to serve in the Israeli army. (15 +)

Jacqueline Bernard, *Journey Toward Freedom: The Story of Sojourner Truth* (Norton). The former slave turned abolitionist, feminist and spokeswoman for nonviolence. (11–15)

Ann Petry, *Harriet Tubman: Conductor of the Underground Railroad* (Crowell). The black woman who personally emancipated hundreds of slaves. (12–15)

Biographical Collections

Alice Fleming, *Great Women Teachers* (Lippincott). Ten pioneers in American education. (12–15)

Harry Gersh, *Women Who Made America Great* (Lippincott). Women in careers ranging from astronomy to engineering. (12–15)

Mary Finch Hoyt, *American Women of the Space Age* (Atheneum). Women scientists, computer technologists, researchers, etc. (10–15)

Dorothy Nathan, *Women of Courage* (Random). Profiles of Susan B. Anthony, Jane Addams, Mary Bethune, Amelia Earhart, Margaret Mead. (10 +)

Kathryn Taylor, *Generations of Denial* (Times Change Press). 75 short biographies of women in history. (12 +) [For a catalog of pamphlets and posters published by this socialist-feminist press send a postcard to Times Change, 1023 Sixth Avenue, N.Y., N.Y. 10018]

The Woman Question—Answered
in Fact and Fiction

Carole Bolton, *Never Jam Today* (Atheneum). A historical novel about a young girl with a raised consciousness who becomes a suffragist against her father's will. (10–15)

Doris Faber, *Petticoat Politics* (Lothrop). How American women won the right to vote. (12–15)

Elizabeth Hall, *Stand Up, Lucy* (Houghton). A historical novel about a young activist during the period before passage of the 19th amendment. (8–12)

Henrik Ibsen, *A Doll's House*. The classic play that brings sexism in marriage out in the open. (14 +)

Lucy Komisar, *The New Feminism* (Watts). The experiences of young women growing up in an age of social and sexual revolution. (12 +)

Janet Lever & Pepper Schwartz, *Women at Yale* (Bobbs Merrill). The impact of 500 women students on the traditional male campus. (15 +)

Eve Merriam, Editor, *Growing Up Female in America* (Doubleday). Diaries, journals and letters that reveal the lives of ten American women, both famous and unknown. (12 +)

Eve Merriam, *After Nora Slammed the Door* (World). A witty dissection of women's roles from the doll's house to the split-level house. (15 +)

Emily James Putnam, *The Lady* (Chicago). Society's definition of her story from the Greek lady to the lady of the slave states. (15 +)

Mary Lou Thompson, Editor, *Voices of the New Feminism* (Beacon). Women in law, labor, politics, education and the church speak out on the issues. (15 +)

Books to Boycott (and Girlcott)—Three examples of what to avoid

Whitney Darrow, Jr. (Windmill). *I'm Glad I'm a Boy! I'm Glad I'm a Girl!* Symptom (from the text): "Boys invent things. Girls use what boys invent." Diagnosis: Rampant sexism. For little girls it's a quick course in second-class personhood.

The Sesame Street Book of People and Things (Preschool Press). In its "Note to Adults" the writers consistently refer to the child as "he." Judging by the book's contents they *mean* he. Nearly all the "People in your neighborhood" are men (the one woman in the group is a hairdresser). And the "Other jobs people do" are without exception done by men. Where are the role models for 51% of the preschool population?

Bobby Simon, *Just Like Daddy/Just Like Mommy*. The All-American division of labor: Mom on the inside with the dishes and dust. Dad on the outside—raking, mowing, hammering, painting. Propaganda to perpetuate role stereotypes.